Gubernatorial Leadership
and State Policy

Recent Titles in
Contributions in Political Science

GUBERNATORIAL LEADERSHIP AND STATE POLICY

EDITED BY

Eric B. Herzik

AND

Brent W. Brown

PREPARED UNDER THE AUSPICES OF THE
POLICY STUDIES ORGANIZATION
Stuart S. Nagel, *Publications Coordinator*

CONTRIBUTIONS IN POLITICAL SCIENCE,
NUMBER 281

Greenwood Press
New York • Westport, Connecticut • London

Library of Congress Cataloging-in-Publication Data

Gubernatorial leadership and state policy / edited by Eric B. Herzik
    and Brent W. Brown.
            p.   cm.—(Contributions in political science, ISSN 0147-1066
    ; no. 281)
        "Prepared under the auspices of the Policy Studies Organization."
        Includes bibliographical references and index.
        ISBN 0-313-27933-0
        1. Governors—United States.   2. State governments—United States.
    3. Policy sciences.   I. Herzik, Eric B.   II. Brown, Brent W.
    III. Policy Studies Organization.   IV. Series.
    JK2447.G78   1991
    353.9'313—dc20   91-11331

British Library Cataloguing in Publication Data is available.

Library of Congress Catalog Card Number: 91-11331
ISBN: 0-313-27933-0
ISSN: 0147-1066

First published in 1991

Greenwood Press, 88 Post Road West, Westport, CT   06881
An imprint of Greenwood Publishing Group, Inc.

Printed in the United States of America

The paper used in this book complies with the
Permanent Paper Standard issued by the National
Information Standards Organization (Z39.48–1984).

10 9 8 7 6 5 4 3 2 1

Contents

Illustrations

FIGURES

Preface

Governors are the most salient political actors in state government. Whether the true power center of a state rests with the particular occupant or resides elsewhere, the office of governor is the focal point of state government organization and policymaking. At a minimum, governors set the mood or tone of the state political environment. More commonly, governors take the lead in setting the agenda for public debate, framing issues, setting policy priorities, and influencing policy outcomes by using any number of powers or tools at their disposal.

The power and respect accorded governors has varied over time. Over the past three decades governors have assumed an ever greater role in the state policy process. Governors and states have always addressed policy issues that directly affect the quality of life of citizens. As a group, state governments develop and implement a wider range of policies than the national government. These traditional or perennial state policy concerns include most of the basic services such as education, highways, welfare, healthcare, and public safety utilized by citizens on a daily basis. However, the policy role of governors has also expanded significantly to meet new social needs and citizen demands in areas such as environmental quality, economic development, and consumer protection. Indeed, policy innovation across a wide spectrum of state policies is often the result of gubernatorial leadership. Several factors have influenced the increasing importance of gubernatorial leadership in the policymaking process. Nearly all governors now enjoy a fairly extensive array of formal powers that help them mold policy and guide it through the political process. Increased staff support allows governors to more actively develop policy and oversee its implementation. At a more macropolitical level, changes resulting from the Reagan era's New Federalism have expanded state policy responsibilities and forced governors to assume a greater policy leadership role.

This book addresses various aspects of the roles governors play in the state policymaking process. We have organized the chapters to address chronologically the gubernatorial role. Thus, chapter 1 outlines the general position of governors in the policy process. Chapters 2 and 3 address the governor's role in agenda setting and getting started in developing policy. Chapters 4, 5, and 6 examine how governors interact with other key state government actors and elements in the policy process: administrators, legislators and the budget. Chapters 7 through 11 are then more specific case studies of governors providing leadership in distinct policy areas.

As with most scholarly endeavors, this book results from the work of a great many individuals. The cooperation and expertise of the chapter authors made our task of editing and organizing all the easier. Stuart Nagel provided general assistance and encouragement throughout the process. The Department of Political Science at the University of Nevada, Reno, provided material support. Helpful editorial and substantive comments came from a number of individuals, including Mel Dubnick, David Rosenbloom, Thad Beyle, Pete Haas, and Robin Pulliam. The book would have never seen the light of day, however, without the work and good humor of Marilyn Woosley to whom we extend thanks and dedicate this book.

Eric B. Herzik
Reno, Nevada

Brent W. Brown
Tempe, Arizona

Gubernatorial Leadership and State Policy

1   The Policy Role of Governors

Donald A. Gross

The twentieth century is, in many respects, an "executive era" of American politics. The importance of political executives continued to grow as the policy implications of an expanding governmental sector affected more and more citizens. Despite the apparent setbacks of Watergate and Vietnam, the American president remains at the center of the federal government. In a similar vein, governors are the central figures in state governments.

The importance of governors has increased for two interrelated reasons. First, over the last thirty years numerous states have initiated reforms to enhance the power of the governor. Second, states have continued to expand their role in the development and implementation of policy initiatives that affect the lives of an increasing number of citizens. As a result of these developments we have seen public recognition of the governor increase as has the public's overall image of state government. In addition, contemporary governors appear to be more qualified, innovative, and powerful (Sabato, 1983; Beyle and Muchmore, 1983).

Within this context of a perceived growth in gubernatorial quality and power, a clear understanding of the governor's role in policymaking remains elusive. In many respects, much of the difficulty in understanding the executive's role in policymaking results from two separate, but interrelated, problems. First, how do we study the gubernatorial role in policymaking? Second, how do we evaluate and/or measure executive performance? Any attempt to begin to answer these questions depends upon philosophical assumptions concerning the "proper" roles of executives, legislatures, and government in general. Moreover, one must also consider the way in which the policy process is characterized and how policy success is thus determined.

To assess the gubernatorial policymaking role, this chapter examines the governorship as an institution. Individual case studies of governors or specific policies will not receive a great deal of attention. Rather, it is the systematic and/or quantitative study of governors and policymaking that receives prime consideration. I begin by discussing theoretical and analytical problems associated with the study of gubernatorial power, success, and achievement. Not only is there a large volume of literature on gubernatorial power, but, more importantly, power, success, and achievement are concepts that are often central to an evaluation of executive performance in the policymaking process. Central to this discussion is the importance of analyzing power, success, or achievement in terms of the structure of coalitions and cleavages within a particular state. Next, I examine the literature on policymaking and the executive branch in terms of the importance of power, coalitions, and cleavages with particular emphasis on the role of the governor, the state cabinet, and the governor's staff. Finally, I discuss legislative-executive interaction in the areas of agenda setting and legislative enactment.

GUBERNATORIAL POWER, SUCCESS AND ACHIEVEMENT

Evaluations of executive performance are usually based upon an activist view of government and executives. Presidents traditionally labeled as "great" tend to be those who are perceived as having expanded the power of the president vis-à-vis Congress, expanded the power of the federal government, and/or expanded American power overseas. In contemporary state affairs there is a similar bias in favor of activist governors. Reforms in recent years have been aimed at increasing gubernatorial power (Young, 1958; Rich, 1960; Ransone, 1982). Subjective evaluations or listings of "better" governors tend to be headed by activist governors who are described by words such as innovative, dynamic, and energetic (Sabato, 1983; Peirce, 1972; Weeks, 1981).

Even though this bias in favor of activist governors is likely to remain, it is important to recognize that achievement or success need not imply a positive subjective connotation in favor of governmental expansion. It is only necessary for the analyst to consider that success can involve either the expansion or contraction of either executive or state power. For example, an evaluation of the Reagan presidency must consider the administration's ability to reduce federal power which is action traditionally associated with "weak" presidents. While such action would traditionally be associated with "weak" presidents, reduction of federal power would have to be judged as a success because it conforms with the philosophical thrust of Reagan's administration. As such, achievement or success of policy goals should form the basis for evaluating executives.

Even an acceptance of achievement or success as a legitimate basis for evaluation, however, does not simplify greatly our task. All governors enter office in different state cultures, institutional settings, partisan alignments, and economic settings. Most importantly, power and success are not coterminous.

An examination of the literature on gubernatorial power indicates a disproportionate emphasis on an absolute or legalistic approach to the study of power (Schlesinger, 1965; Crittenden, 1967; Sharkansky, 1968; Dye, 1969; Beyle, 1968; Dometrius, 1979; Gross, 1983). Gubernatorial power indices generally include factors such as the governor's tenure potential, appointive powers, budgetary powers, and veto powers. Yet, as Sigelman and Dometrius (1988) point out, formal gubernatorial power is best interpreted as a "necessary but not sufficient condition" for the actual exercise of power by the governor. A more appropriate approach to the study of gubernatorial power requires the analysis of power relationships. That is, one must not only consider a governor's ability and willingness to utilize his or her formal power but one must also consider the powers of the other important institutional actors such as state legislatures. For example, while the formal powers of governors have generally increased over the last thirty years, so too have the powers and professionalism of state legislatures (Jewell, 1982; Gosling, 1985). It simply remains unclear how these concomitant increases in formal powers in both institutions have fundamentally affected the power balance or relationship between the two institutions.

In a similar view, the federal/state relationship has changed significantly in recent years. Changes such as the New Federalism of the Reagan administration can be seen as having both expanded and limited the latitude of action of contemporary governors. As Schneider's analysis in this volume points out, changes in federal policy on health care have allowed the states, and therefore the governors, to take on a more active role as policy initiators. At the same time, federal mandates, whether legislative or judicial, continue to constrain gubernatorial actions.

It makes little difference whether one is interested in analyzing governors, legislatures, court systems, interest groups, or other institutional actors; an examination of the formal power of any one institutional actor, without an examination of the powers of other institutional actors, can be misleading. The potential to utilize political power does not exist in a vacuum. The importance of political power must be evaluated in terms of the political power of other institutional actors attempting to affect the political phenomena of interest.

Yet a singular focus on even relative power still cannot form the basis for a fully developed understanding of gubernatorial achievement or success in policymaking because the ability and willingness to exercise gubernatorial power are simply never in a one-to-one relationship with success unless there is total and absolute disagreement between the governor and the other institutional actors in the policymaking process. A simple example can be used to illustrate this point.

Define a gubernatorial bill as a bill that is supported by the governor. Define the level of gubernatorial-legislative congruence as the percentage of all gubernatorial bills that will pass a legislature because of fundamental policy or partisan agreement between the governor and the legislature. When there is fundamental agreement, there is no need for the exercise of gubernatorial power. For simplicity, gubernatorial power can be defined as the percentage of all gubernatorial bills that will pass a legislature when there is fundamental partisan or policy disagreement between the governor and legislature.[1] If there are 100 bills on which the governor and legislature disagree and gubernatorial power is 20 percent, then 20 bills will pass because of the governor's exercise of power.

Table 1.1 indicates the number of gubernatorial bills that will pass a legislature, out of a possible 100, for various levels of gubernatorial power and gubernatorial-legislative congruence. The contribution of gubernatorial-legislative congruence is constant across all levels of gubernatorial power. The added increase in the number of bills passed because of the use of gubernatorial power, however, is dependent upon the level of congruence. If congruence is 20 percent, then every 10 percent increase in power results in eight more bills being passed. If congruence is 80 percent, then every 10 percent increase in power results in only two more bills being passed.

The data in table 1.1 can be generated in terms of a simple equation:

$$(1)\ Y = X + Z - (XZ/100)$$

where:

Y = the total number of bills passed by a legislature;
X = the level of gubernatorial–legislative congruence; and,
Z = the level of gubernatorial power.

One can specify the number of bills that will pass a legislature because of gubernatorial power, therefore, in terms of equation 2:

Table 1.1
The Number of Bills that Will Pass a Legislature (Out of a Possible 100, for Various Levels of Gubernatorial Power and Gubernatorial-Legislative Congruence)

100	100	100	100	100	100	100	100	100	100	100	100
90	90	91	92	93	94	95	96	97	98	99	100
80	80	82	84	86	88	90	92	94	96	98	100
70	70	73	76	79	82	85	88	91	94	97	100
60	60	64	68	72	76	80	84	88	92	96	100
50	50	55	60	65	70	75	80	85	90	95	100
40	40	46	52	58	64	70	76	82	88	94	100
30	30	37	44	51	58	65	72	79	86	93	100
20	20	28	36	44	52	60	68	76	84	92	100
10	10	19	28	37	46	55	64	73	82	91	100
0	0	10	20	30	40	50	60	70	80	90	100
0	0	10	20	30	40	50	60	70	80	90	100

Levels of Gubernatorial-Legislative Congruence

$$(2)\ Y - X = Z - (XZ/100)$$

Equation 2 establishes the importance of analyzing gubernatorial power in terms of its interaction with gubernatorial-legislative congruence. As gubernatorial-legislative congruence increases, the importance of gubernatorial power decreases because of the "XZ" interaction term. In a sense, this seems counterintuitive: The effect of gubernatorial power is maximized by decreasing the congruence between the governor and the legislature. However, what governor would desire or work for such a reduction in congruence? None, for the simple but often seemingly ignored principle that the exercise of power for most governors is not an end in itself. Achievement or success in any phase of the policymaking process remains the prime concern of a governor and it is most likely to occur in an atmosphere of agreement or congruence and not in an atmosphere of confrontation.

Equation 2 can also help one understand why it has been so difficult to find statistically significant relationships between executive power and policy outcomes on either the federal or state level. When there is a high degree of gubernatorial-legislative congruence there are a large number of gubernatorial bills passed; but, most pass because of gubernatorial-legislative congruence. Since most statistical techniques focus on explaining variance and gubernatorial-legislative congruence explains most of the variance, traditional statistical techniques may not be sufficiently robust to establish the importance of gubernatorial power. When gubernatorial-legislative congruence is low, there may simply be an insufficient number of bills passed to undertake an appropriate statistical analysis.

The inability to find significant relationships between gubernatorial power and various aspects of the state policymaking process can be seen, therefore, as a consequence of not only failing to evaluate gubernatorial power in relationship to the powers of other institutional actors, but also a consequence of failing to consider the fact that the importance of power is dependent upon the level of partisan or policy congruence between the governor and other major political actors. It is of prime importance to avoid a singular focus upon gubernatorial power when evaluating the governor's role in the state policymaking process. Any such evaluations must depend upon the simultaneous consideration of both confrontation and communality of interests (Ransone, 1982; Gosling, 1985).

It seems clear that a fully developed understanding of the governor's role in policymaking depends on an understanding of the governor's position in the matrix of actors attempting to influence governmental policy. The number of such actors can be quite expansive and may differ by policy area. For simplicity, however, four types of relevant actors may be considered: executive actors, legislative actors, political party actors, and other nongovernmental actors such as interest groups and the mass population. To ease future discussion, figure 1.1 can be used to examine the interaction within and among these types of actors.

Each type of actor in figure 1.1 can be seen as having his or her own political power base. In this sense, the study of the constitutional/legal authority of the governor can be seen as an analysis of the constitutional/legal power base of the most important individual in the executive sphere.

As figure 1.1 and equations 1 and 2 point out, of greater importance to the study of policymaking is the structure of cleavages and coalitions within and among spheres of actors. Within each sphere one needs to analyze the nature of cleavage and/or coalitional structure. Are coalitions highly structured with power centralized in the leadership or are they loose

Figure 1.1
Spheres of Interaction Among Relevant Policymaking Actors

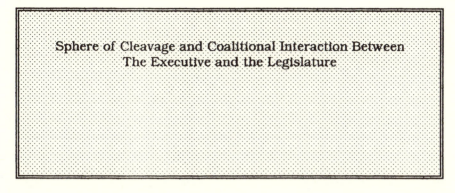

decentralized coalitional structures? Are particular coalitions based upon partisan or ideological factors or are they based more upon the character-istics of individual leaders? Is a particular sphere of action, such as the executive sphere, dominated by a particular coalition or are there multiple cleavage structures?

The cleavage/coalitional structure of any one sphere may reflect or contradict to varying degrees the cleavage/coalitional structure in the other spheres. Of fundamental importance is an understanding of how these spheres are linked. For example, is the nature of cleavages and coalitions outside of the government reflected in the party system and the govern-ment? Is the nature of the cleavages and coalitions in the legislature similar to that in the executive sphere? Is there a similar dominant coalition in both the legislature and the executive? To use earlier terminology, is there a high degree of gubernatorial-legislative congruence? Is the coalition structure in any one of these spheres so powerful so as to dominate all other spheres?

The importance that I have placed upon examining the linkages and interactions among the various cleavage/coalitional structures of various policy relevant actors is implicit in much of the literature on policymaking and explicit in other literature. For example, the literature on "Iron Triangles" or "Issue Networks" explicitly focuses on the importance of analyzing the interaction among interest groups, bureaucrats, and legislative committees (Fritschler, 1983; Heclo, 1978; Ripley and Franklin, 1980; Rose, 1980). Furthermore, a number of the works in this volume, Durning, Grady, and Medler for example, emphasize the importance of analyzing the interaction among policy relevant actors when examining the role of the governor in policymaking. It is within this overall framework emphasizing the importance of coalitions and cleavages within and among policy relevant actors, therefore, that I now turn to a consideration of the literature on policymaking and the executive branch.

THE EXECUTIVE BRANCH

The governor is clearly the most visible actor in the state executive branch. In many respects, the individualized nature of the governorship has hindered research on state executives. Most would agree that the personality of the governor helps determine his or her leadership capabilities. With the exception of individual biographical accounts and the ongoing lists of supposed leadership traits, however, there has been no systematic attempt to develop a conceptual framework for the comparative study of gubernatorial personality. Furthermore, given the numerous problems associated with conceptual frameworks for analyzing presidential personality (Barber, 1977; Qualls, 1977; George, 1974), it seems unlikely that a theoretically appropriate framework for the comparative analysis of gubernatorial personality will be forthcoming.

Within the general framework of political ambition as originally suggested by Schlesinger (1966), there have been a number of analyses of gubernatorial career patterns. In general, these analyses have found that, compared to their predecessors, contemporary governors tend to be younger, better educated, more likely to have had U.S. congressional experience, more likely to have served in state legislatures, and more likely to have significant political careers after their gubernatorial careers (Sabato, 1983; Beyle, 1983). It has also been established that, although there is a historical tradition of high turnover, there has been a trend in recent years toward longer tenure. While there are clear interstate differences, we find that contemporary governors have fewer legal restrictions on seeking reelection, generally have little difficulty receiving renomination, and usually win reelection (Beyle, 1986).

These changes in career patterns have led some to conclude that we are now more likely to have governors of greater capacity and governors who are more likely to be in a better position to exert leadership (Sabato, 1983). At the present time, however, there appears to be little evidence to support the hypothesized link between changes in career patterns and gubernatorial success in the policymaking process. For example, the analysis of Grady, which is found in this volume, found no relationship between experience variables and self-evaluations of economic development policymaking effectiveness. Morehouse's (1981) analysis did indicate a link between tenure potential and legislative support for the governor's program; but, the analysis was limited in a number of ways. Tenure potential was not examined independently of other formal gubernatorial powers; rather, it was treated as one factor in a composite index. More importantly, data limitations prohibited Morehouse from examining tenure potential in respect to a number of confounding factors such as partisan support in the legislature.

Edwards's (1980) analysis of presidential influence in Congress can be considered instructive when considering the importance of changes in gubernatorial career patterns. Edwards found no simple relationship between presidential tenure and presidential success in Congress. In fact, it is often the case that presidential success declines the longer a president is in office (Olson, 1985). It is argued that since governors now tend to have more legislative experience before coming into office, they have greater legislative skills and are more likely to be successful governors. Edwards's conclusion is very straightforward: "Presidential skills do not seem to affect support for presidential policies, despite what conventional wisdom leads us to expect" (Edwards, 1980: 202). It may be the case that one is more likely to find a direct link between an executive's tenure or legislative skills and success at the state level than at the national level. Less professionalized legislatures do tend to be more dependent upon leadership. Until these linkages are analyzed directly at the state level, however, these hypothesized relationships between changes in career patterns and gubernatorial success must be considered suspect and untested.

Earlier I argued that a fully developed understanding of the governor's role in policymaking depends upon an understanding of the governor's position in the matrix of actors attempting to influence governmental policy. Thus, it is necessary to examine the linkages among relevant actors that comprise the coalitional and/or cleavage structures within the executive branch itself. Immediately below the governor in the executive establishment are the heads of the primary administrative units in the state. For convenience, we can refer to these individuals as the state cabinet.[2]

One of the unique aspects of many state governments is that many individuals in the state cabinet are elected to their positions and are not appointed by the governor. Even in those states where these are appointive positions, the limitations on the governor's appointive power differ greatly. In addition, Beyle and Mouw (1989) note that states differ greatly as to constraints on the governor's power to remove individuals in the executive branch. This is in direct contrast to the federal government where the president's authority to appoint and remove individuals from the cabinet is almost unquestioned.

The possible difficulties for a governor confronting a fractionalized executive are clearly evident. The governor cannot readily be assured of policy compliance between him or herself and the cabinet. There is no assurance that cabinet officials will be willing to join the gubernatorial coalition. The potential problems are compounded when the lieutenant governor is also elected independently from the governor. Most texts are able to provide the reader with a number of examples of independently elected executives creating difficulties for the governor. At the same time, systematic analyses of fractionalized executives have provided mixed results. Sharkansky (1968) and Turnbull (1969) found that plural executives diminished gubernatorial budget control. More recently, Gosling (1985) found systematic differences between administrative units headed by elected officials as opposed to those headed by appointive individuals. Dye (1969), however, found little evidence to support the notion that a fractionalized executive, in itself, affected the types of policies in a state. Lauth (1984) found that agencies with elected heads were no more or less successful in budgetary matters than agencies headed by appointive individuals. And, while Beyle (1968) indicated that approximately two out of every three governors stressed the importance of the appointive power, Sabato's (1983) analysis seemed to indicate that most governors do not perceive any major problems with their independently elected officials. Furthermore, Blair (1983) indicates that governors often find a focus on appointing many state officials to be unproductive.

Although there seems to be no consistent evidence to suggest that a fractionalized executive fundamentally affects policymaking in a state, it is clearly too early to discount the potential importance of a fractionalized executive. First, in respect to Dye's analysis, there is no inherent reason why a divided or united executive should favor a particular type of policy (in Dye's analysis, the type of policy being increased was social welfare spending). The type of policy enhanced or diminished is necessarily dependent upon the policy orientations of the executive officials in question. Second, it is clearly inappropriate to consider all types of fractionalization in the executive to be equally important. An independently elected attorney general cannot be assumed to be equally important as an independently elected auditor. Third, the structural potential for a fractionalized executive is not the same thing as an actual fractionalized executive. One would expect different policy consequences when there are fundamental partisan and/or policy cleavages between the governor and other elected executives versus a situation where there is fundamental partisan and/or policy agreement. In fact, it is reasonable to suggest that when an independently elected executive supports a governor's program, the program's chance for success is greater than when an appointed executive supports it. Finally, it seems inappropriate to consider the effect of a fractionalized executive independent of specific policy considerations. It is simply unreasonable to expect a state's social welfare programs to be affected by a fractionalized executive unless the state's social welfare programs are under the purview of an independently elected official. In such a case the interaction between the governor and that one elected official would be of prime importance. There is simply no guarantee that the structure of coalitions and/or cleavages within the executive branch will be the same for all policy areas.

Even in the context of an appointive cabinet system, it remains necessary to distinguish between two types of officials: executive partisans and administrators. Executive partisans are those who receive their positions on the basis of personal loyalty to the governor and his or her program. Such individuals function very much as gubernatorial advocates and, as such, are central to the governor's executive branch coalition. In the case of administrators, partisanship remains a major consideration in their appointment; however, administrative or policy expertise is an equally important consideration. On the gubernatorial level little is known about the degree to which gubernatorial appointees on the cabinet level adopt or are recruited in terms of an executive partisan model or an administrative model. The evidence that is available (Wright, 1967; Dometrius, 1981; Flentje, 1981; Weinberg, 1977; Abney and Lauth, 1983) seems to indicate that, although there appears to be more executive partisans at the state level than what one finds at the national level, there are wide variations among the states.

On the federal level there seems to have been a shift in recent years toward more administrative-type cabinet officials (Polsby, 1978; Heclo,

1978). As suggested by Heclo, the use of administrative-type cabinet officials can actually inhibit presidential policy leadership because such individuals tend to be intimately linked to the various clienteles interested in a given policy area. As such, they tend to become advocates for the very programs over which they chair administrative responsibility. This line of reasoning also underlies much of the contemporary thought on the role of the cabinet vis-à-vis that of the executive office of the president. As cabinet officials become linked to specific interests that are not necessarily an integral part of the president's governing coalition, presidents have been forced to rely more and more upon their personal advisors within the executive office. Given this evidence at the national level, and Abney and Lauth's (1983) evidence that state administrators tend to use the governor to gain departmental advantage more than the governor uses the administrators to gain policy advantage, it seems most important to investigate further how different types of appointed administrators interact with the governor and other executive actors in the development and implementation of policy.

One group of individuals that can be seen as an integral part of the governor's executive branch coalition is the governor's staff. A number of analyses have indicated that, while there continues to be a great deal of difference among the states in the size of the governor's staff, in almost every state the size of the governor's staff has increased significantly over the last twenty years. Other analyses of staff have focused on their background characteristics (Sprengel, 1969); their perceptions of role responsibilities (Wyner, 1972; Williams, 1980; Flentje, 1981); and "significant others'" perceptions of the gubernatorial staff (Wyner, 1972; Abney and Lauth, 1983; Elling and Schottenfels, 1980; Daley, 1984). In general, these studies tend to be highly descriptive or tabular. Explanations for staff characteristics, whether they be role orientations or background information, tend to be highly speculative or individualized. This tendency to rely upon individualized or descriptive analysis is not particularly surprising given that analyses of presidential staff, where information tends to be more readily available, also tend to be individualized, descriptive, and highly speculative.

The final group of executive actors that needs to be mentioned are those individuals who comprise the state bureaucracy. The bureaucracy performs a number of key roles in the policymaking process of any political system. The bureaucracy's importance can be evaluated in terms of program and budgetary initiatives, program enactment because of linkages to clientele groups and legislative committees, program implementation due to what Davis (1969) calls discretionary authority, and program evaluation. Most of the literature on this subject has viewed the bureaucracy rather than the governor as its theoretical focus.[3] There has also been a growing literature on legislative oversight that examines the interaction between administrative agencies and state legislatures as it affects policymaking (Moe, 1985; Rockman, 1984). This literature primarily focuses on state legislatures. Therefore, given the gubernatorial focus of this essay, I will not comment further on these subjects.

Numerous actors within the executive branch can affect the nature of policymaking in a state. While the governor is the central figure in the executive branch, his or her interactions with other executive branch actors can be critical to an understanding of the state policymaking process. As should be apparent in this review of much of the literature, we are only now beginning to understand many of the complexities associated with these interactions.

GUBERNATORIAL-LEGISLATIVE INTERACTION

There are numerous approaches to the study of executive-legislative interaction. There are historical/legal analyses best exemplified at the national level in the works of Fisher (1972, 1975) and Schlesinger (1974). There are case studies that focus on single executives or particular policies. There are systematic empirical analyses that examine executive influence in the legislature during certain stages of the policymaking process. I focus my attention on systematic and empirical analyses of executive influence in agenda setting and legislative enactment. I begin with agenda setting.

Agenda Setting

How broadly does one define the agenda-setting process? How one answers this question is clearly going to affect the conclusions of one's analysis. Since ideas for legislation come from various sources (interest groups, constituents, legislators, executives, bureaucrats), analyses of agenda setting often seem to become bogged down by attempting to answer what I would consider an impossible question to answer: Who thought of the idea first?

Probably the most widely used, and most fruitful way to analyze agenda setting, is to focus upon the chief initiator of legislation before the legislature. Given such a focus, it is clear that the president is the chief initiator of legislation before Congress (Neustadt, 1976; Huntington, 1973). It is also clear that members of Congress and the bureaucracy are often active innovators and involved directly in the generation of legislation (Moe and Teel, 1970; Orfield, 1975; Cobb and Elder, 1972).

Our understanding of the governor's role in agenda setting is much less clear than our understanding of the president's role in agenda setting. Primary responsibility for budgetary preparation is given to the governor and the budgetary staff in most states. Sharkansky's (1968) seminal work and a number of subsequent studies continue to indicate the central importance of the governor to the budgetary priorities of a state (Garand, 1984; Moncrief and Thompson, 1980; Gross, 1980; Gosling, 1986; Abney and Lauth, 1985; Lauth, 1984). At the same time, there is growing recognition of the limits of gubernatorial influence in the budgetary process. There is evidence to suggest that the legislature's role in the budgetary process does increase when both chambers are controlled by the party opposite that of the governor (Moncrief and Thompson, 1980) and when the governor requests appropriations that appear to depart dramatically from past incremental patterns (Hale, 1977). One is more likely to see interchamber disputes on appropriation bills when there is split control of the legislature suggesting differential gubernatorial support in each chamber (Gross, 1983). Others have suggested that state legislatures are becoming increasingly more influential in the budgetary process (Gosling, 1985). Finally, the incrementalist literature clearly suggests that the governor's discretionary authority over the budget is limited (Lowery, Konda, and Garand, 1984). This appears to be the case whether or not the incremental process is a result of stable role orientations (Davis, Dempster, and Wildavsky, 1966), mandatory expenditures (Gist, 1974), or boundaries induced by mandatory expenditures and fiscal constraints (Wanat, 1974).

Once one moves beyond a consideration of budgetary affairs, there are only a limited number of systematic studies that focus on the governor's role in agenda setting. This state of affairs seems very much to be a result of data considerations because there is simply no systematic and readily available means for specifying gubernatorial programs for each state. In this context, Herzik (1983) used the governors' state-of-the-state addresses, in lieu of actual legislation, to analyze the issues emphasized by governors in all fifty states. He found that there were three categories into which most issues could be classified. Perennial issues represented about three-fourths of the state budget and included such issues as education, highways, health care, welfare, and law enforcement. Cyclical issues such as consumer protection and tax reform are those that quickly grow in concern and then steadily decline. Transitory issues tend to often be emotionally based quick responses to a sudden development.

The analyses of Bell (1984) and Morehouse (1973 and 1981) are excellent examples of the difficulty associated with any attempt to analyze systematically the governor's role in agenda setting outside of the budgetary area. Bell's analysis indicated that only about 10 percent of the bills introduced in California could be traced directly to the governor and that the single greatest source of legislation was private interest groups. What is perhaps most instructive from her work is that to analyze the initiation of only 12 percent of all bills in one state for one session, the analyst had to interview hundreds of state officials. In a similar vein, what is perhaps most instructive in Morehouse's work are the difficulties that she encountered when attempting to specify gubernatorial initiatives.

The cases in gubernatorial policymaking that are included in the final section of this text also offer insight into the difficulty of systematically analyzing the governor's role in agenda setting. Each of these analyses emphasizes the importance of the governor's role in focusing attention on specific types of policies. At the same time, they also point out how governors are constrained in this role. They are constrained by the parameters of public opinion, the coalitions and cleavages in the legislature, state and national political and economic trends, federal policy, and perennial state needs. In a sense, the governor is controlled by the very same forces that he or she needs to influence in setting priorities.

Legislative Enactment

As was the case in agenda setting, it is best to begin an examination of executive influence over legislative enactment by considering briefly what we know about presidential influence over Congress. This literature is much more extensive than similar literature on the governor and state legislatures; thus, it can provide a context in which to judge the literature on gubernatorial influence over state legislatures. Systematic attempts to evaluate presidential influence in Congress generally have relied upon the use of one or more types of data: presidential success scores, presidential support scores, other sets of roll call votes, vetoes, and appointments. Each of these types of data can be seen as specifying a presidential position. Therefore, the analytical question typically focuses on the degree to which Congress supports presidential positions.

There is a massive literature that examines presidential support scores, presidential success scores, and the relationship between president and congressional voting behavior in general. It is clear that the president's party affiliation is the prime factor in explaining presidential success in Congress but that this level of success is dependent upon the policy area being analyzed (Clausen, 1973; Olson, 1985). It is not clear, however, whether the importance of the president's party affiliation is a result of "pure partisanship," party affiliation as a surrogate measure of other considerations such as policy congruence, or some combination of these factors. In any case, what this literature suggests is the importance of the point made in an earlier section of this chapter: Executive success in the legislature is primarily dependent upon the level of executive-legislative congruence not upon the use of executive power.

Additional characteristics that have been considered when analyzing presidential influence on roll call voting are presidential popularity, the joint electoral outcomes between congresspeople and the president, and the president's legislative skills. There seems to be sufficient data to indicate that there is a positive relationship between presidential popularity and support in Congress (Edwards, 1980). A positive relationship between presidential and congressional electoral outcomes and the presidential support scores of congresspeople has been found by a number of authors (Flinn and Wolman, 1966; Weinbaum and Judd, 1970; Edwards, 1980; Harman and Brauen, 1979). Finally, although numerous case studies have indicated the importance of presidential legislative skills to presidential success in the legislature (Holtzman, 1973; Caro, 1981, Evans and Novak, 1966; Arnold, 1979), analyses of aggregate roll call votes provide little evidence to suggest that legislative skills significantly improve support in Congress (Edwards, 1980).

The apparent contradiction between the importance of legislative skills found in case studies and the findings of aggregate studies is not as surprising as one might suspect if one again remembers the lessons shown in table 1.1 and equations 1 and 2. Executive-legislative congruence should explain most of the variance in the amount of executive success in the legislature. The amount of residual variance to be explained by factors other than congruence is likely to be quite small. It may simply be the case that it is this small unexplained residual variance in aggregate studies that is explained in the case study approach as legislative skills.

If we consider the literature on presidential vetoes, analyses indicate that vetoes are not widely used and are rarely overturned. Most presidential vetoes are of private bills (Cronin, 1975) with Congress more likely to override a veto when it is controlled by the party opposite to that of the president, after a midterm election, during economic instability, and when there is no military involvement (Lee, 1975). Presidents are more likely to veto legislation when they enter office after a major electoral victory, with contemporary presidents being heavily influenced by the advice of the Office of Management and Budget (OMB) and the department most affected by the bill (Wayne, Cole, and Hyde, 1979). Once again, the importance of the coalitions and cleavages in Congress to presidential success is evident. However, there are two points of fundamental importance to consider when examining vetoes as compared to voting on legislation in general. First, the mere fact that one is analyzing vetoes means that one is focusing on situations involving confrontations, not congruent behavior. Second, the structural parameters defining the interaction between the executive and the legislature are fundamentally different because of the two-thirds requirement in Congress to override a veto. Thus, the importance of the structure of coalitions and cleavages in Congress is fundamentally altered.

When one moves to a consideration of gubernatorial success in the legislature one finds that, unlike presidential analyses, much more attention has been focused on gubernatorial vetoes and legislative attempts to override them (Prescott, 1950; Wiggins, 1980; Morehouse, 1966, 1973, 1981). As in the case of the federal government, only a small percentage of the bills vetoes by a governor is ever overridden. There is evidence, however, that the percent overridden has increased in recent years (Wiggins, 1980). However, a clear specification of the factors that explain differing levels in the use of gubernatorial vetoes and legislative overrides remains elusive (Herzik and Wiggins, 1989).

In recent years attention has been focused on the use of item vetoes by governors. In order to support their desire for the adoption of the item veto at the federal level, the Reagan administration liked to point out that most governors have this authority. The Bush administration continues this effort. Two recent works have shed light on this controversy. Both Gosling (1986) and Abney and Lauth (1985) indicate that although the item veto does likely result in less state spending, it is used by governors as a tool of partisanship and policy preferences. The item veto is not used primarily as a tool of of fiscal constraint.

Once one moves beyond a consideration of vetoes, most analyses of gubernatorial influence on legislators' voting behavior focus on budgetary matters. Since most of this literature has already been mentioned when discussing agenda setting, I will not comment further on these works. Systematic analyses of gubernatorial influence on legislative behavior in the nonbudgetary area are few. A number of studies have asked different types of individuals (department heads, state bureaucrats, or others) to indicate their perceptions of the influence of certain actors in the policy process. As opposed to the governor, it is the legislature that is typically seen as most influential or too influential (Abney and Lauth, 1983; Miller, 1987; Wright, 1967).⁴

Other studies of gubernatorial influence in the legislature include the analyses of Wyner (1968), Ransone (1982), and Morehouse (1966, 1973, 1981). The best of these are probably the analyses of Morehouse. The conclusions of Morehouse can be summarized as follows. First, industrialization is weakly associated with support for the governor. Second, the formal powers of the governor are related to legislative support. Third, the governor's party leadership (measured in terms of electoral support in the primary) is significantly related to support in the legislature. Finally, inferential evidence indicates that it is the governor's outside party organization that is important to the generation of discipline within the legislative party.

In relation to these last two points, numerous gubernatorial scholars have argued that the key to understanding gubernatorial success in the legislature is an understanding of the role of the governor in the state party organization. Thus, it is not only important to determine whether the two legislative chambers are both controlled by the governor's party, by the opposition, or split in their partisan control; but, it is also important to specify the cohesion and factional basis of the governor's party in both chambers. Gubernatorial support is likely to be much different when party factions are based upon personalities as opposed to issues and ideology. It is most important, however, to point out that the relationships among the governor, his party, and support for the governor in the legislature remain controversial and poorly specified. For example, Beyle and Muchmore (1983:50) argue that "the governorship seems to have developed in such a way that the party is no longer the most important instrument of political action." Over the last twenty to thirty years we have seen major changes in state parties, state legislatures, governors, and other actors interested in affecting state policy. These changes have likely changed the relationship among governors, their parties, and their legislatures. These changes have also likely affected different policy areas in different ways. Systematic analyses of the relationships among these various groupings are essential if we are to understand the contemporary governor's ability to gain success in the legislature.

As should be apparent by now, as compared to the literature on the American presidency, very little has been done to analyze systematically gubernatorial success in state legislatures. As such, our understanding of the governor's role in affecting legislative action and policymaking in general remains highly speculative and individualized.

CONCLUSION: COALITIONS, CLEAVAGES, AND
SUCCESS IN POLICYMAKING

I began this essay by stating that much of the difficulty in understanding the executive role in policymaking results from two separate, but interrelated, problems. First, how do we study the gubernatorial role in policymaking? Second, how do we evaluate and/or measure executive performance? The literature exemplifies multiple answers to each of these questions. It would simply be impossible, and indeed inappropriate, for me to suggest a single answer to each of these questions. At the same time, it seems important to address some fundamental points regarding each of these questions.

Power, success, and achievement are illusive terms. It is clear that the application of gubernatorial power and gubernatorial success is linked together. However, in many cases, the application of power may have little to do with success. The legislation supported by a governor may often pass a legislature merely because a sufficient number of legislators are in fundamental agreement with the policy implications of the legislation. It seems that we often have a tendency to assume that it was the governor who used his or her influence to get the legislation passed. At the same time, such legislation may never have reached the stage of legislative action if the governor had not acted to get the item on the public agenda. But, the governor may have felt compelled to place the item on the public agenda because of political forces, many of which might be the same as those resulting in legislative support. How do we evaluate the success of a governor, legislature, or any institutional actor in such a complex matrix of potential interactions?

When discussing agenda setting I suggested that analyses often seem to get bogged down in what is probably a question without an answer: Who thought of the idea first? Given our current state of understanding, traditional modes of specifying gubernatorial power, success, and achievement may also be attempting to deal with a question that we currently cannot answer: Who or what is more powerful or successful? The question implies confrontation and this may seem reasonable because politics is, in a sense, about conflict. However, political cleavages and the conflict surrounding them occur in different spheres of political action. The cleavages and coalitions associated with a conflict in one political sphere may or may not be reflected in another sphere of political action.

In this sense, gubernatorial action is often undertaken in an atmosphere that is not dominated by confrontation but one dominated by linkages to political actors with similar policy orientations. This is not to suggest that political disputes do not exist in multiple spheres of political action. In the legislature, for example, there may be a number of cleavages and political disputes resulting from these cleavages. However, governors are not likely to receive support for their programs by confronting those forces in opposition to their programs in a direct power struggle. Instead, their success depends upon establishing linkages with those legislators who have similar policy orientations. It is for this reason that executives who are most successful in having their programs passed are typically those who have a majority coalition in the legislature.

The question of who or what is more powerful or successful, therefore, may simply not have a readily apparent answer that can be considered theoretically satisfying. The application of power, as I have used the term in this chapter, may simply not be very useful or applicable in most policymaking situations. Of course, these may, in some sense, be critical situations. A definition of success may also be difficult to specify outside the parameters of a particular contextual situation or narrowly defined research project.

Multiple approaches to the study of the role of the governor in policymaking are likely to continue to be seen in the literature. As research continues to add to our knowledge, it is imperative to recognize the limitations associated with the particular approach utilized to study the phenomena of interest. The policymaking process involves complex interactions among multiple political actors at numerous time points. Thus, particular research conclusions must ultimately be viewed in the context of this complexity.

NOTES

1. This is a restrictive notion of power; however, I think that it is a reasonable definition for use in this example. Most power sources examined in the literature tend to emphasize factors that are most useful in an atmosphere of confrontation. An example of this is the veto authority of a governor. One must note that in this example, gubernatorial power is not equal to one minus gubernatorial-legislative congruence. It is also assumed that power is only usually applied if it is needed; that is, when gubernatorial-legislative congruence will not achieve the passage of legislation. Furthermore, while this example is developed in terms of the entire legislature, one could just as easily think of this example in terms of just one legislator. Instead of specifying the percentage of bills that will pass a legislature, one just specifies the percentage of bills for which a particular legislator will vote.

2. I use the term *cabinet* for ease of expression. Actual forms of departmental structures and their leadership differ among the states (Bodman and Garry, 1982).

3. For a solid discussion of the bureaucracy's role in policymaking see Elling (1983). A general model of executive control of the bureaucracy can be found in Garand and Gross (1982).

4. Throughout this chapter I have argued the importance of examining the governor's role in policymaking in terms of the matrix of interactions among policy relevant actors and avoiding a singular focus on the absolute power of specific actors. In this sense, to ask respondents which actor or institution is more influential may simply be asking the wrong question. It may be the wrong question for two reasons. First, in many policymaking situations actors may not be confronted with a situation of the governor versus the legislature or the governor versus other actors. Relevant actors may have similar preferences or there may be specific types of coalitions among the relevant actors. Second, it is simply not legitimate to assume that the effect of specific actors is additive. If, as I have argued, respondents are likely to respond in terms of specific coalitions trying to influence policy, then the effect of coalitions ought to be modeled in terms of interaction not additivity.

REFERENCES

Abney, Glenn, and Thomas P. Lauth. 1983. The Governor as Chief Administrator. *Public Administration Review*, 43, 1:40–49.

_____. 1985. The Line Item Veto in the States. *Public Administration Review*, 45, 1:372–77.

Arnold, R. Douglas. 1979. *Congress and the Bureaucracy*. New Haven, CT: Yale University Press.

Barber, James D. 1977. *Presidential Character*. Englewood Cliffs, NJ: Prentice-Hall.

Bell, J. D. 1984. Legislative Genesis, Agenda Setting, and Gatekeeping: A Study of the California State Legislature. Paper presented at the 1984 annual meeting of the American Political Science Association, Washington, D.C.

Beyle, Thad. 1968. The Governor's Formal Powers: A View from the Governor's Chair. *Public Administration Review*, 28, 4:540–45.

_____. 1983. Governors. In Virginia Gray, Herbert Jacob, and Kenneth Vines, eds. *Politics in the American States*. Boston: Little, Brown and Company.

_____. 1986. *Re-Electing the Governor*. New York, NY: University Press of America.

Beyle, Thad, and Lynn Muchmore. 1983. *Being Governor: The View from the Office*. Durham, NC: Duke University Press.

Beyle, Thad and Scott Mouw. 1989. Governors: The Power of Removal. *Policy Studies Journal*, 17, 4: 804–28.

Blair, Diane K. 1983. The Gubernatorial Appointment Power: Too Much of a Good Thing? In Thad Beyle and Lynn Muchmore, *Being Governor: The View From the Office*. Durham, NC: Duke University Press.

Bodman, Lydia and Daniel Garry. 1982. Innovation in State Cabinet Systems. *State Government*, 55, 3:93–97.

Bunce, Valerie. 1981. *Do Leaders Make a Difference*. Princeton, NJ: Princeton University Press.

Caro, Robert. 1981. *The Path to Power*. New York, NY: Vintage Books.

Clausen, Aage. 1973. *How Congressmen Decide*. New York, NY: St. Martin's Press.

Cobb, Roger, and Charles Elder. 1972. *Participation in American Politics*. Boston, MA: Allyn and Bacon.

Crittenden, John. 1967. Dimensions of Modernization in the American States. *American Political Science Review*, 61, 4:989–1001.

Cronin, Thomas. 1975. *The State of the Presidency*. Boston, MA: Little, Brown and Company.

Daley, Dennis. 1984. Controlling the Bureaucracy Among the States: An Examination of Administrative, Executive, and Legislative Attitudes. *Administration and Society*, 15, 4: 475–88.

Davis, Kenneth. 1969. *Discretionary Justice: A Preliminary Inquiry*. Urbana, IL: University of Illinois Press.

Davis, Otto, M. Dempster, and Aaron Wildavsky. 1966. A Theory of the Budgetary Process. *American Political Science Review*, 60, 3:529–47.

Dometrius, Nelson. 1979. Measuring Gubernatorial Power. *Journal of Politics*, 41, 2:589-610.

_____. 1981. Some Consequences of State Reform. *State Government*, 54, 2.

Dye, Thomas. 1969. Executive Power and Public Policy in the States. *Western Political Quarterly*, 27, 4:926–39.

Edwards, George. 1980. *Presidential Influence in Congress*, San Francisco, CA: W. H. Freeman.

_____. 1981. The Quantitative Study of the Presidency. *Presidential Studies Quarterly*, 11, 2: 146–50.

Elling, Richard. 1983. State Bureaucrats as Policy Shapers. In Virginia Gray, Herbert Jacob, and Kenneth Vines, eds. *Politics in the American States*. Boston, MA: Little, Brown and Company.

Elling Richard, and D. Schettonfels. 1980. The State Administrative Influence Matrix. Paper presented at the National Conference of the American Society for Public Administration.

Evans, Rowland, and Robert Novak. 1966. *The Exercise of Power*. New York, NY: New American Library.

Fisher, Louis. 1972. *President and Congress*. New York, NY: Free Press.

_____. 1975. *Presidential Spending Power*. Princeton, NJ: Princeton University Press.

Flentje, H. 1981. The Governor as Manager. *State Government*, 42, 2.

Flinn, T., and H. Wolman. 1966. Constituency and Roll Call Voting: The Case of the Southern Congressmen. *Midwest Journal of Political Science*, 10, 2.

Fritschler, A. Lee. 1983. *Smoking and Politics*. Englewood Cliffs, NJ: Prentice-Hall.

Garand, James, and Donald Gross. 1982. Toward a Theory of Bureaucratic Compliance with Presidential Directives. *Presidential Studies Quarterly*, 12, 2:195–207.

_____. 1984. *Incremental Budgeting in the American States: The Impact of Partisan Factors*. Unpublished Ph.D. dissertation: University of Kentucky.

George, Alexander L. 1974. Assessing Presidential Character. *World Politics*, 26, 2:255–59.

Gist, John. 1974. *Mandatory Expenditures and the Defense Sector*. Beverly Hills, CA: Sage Professional Series in American Politics.

Gosling, James. 1985. Patterns of Influence and Choice in the Wisconsin Budgetary Process. *Legislative Studies Quarterly*, 10, 4:457–82.

_____. 1986. Wisconsin Item Veto Lessons. *Public Administration Review*, 46, 4:292–300.

Gross, Donald. 1980. House-Senate Conference Committees: A Comparative State Perspective. *American Journal of Political Science*, 24, 4:769–78.

_____. 1983. Conference Committees and the Levels of Interchamber Disagreement. *State and Local Government Review*, 15, 3:130–33.

Hale, G. 1977. Executive Leadership versus Budgetary Behavior. *Administration and Society*, 9, 4.

Harman, Kathryn, and Marsha Brauen. 1979. Joint Electoral Outcomes as Cues for Congressional Support of U.S. Presidents. *Legislative Studies Quarterly*, 4, 2:281–300.

Heclo, Hugh. 1978. Issue Networks and the Executive Establishment. In Anthony King, ed. *The New American Political System*. Washington, DC: American Enterprise Institute.

Herzik, Eric. 1983. Governors and Issues: A Typology of Concerns. *State Government*, 54, 3:58–64.

Herzik, Eric, and C. Wiggins. 1989. Governors vs. Legislatures: Vetoes, Overrides, and Policymaking in the American States. *Policy Studies Journal*, 17, 4:841–62.

Holtzman, Abraham. 1973. *Legislative Liaison: Executive Leadership in Congress*. Chicago, IL: Rand McNally.

Huntington, Samuel. 1973. Congressional Responses to the Twentieth Century. In David Truman, ed. *The Congress and America's Future*. Englewood Cliffs, NJ: Prentice-Hall.

Jewell, Malcolm. 1982. The Neglected World of State Politics. *Journal of Politics*, 44, 3: 638–57.

Lauth, Thomas. 1984. Impact of the Method of Agency Selections on Gubernatorial Influence Over State Agencies. *Public Administration Quarterly*, 7, 4:396–409.

Lee, Jong. 1975. Presidential Vetoes From Washington to Nixon. *Journal of Politics*, 37, 2: 522–46.

Lowery, David, Thomas Konda, and James Garand. 1984. Spending in the States:A Test of Six Models. *Western Political Quarterly*, 37, 1.

MacKenzie, G. Calvin. 1981. *The Politics of Presidential Appointments*. New York, NY: Free Press.

Miller, Cheryl. 1987. State Administrator Perceptions of the Policy Influence of Other Actors: Is Less Better. *Public Administration Review*, 47, 3:239–45.

Moe, Ronald, and Steven Teel. 1970. Congress as Policymaker. *Political Science Quarterly*, 85, 3.

_____. 1985. Congressional Control of the Bureaucracy: An Assessment of the Positive Theory of Congressional Dominance. Paper presented at the annual meeting of the American Political Science Association.

Moncrief, Gary, and Joel Thompson. 1980. Partisanship and Purse Strings: A Research Note on Sharkansky. *Western Political Quarterly*, 33:336–40.

Morehouse, Sarah McCally. 1966. The Governor and His Legislative Party. *American Political Science Review*, 60, 4:923–942.

_____. 1973. The State Political Party and the Policy-Making Process. *American Political Science Review*, 67, 1:55–72.

_____. 1981. *State Politics, Parties, and Policy*. New York, NY: Holt, Rinehart, and Winston.

Neustadt, Richard. 1976. *Presidential Power*. New York, NY: John Wiley and Sons.

Olson, David. 1985. Success and Content in Presidential Roll Calls: The First Years of the Reagan Administration. *Presidential Studies Quarterly*, 15, 3:602–10.

Orfield, Gary. 1975. *Congressional Power: Congress and Social Change*. New York, NY: Harcourt, Brace, Jovanovich.

Peirce, Neal. 1972. *Megastates of America*. New York, NY: Norton.

Polsby, Nelson. 1978. Presidential Cabinet Making. *Political Science Quarterly*, 93 (Spring).

Prescott, Frank. 1950. The Executive Veto in American States. *Western Political Quarterly*, 3, 1: 97–111.

Qualls, James. 1977. Typological Analysis of Political Leaders. *American Political Science Review*, 71, 1:182–211.

Ransone, Coleman. 1982. *The American Governorship.* Westport, CT: Greenwood Press.

Rich, Bennett. 1960. *State Constitutions.* New York, NY: National Municipal League.

Ripley, Randall, and Grace Franklin. 1980. *Congress, the Bureaucracy, and Public Policy.* Homewood, Il: Dorsey Press.

Rockman, Bert. 1984. Legislative-Executive Relations and Legislative Oversight. *Legislative Studies Quarterly*, 9, 3:387–440.

Rose, Richard. 1980. Governments Against Sub-governments. In Richard Rose and Ezra Suleiman, eds, *Presidents and Prime Ministers.* Washington, DC: American Enterprise Institute.

Sabato, Larry. 1983. *Goodbye to Goodtime Charlie.* Washington, DC: CQ Press.

Schlesinger, Arthur. 1974. *The Imperial Presidency.* New York, NY: Popular Library.

Schlesinger, Joseph. 1965. The Politics of the Executive. In Herbert Jacob and Kenneth Vines, eds, *Politics in the American States.* Boston, MA: Little, Brown and Company.

Schlesinger, Joseph. 1966. *Ambition and Politics.* Chicago, Il: Rand McNally.

Sharkansky, Ira. 1968. Agency Requests, Gubernatorial Support and Budget Success in State Legislatures. *American Political Science Review*, 62, 4:1220–31.

Sigelman, Lee, and Nelson Dometrius. 1988. Governors as Chief Administrators. *American Politics Quarterly*, 16, 2:157–70.

Sprengel, Donald. 1969. *Gubernatorial Staffs: Functional and Political Profiles.* Iowa City, IA: Institute of Public Affairs.

Turnbull, Augustus. 1969. Budget-Making in Georgia and Wisconsin. *Midwest Journal of Political Science*, 14, 4:631–45.

Wanat, John. 1974. Bases of Budgetary Incrementalism. *American Political Science Review*, 68, 3:1221–28.

Wayne, Steven, Richard Cole, and James Hyde. 1979. Advising the President on Enrolled Legislation. *Political Science Quarterly*, 94, 2:303–18.

Weeks, G. 1981. Statehouse Hall of Fame. Paper presented at the annual meeting of the Southern Political Science Association.

Weinbaum, Marvin, and Dennis Judd. 1970. In Search of the Mandated Congress. *Midwest Journal of Political Science*, 14, 2:276–302.

Weinberg, Martha. 1977. *Managing the State.* Cambridge, MA: MIT Press.

Wiggins, Charles. 1980. Executive Vetoes and Legislative Overrides in the American States. *Journal of Politics*, 42, 4:1110–17.

Williams, Charles. 1980. The Gatekeeper Function of the Governor's Staff. *Western Political Quarterly*, 33, 1:87–93.

Wright, Deil. 1967. Executive Leadership in State Administration. *Midwest Journal of Political Science*, 11, 1.

Wyner, Allen. 1968. Gubernatorial Relations with Legislators and Administrators. *State Government*, 41: 199–203.

_____. 1972. Staffing the Governor's Office. In Thad Beyle and J. Oliver Williams, eds. *The American Governor in Behavioral Perspective.* New York, NY: Harper and Row.

Young, William. 1958. The Development of the Governorship. *State Government*, 31: 178–83.

2 Policy Agendas and Gubernatorial Leadership

Eric B. Herzik

Every citizen is affected by the policy decisions of state government. As a group, state governments develop and implement a wider range of policies than the national government. State governments are most active in providing basic services, especially such items as education, highways, healthcare, and welfare. The policy role of state government has also expanded over time to meet new social needs and demands in areas such as environmental protection and consumer protection. In addition, state governments play a central role in coordinating the delivery of federal and local government policies and services. Thus, the quality of life enjoyed, and indeed expected, by most Americans is in large part a function of state government policy.

The sources of state policy initiatives and centers of decisionmaking are diverse. Yet the central figure in each state's political and governmental hierarchy is the governor. The role and importance of the governor in the state policy process is best summarized by Terry Sanford:

The governor, by his very office embodies his state. He stands alone at his inauguration as the spokesman for all the people. . . . He must, like the President of the United States, energize his administration, search out the experts, formulate the programs, mobilize the support, and carry new ideas into action. . . . Few major undertakings ever get off the ground without his support and leadership. The governor sets the agenda for public debate; frames the issues; decides on the timing; and can blanket the state with good ideas by using his access to the mass media. . . . The governor is the most potent political power in the state (1967: 185–88).

The governor's role in developing state policy has, if anything, increased in importance since Sanford's observation of the late 1960s.

Changes resulting from the Reagan era's New Federalism have expanded state policy efforts and responsibilities. State governments now have more administrative flexibility for tailoring programs, although they are also faced with greater financial burdens with the lessening of federal grants-in-aid. This combination has led to a number of state initiated policy innovations: innovations often emanating from the governor's office.

Governors are aided in coping with their expanded policy role by several recent developments involving state administration. Gubernatorial staff have been expanded and the ability of governors to better oversee executive branch administrative operations improved (Beyle, 1990). The formal powers of governors have been upgraded across the states to the point where little variation exists between so-called strong and weak governor states (Dometrius, 1988). Indeed, the general trend of professionalizing state executive, administrative, and legislative operations serves to strengthen the ability of governors to successfully develop, present, and implement state policy.

While the policymaking role and tools of gubernatorial leadership have expanded, there are still important constraints on governors in the state policymaking process. Formal powers, even as strengthened during the past twenty years, have distinct limitations in dealing with the multiple independent sources of executive decisionmaking still found in most states. Federal aid cutbacks may promote innovative behavior, but dollars lost must still be covered and state services often suffer in the competition for scarce resources. Broader political trends and internal state policy needs also work to shape gubernatorial policy agendas. Thus, governors may be cognizant of state policy shortcomings needing attention or have individual policies they would prefer to pursue. However, such needed or preferred policy courses may be at odds with prevailing state politics or prevailing issue-attention cycles (Herzik, 1983; Herzik, Brown, and Mushkatel, 1989).

This chapter addresses various aspects of the policymaking role of governors, in particular, the analysis centers on how gubernatorial policy agendas are shaped and how policy priorities evolve over time. The chapter is divided into three sections, beginning with a discussion of the political and structural context of gubernatorial policymaking. The second section examines how gubernatorial policy priorities develop and illustrates a basic patterning and typology in gubernatorial policymaking. The chapter concludes by considering the future role of governors in guiding state policy.

THE CONTEXT OF GUBERNATORIAL POLICYMAKING

Governors are the most central and visible individual actors influencing state policy. However, gubernatorial influence on state policy unfolds within the larger political and structural environment surrounding state policymaking. Thus, gubernatorial policymaking is dependent on several factors, many over which governors have little direct control. Based on prior research, the primary factors affecting gubernatorial influence over state policymaking include the formal and informal powers each governor possesses, partisan organization of the legislature, the fragmentation of state government policymaking and administration, intergovernmental relations, and personal interest (Gross, 1989).

Formal gubernatorial powers have long served as the basic measures of gubernatorial influence in state policy research. However, despite the intuitive idea that such formal powers should enhance gubernatorial influence, most research suggests they have little effect on policy (Dye, 1969; Lester, 1980) or the ability of governors to control state policy administration (Hebert, Brudney, and Wright, 1983; Abney and Lauth, 1983; Haas and Wright, 1989).

Yet abandoning the idea that formal powers play a role in strengthening gubernatorial influence over state policy is premature. Some modest effects are attached to gubernatorial budgetary powers (Sharkansky, 1969; Hedge, 1983). More importantly, formal powers appear to have policy significance when conceptualized as mediating or interactive (Morgan and Brudney, 1984; Sigelman and Dometrius, 1988). As Sigelman and Dometrius argue, "[F]ormal powers give a governor the *opportunity* to wield influence, but that opportunity is likely to become *reality* only under certain conditions" (1988: 159, emphasis in the original). Sigelman and Dometrius then demonstrate that formal powers are potentially potent policy tools when combined with key informal political resources, most notably the electoral mandate enjoyed by the governor and the size of the same party representation in the state legislature.

The strength, ideological cohesion, and structure of state parties and legislatures are thus other factors that complicate gubernatorial policymaking efforts. Governors almost by default become party leaders (Morehouse, 1976). The singular nature of the governorship and the partisan organization of most state legislatures provide governors an ideal opportunity to marshall partisan and legislative support for executive policy efforts. However, the ability to marshall such support is not a function of formal powers and executive command. Instead, governors must recognize the independence, differing goals, and needs of party and legislature in developing state policy.

The coordination of such differing goals and needs is made more difficult to the degree the governor, legislature, and state parties are separately controlled or ideologically factionalized. Governors often face the situation where one or both of the legislative houses are controlled by another party. This "perversion of separation of powers" (Key, 1956: 52) allows partisan differences to blend with constitutional differences and can create a type of policy gridlock. However, ideological factions that splinter a majority party's control can be equally debilitating to gubernatorial policy efforts. Michael Dukakis found himself under greatest fire from his own party members in Massachusetts and was denied renomination as the party's standard bearer after his first term (Beyle, 1983a). In a more extreme case, Arizona's Evan Mecham so totally alienated himself from the mainstream of the Arizona legislature that he was impeached and convicted by a majority vote of fellow Republican legislators (Herzik, Brown, and Mushkatel, 1989).

The fragmentation of state government administration is another factor that generally constrains gubernatorial policymaking efforts. Governors, while nominally labelled chief executives, must interact with a variety of independent sources of state policymaking authority. Beyond the basic separation of powers (legislative, judicial, and executive), states empower differing numbers of separately elected executive officials and administrative boards. The governor may influence such independent actors to some extent through formal budget, veto, and appointment powers, but the ability to simply command action is generally denied either by statute or constitutional provisions. Just as with governors facing separately controlled legislatures, policy leadership must involve large measures of compromise and consultation with independent sources of state administrative power or face policymaking paralysis.

The gubernatorial policymaking role is not constrained solely by factors internal to individual states. State policies are often intertwined with national and local efforts. Federal grant-in-aid monies may encourage development of particular policy initiatives, and congressional mandates often force states to divert resources to achieve legal compliance. Changes in the structure of program funding and administration also alter state policy efforts. The "devolution" of administrative responsibility (without corresponding funding) during the Reagan era's New Federalism often forced governors to develop innovative policy responses (Schneider, 1989). Pressing local government needs also draw attention and policy response from governors. For example, recognizing a continuing problem with educational quality that exceeds local government revenue and legal capacities, governors have become increasingly involved with expanding state policies for educational assistance (Herzik, 1988; Florestano and Boyd, 1989). Regardless of the specific substance of federal policy changes or local government needs, intergovernmental relations will continue to influence the gubernatorial policymaking role.

In addition to structural and political factors shaping state policy agendas, every governor brings specific policy goals to the statehouse. North Carolina's Terry Sanford made primary education the centerpiece of his administration in the early 1960s, pursuing added taxes for proposed improvements. In California, Ronald Reagan targeted and achieved welfare reform. Michael Dukakis focused particular efforts on healthcare financing in Massachusetts. Yet even these personal policy goals are tempered by political realities and ongoing state needs.

The foregoing analysis indicates gubernatorial influence on state policy flows from, and is constrained by, numerous factors. Despite a seemingly extensive supply of formal powers, governors can rarely command or totally redirect policy in the complex political environment of state government. Accordingly, gubernatorial leadership appears to largely mirror Neustadt's aphorism describing presidential power based on the power to persuade. Indeed, this more limited view of gubernatorial leadership is recognized by most governors. As Beyle summarizes a series of interviews with former governors, "[M]ost saw their role as an issue catalyst, picking the issue up from the public, focusing it, and seeking to take action on it" (1983a: 205). It is to how and why particular types of issues are picked up and catalyzed as part of the governor's policy agenda that we now turn.

DEVELOPING POLICY PRIORITIES

Despite the constraints noted above, governors can have a real impact in formulating the course of governmental action. Dye (1981) notes that public expectations of the governor as both political leader and administrator are exceeded only by expectations of the president. Francis and Weber (1980), noting the constancy of issue concerns for state legislatures, find that gubernatorial interest in specific issues is more variable and conclude that gubernatorial policy agendas are indicative of major trends and state problems. The primacy of gubernatorial leadership in setting state priorities is also acknowledged by governors themselves (NGA, 1978; 1981).

Prior research has employed several approaches for determining how gubernatorial issue agendas are fashioned. Numerous surveys of governors have been conducted (primarily through the National Governor's Association) asking governors what their concerns are at a specific point during their administrations (See: NGA 1983; Beyle, 1983a; Grady, 1989). Other analysts have examined those issues raised in gubernatorial campaigns (Tidmarch, Hyman, and Sorkin, 1984). However, political campaigns often generate "more heat than light," with an aim at the political consciousness of voters rather than the concerns governors may face as they lead state government. A third approach analyzes those issues governors raise in their major address to their legislatures and citizens: the state-of-the-state address. As these addresses generally come at the outset of legislative sessions and contain specific policy and budgetary proposals the governor will pursue, they best approximate the governor's actual policy agenda.

The analysis for this chapter is thus based upon a content analysis of gubernatorial state-of-the-state addresses as summarized by *State Government News*. The specific methodology employed is discussed in prior works of the author (See: Herzik, 1983; 1988). In essence, the analysis excludes rhetorical appeals and codes only those items associated with specific legislative proposals or budgetary outlays. Building on previous research, content summaries are developed on a three-year cycle beginning with 1970. This sampling procedure ensures that all significant phases of gubernatorial terms (i.e., general election years, midterm election years, off-years) are analyzed. The three-year cycle also allows sufficient time for an issue to either develop-and-persist or disappear from gubernatorial agendas. This temporal nature of policy agendas is critical in developing any typology of issues and allows for a comparative analysis of state policy trends.

Table 2.1 lists the rank ordering of gubernatorial policy concerns for the seven time periods in the data cycle. The data are of interest for showing both variability in gubernatorial attention toward some policy areas and relative constancy in others. Following Francis and Weber (1980), governors are often the focal point for major policy themes that condition state policymaking during any given term or era. For example, environmental policy topped the list of gubernatorial concerns in 1970 but gradually fell away as attention shifted to tax cut initiatives and deteriorating economic conditions. As tax-cut fever subsided and state economies rebounded, the agendas during the 1980s see a return to more expansive policy initiatives (supported by tax increases) in the areas of child care, economic development, and, again, environment (largely through hazardous waste and water quality acts). Gubernatorial policy agendas are also highlighted by the constancy of policy attention directed to key state services such as highways, education, and healthcare. These key state service responsibilities reflect the administrative role every governor plays in providing policy leadership.

The variation and change of gubernatorial policy agendas have been analyzed previously and a typology of issues found in gubernatorial agendas developed (Herzik, 1983; Beyle 1990). Three distinct issue types are identified. Every governor must deal with "perennial" issues concerning delivery of traditional state services. These perennial policy concerns are distinguished by the consistent ranking of particular policy areas in nearly every year of the sample. The most notable representatives of this policy type are education, highways, corrections, healthcare, law enforcement, and welfare.

It is hardly surprising that these policy areas receive such constant attention from governors. The six policy areas listed earlier account for nearly 75 percent of average state expenditures. There is also broad consensus on the legitimacy of state effort in promoting these policy areas. Crises in funding or quality in any of these services will force a governor to devote time and resources in developing corrective policy action as so much of state's population, economic well-being, and quality of life is tied directly to the adequate and efficient delivery of these services.

A second set of policies found on gubernatorial agendas are labelled "cyclical." Cyclical policies are those in which interest grows, peaks, and then declines. They are indicative of broad political themes that shape politics and policymaking. Governors must fashion policy initiatives to both capture the political sentiment embodied in these items and are forced to modify other policies in line with them. The ebb-and-flow of "tax-cut fever" during the 1970s best illustrates the cyclical issue. While governors in the 1960s could often propose tax increases to expand and improve state services, their counterparts in the 1970s had to develop policies in response to tax cut initiatives. Significantly, the cyclical nature of an item such as taxes is evident by the cautious move by many governors in the 1980s to once again pursue policies of limited tax increases for state services. Unfortunately for state finances, the cycle in federal grants-in-aid to states is reversing itself from higher levels of the 1960s and 1970s. Thus, cyclical issues often incorporate the effects of intergovernmental policy actions (both from the federal government and in other states) as yet another constraint on gubernatorial policy leadership.

Other cyclical policy concerns are environmental policy, economic development, consumer protection, and government reorganization/efficiency. Environmental policy shows a clear ebb-and-flow during the time period, peaking in the early 1970s, dropping off in the later 1970s and

Table 2.1
Gubernatorial Issue Agendas: 1970–1988 (By Rank, Percent Governors Mentioning)

1970		1973		1976		1979	
Environment	65.2	Tax Relief	73.2	Tax Relief	61.5	Tax Relief	61.5
Tax Increases	52.1	Property	66.6	Property	46.0	Property	40.0
Education Aid	47.8	Income	8.6	Income	15.3	Income	32.5
Government Reorg.	39.1	Education Aid	46.6	Sales	7.6	Sales	20.0
Health Care	30.4	Environment	35.5	Education Aid	38.0	Education Aid	55.0
Drug Control	26.0	Gov't. Reorg.	33.3	Law Enforce.	38.0	Energy Dev.	30.0
Drunk Driving	26.0	Consumer Aff.	31.1	Energy Dev.	23.0	Aid to Elderly	27.5
Mass Transit	26.0	Mass Transit	26.2	Consumer Aff.	20.5	Health Care	25.0
Highways	26.0	Tax Revisions	26.2	Corrections	17.9	Economic Dev.	25.0
Law Enforcement	21.7	Mental Health	24.4	Health Care	17.9	Environment	20.0
Corrections	21.7	Highways	24.4	Highways	15.3	Corrections	20.0
Local Gov't. Aid	21.7	Corrections	24.4	Mass Transit	15.3	Law Enforce.	17.5
Consumer Affairs	21.7	Health Care	22.2	Economic Dev.	15.3	Budget Reform	17.5
Government Ethics	13.0	Tax Increases	20.0	Elect. Law Ref.	17.5	Utility Relief	17.5
Welfare Services	13.0	Unemployment	20.0	Gov't. Reorg.	15.3	Unemployment	15.0
		Court Reform	20.0	State Employee		"Sunset Laws"	15.0
		Restore Death		Reduction	15.3	Elect. Law Ref.	15.0
		Penalty	15.5	Environment	15.3	Local Gvt. Aid	12.5
		Welfare		Medical		Legalized	
		Services	15.5	Malpractice	12.8	Gambling	12.0
				Unemployment	10.2	Welfare	10.0
				Welfare			
				Services	10.2		
				Aid to Elderly	10.2		
N = 23		N = 45		N = 39		N = 40	

Employee Pay Hikes	32.5
Education Aid	30.2
Corrections	30.2
Sentencing Reforms	27.9
Highways	25.5
Tax Reforms	25.5
Tax Incentives for Bus.	23.3
Local Government Aid	23.3
Government Hiring/ Spending Freeze	20.9
Increased Fuel/Oil Taxes	20.9
Increased Teachers Sal.	20.9
Funds for Higher Educa.	18.6
Increased "Sin" Taxes	16.2
Environment	16.2
Drug Crackdown	16.2
Medicaid	16.2
Job Training	13.9
Drunk Driving	13.9
Off-set Lost Fed. Funds	13.9
"High Tech" Training	11.6
Housing	11.6
Welfare/Human Services	11.6
Vocational Education	11.6
Ethics Bill	11.6

N = 43

Education Aid	73.5
Groundwater Protection	44.1
Economic Development	38.2
Child Protection Laws	32.3
Hazardous Wastes	32.3
Tax Reform	26.2
Government Reorg.	26.4
Highways	26.4
Sales Tax Increase	23.5
Corrections	23.5
Health Care	17.6
Employee Hike	17.6
Income Tax Cut	17.6
Human Services	17.6
Job Training	17.6
Alternatives to Prison	17.6
Local Government Aid	14.7
Soil Erosion	14.7
Solid Waste	14.7
Agricultural Aid	14.7
Drunk Driving	14.7
Raise Drinking Age	14.7
Housing	11.7
Parks	11.7

N = 34

Education Aid	53.6
Education Reforms	41.4
Economic Development	39.0
Govt. Productivity	31.7
Job Training	29.2
Highways	26.8
Environment	26.8
Rural Assistance	21.9
Capital Improvements	21.9
Asst. "Children at Risk"	21.9
Child Health Problems	19.5
Funding for Child Care	17.0
International Trade	17.0
Maintain Bal. Budget	17.0
Corrections	14.6
Housing	14.6
Health Care	14.6
Human Services	12.1
Growth Management	12.1
Drug & Alcohol Abuse	12.1

N = 41

early 1980s, and returning to salience in the mid-1980s. Government reorganization, a rallying cry of efficiency minded governors in the 1960s returns with the call for efficiency, productivity, and reorganization efforts in the 1980s. Economic development is listed as a cyclical issue as governors appear to be using economic development policies as part of a broader political effort to reorganize and redirect a whole host of state policies. For example, many perennial policy concerns such as education (creation of high-tech centers, skill training) and highways (linked to industry attraction) are currently being fashioned to buttress state economic development efforts. This is a change from more traditional Department of Commerce efforts where economic development stood as an equal, but not driving force, of other state policies.

Finally, governors may confront "transitory" issues: items that generally appear suddenly to be dealt with in an almost yes–no policy manner. Transitory issues, while by definition short-lived, can be emotionally charged and have polarizing political effects. As Beyle notes, "[S]everal governors have been hurt in the public opinion polls....and by voters in the polling booth" for perceived mistakes in developing or implementing policy responses to such issues (1983a: 205). Over time such issues have included controversies concerning the death penalty, Cuban immigrants, the drinking age, and most recently, drug testing and AIDS. A suggestive listing of policies using this typology is presented in table 2.2

PROSPECTS FOR GUBERNATORIAL POLICY LEADERSHIP

In examining gubernatorial roles in both the 1950s and 1970s, Coleman Ransone noted that "policy formation was the most significant" of a governor's duties (1982: xv). The quote from Terry Sanford at the beginning of this chapter adds to Ransone's observation by focusing on how the governor embodies the needs and aspirations of the state. The analysis of gubernatorial policy agendas presented earlier is further evidence that the governor's policymaking role covers the whole range of state needs and politics.

The sources of state policy initiatives are diverse. However, the governor's role in forming a policy agenda can be synthesized from the elements of the typology I have presented. The governor's policy agenda is a blend of perennial state needs, framed by larger political trends and cycles, and augmented by transitory items that either flow from spikes in public interest, external events, or particularized gubernatorial goals. Thus, governors are not entirely free to choose their policy agenda

Table 2.2
Gubernatorial Issue Types (Percent of Governors Presenting Issue in State-of-State Address)

	1970	1973	1976	1979	1982	1985	1988
N =	23	45	39	40	43	34	41
Perennial Issues							
Education	47.8	46.6	38.0	55.0	30.2	73.5	53.6
Highways	26.0	24.4	15.3	0.0	25.5	26.4	26.8
Corrections	21.7	24.4	17.9	20.0	30.2	23.5	14.6
Health Care	30.4	22.2	17.9	25.0	16.2	17.6	14.6
Welfare/Human Services	21.7	15.5	10.2	10.0	11.6	17.6	12.1
Cyclical Issues							
Tax Increases	52.1	20.0	15.3	0.0	30.2	14.7	4.8
Tax Relief	0.0	73.3	61.5	75.0	16.2	17.6	9.7
Gov't Reorganization/Productivity	39.1	33.3	15.3	7.5	0.0	26.4	31.7
Environmental	65.2	35.5	15.3	25.0	16.2	55.8	39.0
Energy Development	0.0	0.0	23.0	30.0	4.6	8.8	0.0
Economic Development	0.0	0.0	15.3	25.0	23.3	38.2	39.0
Consumer Protection	21.7	31.1	20.5	0.0	0.0	0.0	0.0
Temporal Issues							
Restoration of Death Penalty	0.0	15.5	0.0	0.0	0.0	5.8	0.0
Election Law Reform	0.0	0.0	15.3	15.0	0.0	8.8	0.0
Government Ethics	0.0	0.0	0.0	0.0	11.6	0.0	0.0
Raise Drinking Age	0.0	0.0	0.0	0.0	6.9	14.7	0.0
AIDS	0.0	0.0	0.0	0.0	0.0	0.0	7.3

divorced from such a mix of perennial, cyclical, and transitory concerns. In addition, the gubernatorial policy role must recognize and work with the constraints imposed on the incumbent by factors of state politics, structure, and administration.

There is no single course by which issues get translated into policies on the gubernatorial agenda. As the constraints noted previously indicate, governors are often forced to react to ongoing situational needs, limitations on their powers, and broader political trends that accent any policy initiative. Because there is such a complex mix of factors influencing gubernatorial policymaking, simply strengthening the formal powers of governors or streamlining state government administration will not result in singularly powerful or more effective gubernatorial policymaking. A formally powerful governor, devoid of political sensitivity, will fail as surely as a weak governor in promoting policies.

The policy role of governors thus includes a variety of perspectives. At times the governor must serve as catalyst, translating inchoate public needs and demands into workable policies. In other circumstances, governors must work to educate both the public and fellow state leaders as to true state needs and interests. As federal involvement with and financing of state policy efforts recedes, at least in the short term, governors will play an increasing role in identifying policy needs and formulating viable policy options. The immediate prospect for governors as policymakers, therefore, might thus be summarized as involving a little more of "more of the same."

REFERENCES

Abney, Glenn, and Thomas P. Lauth. 1983. The Governor as Chief Administrator. *Public Administration Review*, 43, 1:40–49.

Beyle, Thad L. 1983a. Governors. In Gray, Jacob, and Vines, eds. *Politics in the American States*, 4th ed. Boston: Little, Brown.

_____. 1983b. Issues Facing the States and Governors, 1982. *State Government*, 56, 2:65–69.

_____. 1990. Governors. In Gray, Jacob, and Albritton, eds. *Politics in the American States*, 5th ed. Glenview, IL: Scott Foresman.

Dometrius, Nelson. 1988. Measuring Gubernatorial Power: The Measure vs. the Reality. *Western Political Quarterly*, 40:319–34.

Dye, Thomas. 1969. Executive Power and Public Policy in the States. *Western Political Quarterly*, 27, 4:926–39.

_____. 1981. *Politics in States and Communities*, 4th ed. Englewood Cliffs, NJ: Prentice-Hall.

Florestano, Patricia, and Laslo Boyd. 1989. Governors and Higher Education. *Policy Studies Journal*, 17, 4:863–78.

Francis, Wayne, and Ronald Weber. 1980. Legislative Issues in the 50 States. *Legislative Studies Quarterly*, 5, 3.

Grady, Dennis. 1989. Governors and Economic Development Policy. *Policy Studies Journal*, 17, 4:879–94.

Gross, Donald. 1989. Governors and Policymaking. *Policy Studies Journal*, 17, 4:764–87.

Haas, Peter, and Deil S. Wright. 1989. Public Policy and Administrative Turnover in State Government: The Role of the Governor. *Policy Studies Journal*, 17, 4:788–803.

Hebert, F. Ted, Jeffrey Brudney, and Deil S. Wright. 1983. Gubernatorial Influence and State Bureaucracy. *American Politics Quarterly*, 11:243–64.

Hedge, David. 1983. Fiscal Dependency and the State Budget Process. *Journal of Politics*, 45, 1:198–208.

Herzik, Eric B. 1983. Governors and Issues: A Typology of Concerns. *State Government* 56, 2: 58–64.

_____. 1988. The Expanding Gubernatorial Role in Education Policymaking. In Samuel Gove and Thad L. Beyle, eds. *Governors and Higher Education*. Denver, CO: Education Commission of the States.

Herzik, Eric B., Brent W. Brown, and Alvin H. Mushkatel. 1989. Policymaking Under Duress. *Policy Studies Journal*, 17, 4:927–40.

Key, V. O. 1956. *American State Politics*. New York: Knopf.

Lester, James. 1980. Partisanship and Environmental Policy: The Mediating Influence of State Organizational Structures. *Environment and Behavior*, 12:101–31.

Morehouse, Sarah. 1976. The Governor as Political Leader. In Jacob and Vines, eds. *Politics in the American States*, 3rd ed. Boston: Little, Brown.

Morgan, David and Jeffrey Brudney. 1984. The Mediating Effect of Gubernatorial Power on State Policies. Paper presented to the Annual Meeting of the Midwest Political Science Association, April 12–14, Chicago, IL.

National Governors' Association. 1978. *Governing the American States*. Washington, DC: NGA.

_____. 1981. *Reflections on Being Governor*. Washington, DC: NGA.

_____. 1983. *Governors' Priorities: 1983*. Washington, DC: NGA.

Ransone, Coleman. 1982. *The American Governorship*. Westport, CT: Greenwood.

Sanford, Terry. 1967. *Storm Over the States*. New York: McGraw-Hill.

Schneider, Saundra. 1989. Governors and Health Care Policy in the American States. *Policy Studies Journal*, 17, 4:909–26.

Sharkansky, Ira. 1969. Agency Requests, Gubernatorial Support and Budget Success in State Legislatures. *American Political Science Review*, 62, 4:1220–31.

Sigelman, Lee, and Nelson Dometrius. 1988. Governors as Chief Administrators. *American Political Quarterly*, 16, 2: 157–70.

Tidmarch, Charles, Lisa J. Hyman, and Jill E. Sorkin. 1984. Press Issue Agendas in the 1982 Congressional and Gubernatorial Election Campaigns. *Journal of Politics*, 46, 4:1226–42.

3 Developing Executive Roles: Gubernatorial Concerns in the Transition Period

Mary D. Herzik, Eric B. Herzik, and James S. Granato

One of the hallmarks of American democratic process is the orderly transition of government. Except in rare instances such as death or impeachment, the tenure of elected officials is well established. But the importance of the transferring of power in American politics goes beyond rather nebulous concerns with system maintenance and governmental legitimacy. As Beyle and Williams note, it is during this crucial period that "new priorities are set and new personnel to run government are chosen, and when, in general, there is a change in the mood and tone of government, which makes new directions in policy and administration possible" (1972: 76).

To begin to sort out the process of gubernatorial role definition, a logical starting place is the period immediately following the election to the first few weeks in office. This is the "transition period," when the kaleidoscopic nature of the campaign challenge gives way to the demands and strains of actually running government. The focus of this chapter is on how governors handle key aspects of the transition to office. Unlike most previous research, however, we adopt a comparative approach utilizing a survey of former governors.

We divide our study into four parts. First is an assessment of current literature, focusing particularly on the uneven attention given to the wide range of concerns confronting governors as they organize their administrations. While much is written about staffing and policymaking, little is known about needs in the area of public relations, communications with various actors surrounding the governor's office, and the tremendous impact felt in the personal life of the new officeholder. Second is a discussion of our data and method. The third section presents our results.

The conclusion places our findings on the process of gubernatorial role definition within the more general context of the executive in American politics.

THE TRANSITION PERIOD

The process of role definition during the transition period has been examined, but largely in the context of case studies (Ahlberg and Moynihan, 1960; Allen, 1965; Schenker, 1969; Beyle and Wickman, 1970; Amalu, 1974). Long (1962) presents a more wide-ranging treatment depicting the general mood and nature of transitions. While rich in suggesting both problems and solutions inherent to the process, the Long piece is devoid of any empirical analysis. More recently, Beyle (1985) organized a series of case studies focusing on gubernatorial transitions following the 1982 elections. The authors included in the Beyle text do a commendable job weaving common themes through each state analysis.[1] Still, the single state case study approach dominates the study of the transition process, emphasizing particularized policy and personnel effects while only secondarily developing more generalized analysis.

Previous literature devotes considerable energy to four general concerns of transition: the development of the administration's mood or tone; staffing and organization; budgeting; and policymaking. The academic literature on transitions has been augmented by research from the National Governors' Association (NGA). NGA prepares two primary guides for new governors (NGA, 1978; 1982) and conducts a New Governors' Conference immediately following any given set of gubernatorial elections. Huefner and Nash (1984) note the NGA guidelines fall into four functional areas that mirror academic concerns: personnel; administrative organization; policy focus; and budget preparation.

Collectively, the conjunction of the academic and practitioner literature has developed fairly extensive analyses of some major concerns of governmental transition. This past research is largely task oriented, however. That is, the transition is generally analyzed as a series of challenges and chores that must be accomplished within a highly constrained time frame and particular political setting. Staffs must be appointed from a massive pool of applicants with an eye on balancing intrastate interests, political factions, personalities, and administrative needs. Budgets and policies are framed within the context of campaign promises and as legislatures are convening. On these points, past studies give us a rich sense of the overall process of the transition into the governor's office.

Beyond these functionally related concerns, there are aspects of the transition process that have been largely ignored by past research. The linkage between the campaign and the transition period needs to be further developed. This can have particular influence in setting the mood or tone of the new administration. Past studies have generally suggested that the governor-elect must quickly change course from campaigning to administering government. However, to consolidate recently won support, might not the transition period be a time of gradual rather than abrupt change? Rather than distinct elements, the campaign-transition-administrative tenure may be best viewed as an organic process, with each period growing from and building upon its predecessor.

Almost completely ignored in past analyses is the tremendous change in the personal life of the new governor and his family. While studies of the transition focus upon structural and political issues, only Long hints at the effects felt by the first family. "Among the many new trials the chief executive and his family must face, few are more difficult than those occasioned by the friction between palace and executive office" (1962: 196).

This suggests that more systematic attention to the personal dimension in executive politics may be warranted. Beyle (1979) has discussed the pressures felt by governors during the course of their tenures to a limited extent. The issue is not without implications, as Bernick and Wiggins (1978) and Blair and Henry (1981) find personal considerations a primary cause in state legislature turnover. An unsuccessful transition in the personal life of a governor may itself lead to problems of equal magnitude (although probably less obvious to outside observers) to those generally identified by political analysts.

Generally missing in past studies is also consideration of broader criteria for evaluating the transition process. This, in part, reflects limitations of the case study approach. Little comparative study of transitions is to be found. A more systemic comparative focus would allow us to address questions germane to all new governors. For example, what constitutes a "good" or "bad" appointment? Specifically, should campaign staffers readily move to administrative positions? With respect to organization, how should the new governor communicate with his or her staff—how frequently and how formally? Can the governor-elect in some way get a jump on developing a policy agenda?

It is to the development of a more specific understanding of transition period concerns that we now turn. Where in the past, analyses focused on a single state or case-type, we utilize a survey of former governors. This approach shifts the unit of analysis from the state to the governor and allows for a more comparative and theoretical assessment of the transition process.

DATA AND METHOD

The data for this study are derived from the results of a mail survey questionnaire sent to fifty-nine former governors. The survey was conducted by the Center for Policy Research of the National Governors' Association in 1982. From the fifty-nine governors polled, fifty-three returned useable survey data and are included in this study.[2] Our research utilizes that part of the survey that asked the former governors to rate advice given to new governors specifically concerning the transition period. The questionnaire consisted of 12 Likert-type (5-point agreement scale) questions, reflecting a diverse set of guidelines for new governors from "hire a good speechwriter" to "keep an open door policy for legislators" (Appendix 1).[3]

We believe this survey data set offers a number of advantages for studying the transition process. First, it offers a comparative perspective on the topic. The fifty-three governors in our sample served in thirty states, are drawn from both political parties (thirty Democrats, twenty-three Republicans), and represent tenures from three different decades (1950s, 1960s and 1970s). This diversity allows us to draw more general conclusions about the importance of various aspects of the transition process. A second advantage is that we can also test for any bias in the views of the former governors by party, era served, circumstances of exit from office, or length of tenure. A third advantage is the perspective the former governors offer. Past studies of transitions have focused upon the direct experience of new administrations, often as they are sorting out the process. Ironically, the new officeholders may be the worst source of information for determining what is important for a successful transition. The former governors, by contrast, are able to offer their advice from a position of experience and reflection. Finally, by asking for advice on particular aspects of the process, we can match the "advised method" with actual behavior of new administrations.

Our research is contained in three primary steps. We begin with a rank ordering of the data. The questions of the survey provide a range of alternatives that past governors feel may be of importance for new governors. The rank ordering, therefore, gives us a preliminary guide to the relative importance of these several items.

The second part of the analysis tests for variations in the rank ordering in light of selected controls. Differences in what is perceived to be important in the transition to office may follow party lines, length of tenure, or other circumstances faced by the former governors of our sample. For example, emphasis on media relations may be less important in the responses of governors who served in the 1950s and 1960s. Similarly, Republican governors, often representing minority parties, may highlight the importance of legislative relations and media use more than their Democratic counterparts. These types of distinctions have never been analyzed in previous works on the transition process.

Thirdly, we probe for further patterns that may exist in our data. If the survey responses are viewed as a range of alternatives available for new governors, then within this range certain patterns of communication or linkages might develop. Former governors may highlight not only specific items of advice, but also whole packages of interrelated topics. This suggests that during the transition governors should work to develop certain role structures. For example, a staff and organization role may coalesce around responses to questions 6, 7, and 8. Similarly, the former governors may highlight a communications role centering on the governor's relationship to the press (questions 1, 5, and 10), legislators (question 9), and the public (question 12). (See Appendix 1 for question content and numbering.)

To accurately portray these relationships, we perform a cluster analysis. This procedure identifies clusters of variables based on a measure of association or similarity between the variables linked to a measure of distance separating the variables (Johnson, 1967; Hartigan, 1975).[4] The advantage of this technique is two-fold. First, it allows us to go beyond simple rank ordering and produce complex factorings of the data. Second, these clusters provide an insight into the interrelationships between the specific pieces of advice offered new governors and their broader theoretical meaning. Thus the clusters may indicate principal components of various roles and concerns that are addressed during the transition period.

ANALYSIS

Several primary concerns for governors during the transition period have been identified. Surveying former governors, we would expect them to highlight staffing, organization, and policy formation. In addition, the survey data include responses to items of press and public relations, as well as selected personal concerns. It is hypothesized that these more diffuse elements should fall below the more specific bureaucratic and policy items, particularly given their lack of attention in the literature.

The results of a simple rank ordering of responses only partly confirm this hypothesis (table 3.1). The ranking based only upon "strongly agree" responses shows a large majority of governors believe that an "open door for legislators" is something that cannot be ignored. This may be interpreted as a traditional policy item, but it is followed by a personal concern for new governors: advice against taking a vacation. The next three items reflect traditional staff and organization concerns, although the advice to "hire a good speechwriter" suggests the importance of maintaining a salient public profile. This public relations role is seen in the next item: have an "advertised/managed process of citizen contact."

When the responses "strongly agree" and "agree" are merged, the ranking of concerns changes only slightly. The dominant concern still centers on interaction with the legislature. Regular meetings with department heads is viewed as slightly more important than regular meetings with staff. The public relations role of citizen contact is recognized by nearly three-fourths of the respondents. Also receiving acknowledgement from a majority of governors is the need to "separate personal from professional life."

The simple ranking of concerns also contains some very specific pieces of advice for new governors. The former governors, while acknowledging the need for a managed process of citizen contact, are less certain about how interactions with the press should be handled. We record a nearly even split on whether there should be regular press conferences or an "open door" for the press.

Other specific advice for the new administration centers on staffing. Many have noted the problems of changing over from campaign to administration (Ahlberg and Moynihan, 1960; Long, 1962; Neustadt, 1983). Loyal campaign workers may be expecting some personal payoff for their efforts, particularly in the form of governmental appointment. This, our respondents suggest, is not the best course to follow. Only 21 percent believe campaign staff should be used in the governor's office. This perhaps reflects the different skills needed for the two types of jobs, skills that any one individual may not possess. Unfortunately, this may be easier advice to give than to follow. Thus, the traditional concerns of transition—staffing, organization, and policy—all appear, but so do other less mentioned items—personal life changes and public relations. The responses from former governors provide a more varied view of the transition process. We believe it is significant that these former governors so strongly highlight the need for maintaining a high public profile. The implication is that the newly won popular support should be consolidated. This links logically to Bernick's (1979) finding that popular support is a

Table 3.1
Rank Order of Transition Concerns (Percentage of Governors)

	Strongly Agree (Only)	Agree and Strongly Agree
Keep an Open Door for Legislators	.64	.96
No Vacation in First Six Months	.40	.83
Hire a Good Speech Writer	.40	.75
Hold Regular Meetings with Staff	.36	.70
Hold Regular Meetings with Dept. Heads	.34	.77
Advertised/Managed Process of Citizen Contact	.30	.73
Separate Personal From Professional Life	.19	.40
No Regular Press Conferences	.19	.60
Use Memos/Letters not Meetings	.11	.41
No Open Door for the Press	.08	.43
Press Secretary from Statehouse Press Corps	.02	.21
Use Campaign Staff for Governor's Office	.02	.21

potent gubernatorial tool. Riding the crest of a popularity wave, new governors may find this makes it easier to accomplish their duties and should therefore seek to hold the ride for as long as possible.

The advice of the former governors is fairly consensual. However, the uniformity at the aggregate may be attenuated by specific contextual variables. Thus, seven control variables were applied to the gubernatorial responses. The variables tested are party affiliation, length of service, strength of formal powers, whether the former governor retired from office or was defeated, era of term, age of governor, and the partisan control of the legislature faced by the governor.[5] All of these variables have been shown to have some effect on aspects of gubernatorial performance, except the era of service. We have included this item for its possible linkage to media/communication issues in the governor's office.

While these control variables can be linked to specific hypotheses, we expect little variation from the general response pattern in table 3.1 as transition concerns are more or less the same for all governors. Testing for party differences is largely descriptive. As the aggregate, Democrat and Republican governors should view the duties and pressures of the transition similarly. Governors serving shorter terms should be less likely to stress media orientation and personal concerns, instead focusing on staffing and organizing to get a jump on the job. Defeated governors should stress communication items, feeling their message was never effectively articulated to the general public. Analysis of era of service might give us an insight as to how the increasing importance of the media and scope of the job have changed gubernatorial perspectives. We would expect, if a difference does exist, those serving in more recent years to highlight communications and the separation of the personal and professional aspects of the job. Strong formal powers allow governors more leeway in performing their jobs. Thus, a more individualistic response pattern might emerge from these governors as they organize the office to suit their particular goals and personalities. Age is included as it is the one personal characteristic linked to "superior" gubernatorial performance (Sigelman and Smith, 1981). Thus, we examine if younger governors perceive the concerns of the transition period differently from their counterparts. Finally, governors facing a legislature controlled by the opposite party might pursue any avenue of communication—with the legislature, press or public—to highlight and gain support for their programs. Conversely, governors with a legislature of the same party are in a more secure position and can focus more attention to details of staffing and organization.

Rank orderings of the gubernatorial response data were calculated for each control variable. These rank orderings were then correlated with the overall ranking percentages of table 3.1. As expected, little variation from the overall pattern is apparent (table 3.2). In twelve of seventeen cases, the correlations (Spearman Rho) are greater than .60. In only two cases are the correlations less than .40, and neither is statistically significant. In fact, both can be explained by exceedingly low Ns. There were just seven governors who served two years and four who served more than eight years.

Two variables had only moderate correlation with the overall ranking: strong formal powers and governors serving in the 1970s. (Both nearly significant at the 0.1 level.) Analysis of the individual item scores for governors in these two categories conforms with our hypotheses above.

Table 3.2
Intercorrelations of Transition Concerns by Selected Controls (Spearman Rho, Significance Level in Parenthesis)

Ranking of Transition Concerns by:	Transition Concerns (from Table 3.1)	
Democrats	.956	(.0001)
Republicans	.928	(.0001)
Retired from Office	.933	(.0001)
Defeated for Re-election	.677	(.134)
Strong Formal Powers	.420	(.173)
Weak Formal Powers	.582	(.046)
Two Years Service	.082	(.798)
Four Years Service	.947	(.0001)
Six to Eight Years Service	.957	(.0001)
More than Eight Years Service	.059	(.854)
Term in 1950s	.866	(.0003)
Term in 1960s	.952	(.0001)
Term in 1970s	.488	(.0002)
Age 45< Time of First Transition	.889	(.0002)
Age >45 Time of First Transition	.957	(.0001)
Legislature of Same Party	.726	(.003)
Divided Control	.701	(.011)

Governors with strong formal powers are more individualistic in their responses. Percentages for most advice items are lower than the overall ranking. Several items also move considerably in the ranking. An "advertised process of citizen contact" ranks second with these governors, while "regular meetings with staff" and "no press conferences" move down to the tenth and eleventh spots, respectively.

Also following our hypotheses, governors serving in the 1970s were more likely to stress items of communication, specifically the holding of regular press conferences and having an open door for the press. The advertised process of citizen contact is also the number two concern for these governors. Overall, however, there are no significant caveats to note when evaluating the advice given by the former governors grouped by these control variables concerning the transition period.

INTEGRATING TRANSITION ADVICE

The results of our rank orderings of the survey responses suggest a broader agenda of transition concerns than usually considered. Additionally, by focusing on the views of former governors rather than any particular transition, the concerns identified have a greater generalizability than many earlier studies. Still, our results, while suggestive of various roles, are confined to single items of advice for new governors to consider. What we pursue now is to link these individual items into more coherent clusters that truly represent general concerns or roles developing during the gubernatorial transition.

The results of our cluster analysis in large part confirm the roles we note earlier. Selecting a similarity value of 65 as a minimum measure of association, three clusters form (table 3.3). (A 65-cluster measure of association is equivalent to a .30 correlation.) A fairly strong cluster forms around the two primary organization variables: holding regular meetings with staff and department heads. This cluster conflates nicely with much of the literature focusing on this traditional concern of drawing the new administration together. The other two clusters, though, center on nontraditional roles. A public relations cluster forms on the variables: "have an advertised/managed process of citizen contact" and "hire a good speechwriter." A third cluster consists of the variables: "separate personal from professional life" and "do not attempt to keep an open door for the press." We label this cluster personal insulation, again noting the need for the new governor to accommodate the changes forthcoming in his or her personal and family life.

Dropping the minimum level of association to 60, two of the three clusters identified above add an additional variable. The organizational cluster picks up the "open door for legislators" variable. Not surprisingly, any new administration must incorporate these key actors of the policy process. Again, this is a primary role long identified in analyses of the transition period. A third variable is also added to the personal insulation cluster: "use memos/letters rather than meetings." This suggests that the governors' time and efforts may be best served by limiting personal contacts to matters of significance. A lesson to draw from this perhaps is that governors should not attempt to solve every problem or become involved in every decision personally.

The cluster results, while instructive, are not definitive. The association levels are, for the most part, relatively modest. In addition, some variables that should have clustered (i.e., the vacation variable on the personal insulation cluster) failed to do so. Still, the clusters do highlight the scope and complexity of the transition process, adding to the more particularized focus of most past analyses.

DISCUSSION

As we have noted throughout the chapter, our results are buttressed by the fact that they are based upon data drawn from governors who have experienced firsthand the transition to office. This makes the concern

Table 3.3
Cluster Analysis of Transition Concerns

Cluster Label and Variables	Association Measure	Equivalent Correlation
Organizational	75.09	.50
-Hold Regular Meetings with Staff		
-Hold Regular Meetings with Dept. Heads		
Public Relations	69.74	.40
-Advertised/Managed Process of Citizen Contact		
-Hire a Good Speech Writer		
Personal Insulation	65.42	.30
-Separate Personal from Professional Contacts		
-No Open Door for the Press		
Expanded Clustering		
Organizational	62.42	.25
-Hold Regular Meetings with Staff		
-Hold Regular Meetings with Dept. Heads		
-Keep Open Door for Legislators		
Personal Insulation	60.38	.20
-Separate Personal from Professional Contacts		
-No Open Door for the Press		
-Use Memos/Letters not Meetings		

with personal life changes noted in both the individual advice rankings and the cluster analysis more cogent. Suggested by Long (1962) as a part of the process that might merit study, our results indicate it may be of more importance than generally thought.

While traditional concerns with staffing, organization, and policy are apparent, our analysis also suggests that the transition period should not be a time to eschew politics. In particular, new governors should maintain a fairly high public profile. To become completely consumed in bureaucratic details risks weakening one of the most important tools a governor has—popular support. A traditional view that separates campaign from transition from administration may perhaps be supplanted by the view that all these processes are related. Indeed, the transition period may be viewed as a concluding phase of the campaign, when newly won support is consolidated.

In addition to these general concerns or roles of the transition, several more specific pieces of advice are offered by the former governors. Nearly all agree that a line of communication should be immediately established with the legislature. This reflects, following Ahlberg and Moynihan (1960), the general equality between the two branches. The use of campaign staff in filling key gubernatorial office positions should also be approached with caution. Again, though, this may be easier said than done. Finally, there is no agreement on how best to handle the press.[6] The observed division of opinion is far from surprising as this relationship has been problematic for executives since before the beginning of the republic.

CONCLUSION

The transition to office for a new governor is an odd mixture of formal and informal requirements, and bureaucratic and personal concerns. At one level, the new governor will gain the statutory responsibility for the job upon inauguration, but this captures only the most formal aspect of the process. Paraphrasing Henry (1961), the executive role is not a tangible thing that can be passed along intact from one individual to another. Rather, all new governors recreate the governorship in unique forms—starting with the materials at hand, but guided by their own concepts and limited by what events their own skills permit to make of the formal office.

Seen in this light, the transition period is that time when so many of the initial decisions that will ultimately shape an administration occur. It is the time when the new officeholder receives a crash course as to what the job of being governor entails and when the shape, style, and content of the administration begin to unfold. As such, the transition period is of importance lasting well beyond its temporal parameters. The initial decisions made during this period hold political ramifications that last throughout the governor's tenure. Indeed, success in ultimately framing and implementing policy agendas may rest upon the foundation set during the transition period. Failure to capture the public's attention or integrate the legislative branch may obscure gubernatorial policy initiatives. While each administration and, hence, each transition will be unique, there are elements similar to all transitions. In this analysis we have highlighted several general concerns that each new governor must in some way address. These concerns are as wide-ranging as the executive function itself, testing the political, administrative, and personal skills of the new governor.

NOTES

1. An introductory chapter by Beyle sets the context of gubernatorial transitions in 1982. The concluding chapter by Huefner and Nash synthesizes some of the themes identified in the individual state analyses. The forerunner of the Huefner and Nash chapter is discussed in the text.

2. The survey was mailed to all former governors believed to be alive in 1982. The 53 useable responses came from a mailing of 215 (.246%). This percentage is an underestimation, however, as some former governors had died and receipt of the survey by others was never verified even with subsequent follow-ups.

3. An open-ended question was also included, soliciting any advice not contained in the twelve specific questions of the survey. As only three governors responded, we have not included this in the analysis.

4. We utilize the BMDP Cluster Analysis of Variables program. The measure of similarity was specified as the value of the correlation. The linkage rule (the criterion for combining two variables) was specified as the average distance or similarity. For a complete description of output and documentation see Dixon (1981).

5. The variables are coded as follows. Party: Democrat/Republican. Electoral Status: Defeated in reelection bid/Retired from office. Formal Powers are calculated on the Schlesinger (1965) 20-point scale. As the Schlesinger scale is time-bound, separate scores were calculated for each governor. A governor was coded as having strong formal powers if he or she scored 12 or higher on the scale. Length of Service has four categories: those serving a total of two years, those serving four years, service of six to eight years, and more than eight years of service. Era of Service is coded by decade in which transition to office occurred. In six cases governors had transitions in two decades. In these cases we coded the decade in which the governor served longest. Age is dichotomous: those 45 or under and those over 45. The age break point is drawn from Sigelman and Smith (1981). The Partisanship of the Legislature is simply coded as being of the same party or opposite party (divided control) of the governor. Partisan control was coded for the legislature faced by the governor at the time of his or her transition to office.

6. Dealings with the press are highlighted in many of the individual case studies of gubernatorial transitions. Here, too, a variety of interpretations and prescriptions can be found. A more systematic analysis of media coverage of gubernatorial transitions is found in Savage and Blair (1985).

REFERENCES

Ahlberg, Clark D., and Daniel P. Moynihan. 1960. Changing Governors and Policies. *Public Administration Review*, 20 (Autumn): 195–205.

Allen, David J. 1965. *New Governor in Indiana: The Challenge of Executive Powers.* Bloomington: Indiana University Institute of Public Administration.

Amalu, Samuel Apolo K. 1974. *Jack Burns: A Portrait in Transition.* Honolulu: Mamalahoa Foundation.

Bernick, E. Lee. 1979. Gubernatorial Tools: Formal vs. Informal. *Journal of Politics*, 41, 2: 656–64.

Bernick, E. Lee, and Charles W. Wiggins. 1978. Legislative Reform and Legislative Turnover. In Leroy Rieselbach, ed. *Legislative Reform*. Lexington, MA: Lexington Books.

Beyle, Thad L. 1979. Governors' Views on Being Governor. *State Government*, 52, 3:103–09.

_____. 1985. *Gubernatorial Transitions*. Durham: Duke University Press.

Beyle, Thad L., and John E. Wickman. 1970. Gubernatorial Transition in a One-Party Setting. *Public Administration Review*, 30, 1:10–17.

Beyle, Thad L., and J. Oliver Williams. 1972. *The American Governor in Behavioral Perspective*. New York: Harper & Row.

Blair, Diane K., and Ann R. Henry. 1981. The Family Factor in State Legislative Turnover. *Legislative Studies Quarterly*, 6, 1:55–68.

Dixon, W. J. 1981. *BMDP Statistical Software*. Los Angeles: University of California Press.

Hartigan, John A. 1975. *Clustering Algorithms*. New York: Wiley.

Henry, Laurin L. 1961. The Transition: The New Administration. In Paul T. David, ed. *The Presidential Election and Transition 1960–1961*. Washington, DC: Brookings.

Huefner, Robert P., and Michael L. Nash. 1984. The Politics of Leadership: The 1982–83 Gubernatorial Transitions. *State Government*, 57, 3:67–72.

Johnson, Stephen C. 1967. Hierarchical Clustering Schemes. *Psychometrika*, 23:141–54.

Long, Norton. 1962. After the Voting is Over. *Midwest Journal of Political Science*, 6, 2:183–200.

National Governors' Association. 1978. *Governing the American States: A Handbook for New Governors*. Washington, DC: NGA.

_____. 1982. *Transition and the New Governor: A Critical Overview*. Washington, DC: NGA.

Neustadt, Richard E. 1983. *Presidential Power*. New York: Wiley.

Savage, Robert L., and Diane D. Blair. 1985. Tales of Two Gubernatorial Transitions: Underlying Scripts for Press Coverage of Political Events. Paper presented at the Annual Convention of the International Communication Association, Honolulu, Hawaii, May 1985.

Schenker, Alan E. 1969. *When Governors Change: The Case of the California Budget*. Davis: Institute of Governmental Affairs.

Scheslinger, Joseph A. 1965. The Politics of the Executive. In Herbert Jacob and Kenneth Vines, eds. *Politics in the American States*. Boston: Little, Brown.

Sigelman, Lee, and Roland Smith. 1981. Personal, Office, and State Characteristics as Predictors of Gubernatorial Performance. *Journal of Politics*, 43, 1:169–80.

Appendix: Survey Question Wording

Below are some samples of advice given to new governors. Please indicate whether you agree or disagree with this advice. (Each question provided space for respondent to Agree Strongly, Agree, No Opinion, Disagree, or Disagree Strongly.)

1. Do not schedule a press conference on a regular basis.
2. Separate personal social life from official contacts.
3. Be prepared not to take a week or more of vacation in the first six months.
4. Hire a good speechwriter.
5. Make sure press secretary has been in statehouse corps.
6. Rely primarily on campaign staff governor's office.
7. Hold meetings of immediate staff on a regularly scheduled basis.
8. Hold meetings with department heads on a regularly scheduled basis.
9. Keep an open door policy for legislators.
10. Do not attempt to keep an open door policy for the press.
11. Use memos and letters rather than meetings where possible.
12. Develop a well advertised and managed process of meeting with citizens.

4 The Management Role of the Governor

Raymond Cox III

While the managerial role of the governor has long been recognized (Ransone, 1956), the breadth of the role has altered considerably over the last two or three decades. The managerial role was traditionally framed in structural and administrative terms. Thus, the problem of managerial capacity was usually presented as a problem of the plural executive (Sharkansky, 1978; Fox, 1974). Since the mid-1960s some twenty-two states have altered the organization and structure of the executive (Muchmore, 1983). This change has reduced the focus on structure, turning instead to leadership and policy aspects of management. Lynn Muchmore summarizes the character of this redefined role as follows: "The governor is looked to as an active and superior force who imposes upon the far-flung bureaucracy a coherent fabric of goals and objectives and then guides the executive machinery toward these. He is more than a problem-solver concerned that government functions smoothly and without corruption; he is a policy-maker who sets the agenda for executive action and shapes priorities that affect decision making at every level" (1983:82).

The shift from a custodial, administrative style to a proactive, policy focused style is key to understanding the modern role of the governor. This change has necessitated the development of a managerial approach that requires both a greater commitment of time and a greater awareness of the interpersonal side of management. The governor must be a "change master," who is not only adept at the politics of change but also the managerial skill to energize state agencies to create new programs (Durning, 1987). The success of the governor, as a manager, is regarded as critical to an assessment of the success of the entire administration

(Flentje, 1981). Further, "managing government" is no longer thought of in terms of span of control, specialization of work tasks, or of the custodial tasks of administration. Rather, managing government requires planning and control systems which can resolve current problems, react to new issues and problems, and define, understand and control such issues and problems.

The primary focus of this chapter is an analysis of the tools of management that make it possible for the governor to be a change master. The analysis is divided into four parts: (1) an overview of the general character of gubernatorial management, (2) the management of staff, (3) working with the bureaucracy, and (4) patterns and styles of policy management. While this analysis is derived from a review of the extant literature, it has been supplemented by information obtained through a questionnaire sent to sitting governors and from personal interviews.[1]

GENERAL MANAGEMENT CHARACTER

Gubernatorial management is different from management practice in the private sector. While the title "chief executive officer" seemingly suggests parallel job responsibilities, the environment, politically and constitutionally, makes the analogy suspect. Michael J. Del Giudice, in reference to Mario Cuomo's administration in New York, comments: "Applying corporate management ideas to state government would not guarantee success. Neither a corporate definition of the role of the chief executive officer, nor a set of corporate management systems can be directly transferred to state government....Managing a state requires its own public management system" (1986:71).

A governor simply lacks the authoritarian command that the private sector presumes is necessary for success and operates within an environment open to public scrutiny.[2] On the other hand, governors are vested with an authority in the public sphere that is quite unlike that found in the private sector.

Governors may not have formal authority comparable to that granted a corporate CEO, but they possess a different kind of authority. That authority comes from the state's citizens who expect the governor to solve problems, make things happen, and get the job done. . . . Whenever the public genuinely expects a governor to get something accomplished, it will invest the governor with sufficient moral authority to see that the job is done (Behn, 1986:55).

The most critical distinction between the public and private sectors is in the structure of government. State governments are not the equivalent of the private corporation. Power in the corporation is centralized and focused in the person of the chief executive officer. Authority in government is widely dispersed. Not only is there no private sector equivalent of the courts, but the legislature is also of considerably more importance to the process of governing than the board of directors of a private company. In addition, while governors are called "chief" executive officers there are numerous other executives with their own responsibilities and constitutional authority.

Gubernatorial leadership and management authority are also limited by the legal environment of state government. With few exceptions the political value that dominates state constitutions is a distrust of government. To protect policy from corrupt legislatures or governors, independent boards and commissions were established and the administration of policy was made more democratic by separately electing (sometimes in nonpartisan elections) executive officials, the use of initiative and referendum, and by permitting the recall of elected officials.

This perspective is not conducive to the creation of strong executive authority. The result is that the ability of the governor to coordinate and administer a coherent set of policy initiatives is limited. Thus, governors often find themselves the nominal leaders of governments that are quite capable of pursuing multiple and conflicting policies simultaneously, but, except under extraordinary circumstances, incapable of concerted action to address a broad range of problems.

Under the circumstances, it should not be surprising that critiques of gubernatorial management initially focused on the structure of government. Beginning in the 1950s, major changes were made in the structure of state government throughout the country. Numerous states attempted to duplicate the efforts of the two Hoover Commissions of the federal government. Notions of span of control, functional differentiation, and other management perspectives set the tone for much of the reorganization agenda. A common view was that the way for governor to exert most fully his or her authority was through the use of a cabinet style government.[3] A second goal was to obtain authority for the governor to reorganize executive agencies.

By the early 1970s the reform of government structure had achieved considerable success. Muchmore (1983) notes that some twenty-two states made such changes during the 1960s and 1970s. Increasingly, however, those inside state government became aware of the limits of a single-minded focus on structure. Although better machinery and processes could make better governments more likely, they do not in themselves guarantee change. Effective policy development and implementation in the public sector suggested a very different approach was needed than the top-down command style of the private sector. The authority to act came not from a legal grant of such powers but in the "moral authority" to lead. As former governor Richard Riley of South Carolina notes, the gubernatorial role "is more a question of leadership instead of mechanics. The mechanics . . . work well if you have leadership that works well. . . .What is really important is hard work and leadership" (Brough, 1987:161).

While the lesson of reform learned during the 1970s was that formal authority was not solely important, constraints on the governor imposed by fragmented governmental structure remained. However, these constraints are increasingly viewed as realities to be "managed," not as problems necessitating structural realignment. The need to coordinate, plan, and manage policy has become more prominent. In this sense the traditionally distinct roles of policymaker and manager have nearly merged. The governor has a central role in planning, organizing, communicating, and implementing public policy (Conant, 1986). The governor, in other words, is a policy "manager" as much as a policymaker.

The governor as an "active and superior . . . policy maker" (Muchmore, 1983) must assume the attributes and qualities of the manager. The question becomes: What are those attributes? The U.S. Office of Personnel Management (OPM) has developed an analytic tool called the Management Excellence Inventory. As part of that tool, OPM defined ten characteristics which constitute the skills, attitudes, and perspectives that underlie effective management. Those ten characteristics are: (1) broad perspective, (2) strategic vision, (3) environmental sensitivity, (4) leadership, (5) flexibility, (6) action orientation, (7) results focus, (8) communication, (9) interpersonal sensitivity, and (10) technical competence (Flanders and Utterback, 1985).

The nation's governors seemingly have taken the policy managers perspective to heart. Concerns about a broad perspective, leadership, flexibility, and an action orientation are expressed in virtually all the responses to the questionnaire sent to governors as part of this research.[4] These expressions of managerial style do not in and of themselves yield success for a governor's agenda. However, these are the characteristics and skills that make success possible. The importance of the ability to manage, then, is that it becomes the foundation for success in other roles.

The key ingredients that emerge from a comparison of the gubernatorial responses and the OPM inventory are:

1. a style that emphasizes creating change opportunities;
2. a style that is trusting of the abilities of others, and
3. a desire to take charge and make decisions, not as an autocrat, but through and with others.

The governors almost unanimously described a management style that encouraged others to assume responsibility for their work. The governor's role is to support that effort by giving them the resources and support needed for the job. The thrust is toward establishing a policy framework and defining goals for the state, not managing in a narrow supervisory sense. As Governor Rudy Perpich of Minnesota comments, "My advice to governors is to find good people to run the day to day operation of government. . . . I strongly believe in delegating responsibilities." Former governor Thomas Kean of New Jersey suggests a similar approach in shaping and managing policy.

I am wary of governors who try to get too involved in the day-to-day details of managing a bureaucracy. We all remember the awful anecdote about President Carter wanting to know who was playing on the White House tennis courts. This is a real danger. The opposite danger, of course, is that you become totally insulated from the bureaucracy for which you are responsible. The only way to guard against that is to choose and trust top-rate managers and maintain informed lines of communication with people in your own office and throughout state government. I often ask three people the same question. In their various answers I can separate the sycophants from the straight-shooters and figure out what is actually happening.

The role of management is not lessened by the decision to turn over basic day-to-day activities to others, rather it is elevated by linking it not to administrative practice but to policy decisionmaking and leadership. The final responsibility for successful management rests with the governor. The governor as manager provides vision, sets an agenda, and then works through others to move the state forward. The governor accomplishes management and policy goals in conjunction with immediate staff and the agencies of government. The next two sections of this study focus on those relationships.

GOVERNORS AND THEIR STAFF

In reshaping the problem of management to that of setting the agenda and priorities, the role of the governor's staff grows. While there has long been the perception of the need for staff to handle constituent services, press relations, and legislative affairs, the modern gubernatorial staff is much more specialized and larger than in earlier years. According to a 1988 National Governors' Association survey, nearly one-quarter of the governors make use of a staff of over 100 professionals (NGA:1988). But even these numbers underestimate the size of the staff resources of governors because of the common practice of "borrowing" agency personnel and the creation of staff agencies for policy, planning, and budgeting that report directly to the governor, even though they are not part of the governor's staff (Beyle, 1983). In fact, two important organizations for reinforcing the gubernatorial managerial role, planning and budgeting offices, are staff agencies often placed outside the office of the governor. While organizations such as budget bureaus and planning offices play a lesser role than those inside these organizations presume, they do have an impact on a wide range of management concerns. Muchmore categorizes the role of such offices as "healthy" in such important areas as developing policy options, "trouble-shooting," and resolving interagency disputes (Muchmore, 1983).

The central feature of these changes is not the numbers of staff working for the governor but the range of activities engaged in by those staff members. The policy management perspective dictates the use of planning staffs, close ties to budget staffs, and better coordination with line agencies. There is no magic formula by which to juggle all these concerns. The common pattern seems to be to rely heavily on both direct and indirect staff organizations. Cabinet officers, their respective staffs, line agencies, even the Washington office and the governor's office play a role. Thus, for example, Governor Garrey Carruthers of New Mexico cut the gubernatorial staff upon assuming office by consciously using cabinet secretaries (and their staffs) to develop policy alternatives and to implement policy. The pattern in Colorado has been to bring the primary policy staffs (planning, budgeting) within the direct orbit of the governor's office. The cabinet officers in Colorado have a policy role but their primary duties involve the day-to-day tasks of administration.

It should not be so surprising that the cabinet officers in California play the same day-to-day administrative role as those in Colorado. As noted by Governor Deukmejian, in a state with 250,000 state employees such intermediaries are vital to the effective management of state programs. The pattern in New York is the same. The "cabinet" itself consists of seventy-five members and therefore is operationally several cabinets or subcabinets. But even these groups are one step removed from governors who have most direct and frequent contact with senior staff of their office (Management Resources, 1988).

In contrast, the smaller governments of Utah and Wyoming permit their governors to operate with a more "hands on" approach. Both use state planning coordinators and planning staff to help formulate and implement public policy. Frequent meetings with agency and even department heads are possible under such circumstances. While neither governor truly has time to "manage" individual departments, they do have the luxury of being more personally and directly involved in day-to-day operations than do governors of larger states. Yet despite the differences found across states, the institutional arrangements are less important than having access to people, information, and ideas when needed.

The distinction between management and administration is important in understanding the role of staff. By management I mean the overall direction and guidance necessary for organizational objectives to be achieved. Administration is the application of specific techniques and technologies to the day-to-day routine of the organization. Administration is both more technical and narrower than management. From this perspective, administration is a "subprocess" of management. No manager can succeed if such administrative subprocesses are neglected, but on the other hand, the role of the manager is broader in that it involves interpersonal, interorganizational, and policy elements.

Just as the head of a line agency must be both a manager and an administrator, the governor's office must attend to both of these matters. Governors, therefore, must concern themselves with both, though the management side is the more critical and politically important. Also, the administrative function is more likely to be undertaken by intermediaries. To the extent that administration refers to the routines of the organization, gubernatorial involvement is most critical at the time of the selection of personnel. The oft noted policy of "find the right people and let them do the job" must be set in this context (Dalton, 1983). Finding and keeping staff and line administrators remains a critical problem for any governor, but most particularly where the "leave them alone" rule operates (NGA, 1988).

The more critical matter of gubernatorial management concerns leadership on policy. It is this management role that is increasingly being emphasized in the literature of the National Governors' Association, Council of State Planning Agencies, and academics (NGA, 1978; Walter and Choate, 1984; Denhardt, 1986). Concerns of planning and budgeting issues and, also, the concern about the relationship of the governor to the bureaucracy must be understood in a management, not an administrative, context. The frequent references to the need for the governor to "lead" reflects this perspective. The central point is that leadership and management are by their nature personal endeavors. This is the meaning of former governor Riley's distinction between "mechanics" and "leadership" cited earlier.

The role of staff in developing and supporting gubernatorial leadership is problematic. The distrust of the "gatekeeper" (Beyle, 1983) role that often falls upon the chief of staff should not be surprising. This problem has been more often confronted in relationship to the role of legislative staff (Hammond, 1985), but the issues are quite similar. The chief danger is that the staff controls the information of and interpersonal access to the governor, possibly to the point where the governor follows the lead of staff, rather than the reverse (Williams, 1980). The reality is that the need for the staff to "filter" information is an inevitable result of the time constraints of the gubernatorial role. The key is that the "inflow of ideas, solutions, [and] opportunities must be varied and diverse" (Beyle, 1983:160). Or, as former governor Kean of New Jersey put it, to "separate the sycophants from the straight-shooters and figure out what is actually happening." The burden rests with the governor. The governor who allows the staff to control the gubernatorial agenda is asking for trouble. While few would necessarily go so far as former governor John Sununu of New Hampshire, who asserted that the role of the governor "is to know more about what is going on in every department than the department heads," the lesson is that "intellectual dominance of the subject" and "a strong gubernatorial staff" are not alternative management styles but complementary components of a single style (Brough, 1986:159). Perhaps the straightforward comments of former governor Ted Swinden of Montana summarize this perspective best, "I'm the boss!"

WORKING WITH AGENCIES

The complexity of the dual role of administrator and manager is equally obvious in exploring the role of the governor vis-à-vis the state bureaucracy. This relationship is often viewed as one based in distrust. Certainly the academic and popular literature prepares a governor to face this relationship as something akin to open warfare. The intransigence and dysfunction of the bureaucracy must, however, be relegated to that of myth. Working with agencies is time consuming, but it can produce results; change does occur. In saying this, it must also be recognized that state bureaucracies, like their federal counterparts, represent a "fourth" branch of government. Bureaucrats are professionals in their own right and, thus, have a perspective that is independent of the governor. Further, the expertise of the bureaucrat means that the flow of information is as likely to go upward as it is downward. And most importantly, other persons and groups, such as legislators and interest groups, influence bureaucrats, possibly in ways contrary to the view of the governor (Abney and Lauth, 1983).

A major difficulty for the governor in working with the bureaucracy is that state agencies and agency personnel are more closely linked by professional background, perspective, and funding to fellow bureaucrats in Washington than to the governor. Harold Seidman comments:

Federal program administrators argue that the administration of joint-action programs is a mutual—and, ideally a professional—undertaking. For them the effective operation of the federal system requires the maintenance of clear and unbroken lines of communication between and among functional specialists and their counterparts in the field. As they see it, successful intergovernmental relations are chiefly successful bureaucratic relations. The major sources of conflict are not to be found between levels of government but among (1) higher level and lower level professionals; (2) professional program administrators and elected policymakers; and (3) professional administrators and intergovernmental reformers (1975:163).

One response of governors to these bureaucratically based sources of conflict was the creation of offices in Washington, D.C., to lobby and to get in at the front end of the "lines of communication." The role of planning and policy staffs in monitoring the then A–95 review process also aided the governor in "keeping up with" the bureaucrats. Ultimately governors have chosen to be more active in shaping state policies as substitutes for federal initiatives. This shift has been accelerated by the reduction in federal financial support for a wide variety of programs forcing the governors to assume control (and the higher tax burden) to prevent the programs from disappearing all together. This area then remains a source of frustration for governors. On the one hand, many would assert that they have moved to respond to state problems in ways unheard of two decades ago, yet they are still held to the federal government programmatically and financially. The days when the state role in the federal-state partnership was to create the bureaucracies necessary to handle federal mandates is past. Today governors assert that the states are again the "laboratories of democracy" where innovative program solutions to social and economic programs are developed; they no longer wait on Washington for direction (Osborne, 1988). Unfortunately, intergovernmental relations are too often primarily bureaucratic relations, and the tension between administrators and elected policymakers remains (Cox, 1984).

The difficulty for the governor is in determining how and when to work with the bureaucracy. Laurence Lynn offers a useful perspective in judging the success of a public executive in introducing change in the bureaucracy. He notes that such change efforts succeed where the executive consciously focuses his or her skill and energy on change, but notes circumstances and opportunity must also be considered (Lynn, 1988). Obviously, the opportunities for change in program areas where the federal government is active are limited. Here the governors have sought to redefine problems so that aspects that are amenable to concepts such as routinization and uniformity of design can be federalized; whereas those program elements that are subject to regional, demographic, and economic variability can be given over to the states. The proposals of the National Conference on Social Welfare, a commission led by former governors Charles Robb of Virginia and Dan Evans of Washington, to reform the federal welfare system are examples of such a policy perspective. The proposed arrangements would permit governors to reassert considerably more control over the policy choices of state agencies, albeit by relinquishing all remaining control over some policy areas. Given that some of the agencies that governors have the least control over, such as welfare, are often the most prone to crisis, this would seem a good choice for governors.

Three factors must be considered in defining gubernatorial involvement with the bureaucracy: time, the importance of the organizational activity, and personnel. Martha Weinberg offers a typology of gubernatorial participation in agency affairs that focuses on the first two concerns.

1. Agencies requiring continual examination; either because of the large expenditures for which the agency is responsible, or because a problem would have serious and immediate consequences.

2. Agencies requiring continual examination because of the personal interests of the governor.

3. Agencies that receive attention only during a crisis.

4. Agencies that receive little or no attention (1977:67–70).

The time and energy of the governor are invariably focused on the first two types of agencies, though increasingly the agencies that are of personal concern to the governor are getting more attention than the Weinberg typology might suggest. Policies covered by agencies in groups 1 and 2 are those that emerge as part of the governor's agenda. The agencies of Weinberg's groups 3 and 4 and the problems associated with them are treated as temporary hindrances that detract from a more critical agenda. But it would also seem difficult to separate attention to a problem agency as problem-qua-problem from attention to a problem agency resulting from personal interest. The comments of Governor Perpich are instructive:

> I employed a variety of strategies to secure jobs for the state during a severe economic slump at the start of my administration in 1983. Beginning at that time and since then I have built new coalitions between [*sic*] government, business, labor and education representatives to help solve many problems in the state. A currently healthy state economy has allowed me to become more focused on job creation efforts, emphasizing a long-term strategy based on research and development.

The agencies that Governor Perpich most closely works with have not fundamentally changed, yet the policy problem and the reason for the interest have changed. The priority is "what do I have to do," then "what do I want to do." The successful governor is the one who can focus on the latter.

The third factor influencing gubernatorial involvement with the bureaucracy is that of personnel. The importance of having the right people in place is critical. The problem of a "bad" appointment is ever present, but is especially troubling in the context of appointments to the numerous boards and commissions for which the governor must take responsibility. With regard to this type of appointment Diane Blair comments that "the decisionmaking process is elaborate and exhausting, the policy consequences may be negligible, and [the] political consequences are frequently a net minus" (1982:88). The qualities that are sought in an appointee are threefold: (1) management skills, (2) experience and competence, and (3) basic commitment to the administration's policy direction (Wyner, 1985). These qualities are important if a governor is to avoid a "bad" appointment that creates a crisis, particularly if the crisis is in an agency that the governor would otherwise ignore.

Another aspect of personnel is that of the relationship between the governor and state employees. James Kee notes that Scott Matheson (Utah governor, 1977–1985) operated upon the philosophy that "the taxpayer gets more for his money out of a positively motivated work force." He further believed that the "motivator" was the governor (Kee, 1986). This need to stay in touch with state employees as outlined by Matheson is echoed in the self-described management styles of Governor Carruthers of New Mexico and former governors Richard Bryan of Nevada and Kean of New Jersey. Durning summarizes this perspective in noting that "[d]espite the heavy demands on a governor's time and attention, it seems prudent for a governor to wage a strategic campaign to win the hearts of the people who can help or hinder implementation of his administrative policies" (1986:81).

THE GOVERNOR AS POLICY MANAGER

It should be clear from these discussions that the gubernatorial role as a policymaker is constrained by three factors: institutional arrangements, personnel, and management style. Institutional arrangements such as the plural executive and gubernatorial-legislative relations are constraints that must be recognized and overcome, but are not amenable to radical alteration in the context of the governor's term of office. As such it need not be discussed further.

The issue of personnel is a question of the desire to find and hold on to the "right people." While this is not an easy task, it too must be recognized as a constraining factor, although not a dominating concern. The choice of appointees is fraught with political peril when the wrong choice is made, but ultimately the issue is one of playing with the cards that have been dealt. Governor Bangartner of Utah offers a particularly telling comment with regard to political appointees when he notes that "you never replace someone until you know you have found a replacement who can improve the situation."

Thus, management style is the overriding factor that both shapes the gubernatorial policymaking role and is amenable to gubernatorial control. It is the one area where the personal style and personal choice of the governor are most apparent. The governor of today is expected to act. The era of "goodtime Charlie," when problems could be ignored or sent to Washington for resolution, ended in the 1950s (Sabato, 1983). Today, the governor must find ways to overcome the constraints of institutional arrangements and personnel because of public expectations. The litmus test of the governor is the policy initiatives he or she takes. The vehicle for such policymaking is an expanded view of management as a tool of policymaking. The governor, as manager, must be knowledgeable in the use of techniques such as planning, policy analysis, management by objective, and strategic management, as well as have the interpersonal skills and awareness needed to get a reluctant or obdurate state government to move toward the policy goals set by the governor. To the extent that governors possess that combination of understanding and awareness of managerial techniques, in conjunction with what was earlier called "moral authority," then the opportunity to seek change is presented. This combination of factors does not guarantee success, but it does seem to represent the minimum necessary conditions for success (Lynn, 1988).

Personal Style

Awareness and effective use of management techniques are critical components of the governor's managerial role. Different governors will emphasize different techniques linked to their background experiences and the policymaking situation confronted. With this individual variation, it becomes apparent that the key ingredient in the analysis of the governor as a manager is personal style. In examining this aspect of the gubernatorial role, it must be recognized that the characteristics presented emerge from the reports of the governors themselves. Others, most particularly those in the legislature or outside state government, see the governors not as managers but often as adversaries or competitors. Thus, for example, the managerial style of former governor Scott Matheson of Utah, as described by James Kee, is quite different from the interpersonal style ascribed to him by opponents in the legislature (Sherman, 1985).

Two common points emerge from the observation of the governors' comments on their personal linkage to the other actors in the state policymaking process: trust and a "common stake" in the organization. Many governors are "people-oriented" in their personal style. Getting involved seems to be a common theme for these governors, particularly those in the smaller states, yet all evoked a viewpoint that, given marching orders, staff would get things done as desired. Implicit in this view is that trust and loyalty are intertwined. This viewpoint also places a heavy burden on the governor to define the parameters of what is to be done, thus creating a common stake. Governor Cecil Andrus of Idaho comments:

As a manager of the executive branch of state government, I keep a hands-on approach to the workings of each department and agency. I'm not involved in each detail or decision because I feel very comfortable and confident in the appointments and staff which I have chosen. The people who are in my administration, however, are very aware of what is expected of them and what they are to do. When I see a change of direction which I don't like, I am actively involved in the resolution.

Later he goes on to add, "I get a dedicated and competent staff and let them do their job. I know if it's getting done or if it's not. If there is a problem then I find a way to solve the problem." What is implicitly downplayed is a reliance on a set organizational structure, or even a set staff configuration in managing policy.

The governors seem quite willing to go outside the normal organizational patterns to get the job done. This is certainly the pattern that Osborne found in examining the changing role of the governors in stimulating economic development. At times this has meant seeking "nonbureaucratic" (but not nongovernmental) patterns of problem solving. It has also meant seeking approval for states to pursue programs less fettered by federal controls. Innovation and creativity in problem solving are more important than older notions of federalism which left the "big" problems to Washington or even notions of capitalism which left the problem to the private sector (Osborne, 1988).

Getting the job done is inevitably the key, particularly in states where the awkward plural executive sometimes still inhibits broad-ranging policymaking. Governor Michael Sullivan of Wyoming summarizes well the emphasis and concern shared by virtually all his colleagues when he comments: "While our administrative structure may seem at times unwieldy, we do have a very hard-working crew of state employees. . . . I would share the observation that developing effective management techniques for government is very important if government is to provide quality services to people."

CONCLUSIONS

The gubernatorial managerial role has indeed changed considerably since the 1950s. At that time the question of management invoked images of restructuring governmental organizations and the capacity of state employees to carry out policy. These issues have faded. Most governors have at the least been given more flexibility with regard to reorganizing state government, and governors are often quite vocal about the abilities of state employees, as well as more distant federal employees, to perform their jobs. But more than this, issues focused strictly on organizational structure have faded because of a redefinition of the governor's managerial role. Most particularly, management skill now is recognized as an interpersonal quality that must be present in the governor, rather than as an attribute of the structure of government. Some would go so far as to suggest that the personal managerial style, in relation to both staff and the state bureaucracy, influences all the roles of the governor. In other words, success as a manager is a necessary, though not sufficient, condition for overall success in office.

This new perspective has changed the approach governors take toward the management of state policy. As a group they are much more aware of management as an aspect of their policymaking and leadership roles. This does not mean that their management styles are identical; differences of personality alone would prevent that. It does mean that there is considerable overlap and commonality in the ways they approach the managerial role. These common approaches include a sensitivity to the need for multiple perspectives on problems, the need for assistance in the analysis of the policy and budgetary implications, and a sense that management is done "with" people not "to" people. The most critical point, however, is in the connection between management and policy. Management is the tool by which to guide and direct policy.

Roadblocks to the success of individual governors exist. The "problem" of the plural executive is a reality for all but the governors of Alaska and Hawaii. Further, state legislatures often jealously guard their prerogatives and powers. Policy is not made exclusively in the governor's office. With the use of the modern tools of management, with an adequate staff, and particularly with the skill and know-how to work with the "fourth branch," the governor can have a considerable impact. Where the managerial role is understood in this broad context, successful policy management is possible.

The central features of the policy management perspective can thus be summarized as follows:

1. recognition of the management element in policymaking;
2. using staff to increase information for decisionmaking;
3. developing an approach to management that encourages flexibility, creativity, and a broad, strategic perspective;
4. a willingness to "get involved" where problems exist; and
5. a proactive style that "makes" opportunities rather than merely reacting to events.

The nation's governors would seem well positioned from a policy management perspective to tackle the institutional and personnel constraints that remain roadblocks to seizing the "opportunity of being a change master." The governors are certainly in a better position than their predecessors of two decades and more ago. Moreover, the perspective that management is central to the accomplishment of policy change seems well accepted. The only question that remains is the highly subjective and speculative one of what use did these governors make of the opportunities for change.

NOTES

1. An initial questionnaire was sent to the thirteen western governors on December 9, 1987; another questionnaire went to the other governors on December 5, 1988. The questions focused on the organization of the office and the management style of the governors, both in relation to their staff and executive agency personnel. Personal interviews with Governor Carruthers of New Mexico (twice) and Governor Bangerter of Utah were conducted on February 8, 1988, January 3, 1989, and March 31, 1989, respectively. Personal interviews were also conducted with Tom Lewis, Senior Executive Assistant to Governor Harris of Georgia (on August 31, 1989) and with

Patrick Cavanaugh of Governor Branstad's Department of Management (on September 25, 1989). These interviews were similarly open-ended, though the primary focus was on the organization and management of the governors' staff. The personal interviews involved a series of open-ended questions concerning each governor's management philosophy. Quotations used in the text attributed to particular governors and not otherwise cited are from survey and/or interview responses.

2. Former governor Kean spoke for a number of governors when he commented, "The major difference, other than monetary compensation, is the degree of public accountability. Most corporate CEO's I know would be traumatized if their every move was chronicled on the front page of local newspapers. The bright spotlight causes you to act with a bit more caution and prudence than if you were running a large corporation or university" (questionnaire response). Some, including Governor Carruthers of New Mexico, disagree with this viewpoint (interview February 8, 1988).

3. In a 1988 survey by the National Governors' Association, thirty-one of the forty states responding use a cabinet system, though only ten of the thirty-one are mandated by constitution or statute to use a cabinet.

4. Specific responses on management skills were given by governors from Nevada, Colorado, Montana, Utah, New Mexico, Wyoming, New York, Georgia, Minnesota, Idaho, Maine, Illinois, Iowa, and New Jersey.

REFERENCES

Abney, Glenn, and Thomas P. Lauth. 1983. The Governor as Chief Administrator. *Public Administration Review*, 43, 1:40–49.

Behn, Robert D. 1986. Getting the Job Done: The Governor's Legal and Moral Authority. *State Government*, 59, 2.

Beyle, Thad L. 1983. Governor's Offices: Variations on Common Themes. In Thad L. Beyle and Lynn R. Muchmore, eds. *Being Governor*. Durham, NC: Duke University Press.

Blair, Diane K. 1982. The Gubernatorial Appointment Power: Too Much of a Good Thing? *State Government*, 55, 2:88–92.

Brough, Regina. 1986. Strategies for Leaders Who Do Not Have a Lot of Power. *State Government*, 59, 4.

Conant, James K. 1986. Gubernatorial Strategy and Style: Keys to Improving Executive Branch Management. *State Government*, 59, 2:82–83.

Cox, Raymond W. III. 1984. *Intergovernmental Relations as an Instrument of Policy Change*. Washington, DC: National Science Foundation.

Dalton, Robert. 1983. Governors' Views on Management. In Thad L. Beyle and Lynn R. Muchmore, eds., *Being Governor*. Durham, NC: Duke University Press.

Del Giudice, Michael J. 1986. Mario Cuomo as New York's Chief Executive Officer. *State Government*, 59, 2.

Denhardt, Robert B. 1986. Strategic Planning and State Government Management. *State Government*, 59, 1.

Durning, Dan. 1986. The Governor's Internal Campaign: Managing State Government by Influencing Attitudes and Values. *State Government*, 59, 2.

_____. 1987. Change Masters for States. *State Government*, 60, 3:145–49.

Flanders, Loretta R., and Dennis Utterback. 1985. The Management Excellence Inventory: A Tool for Management Development. *Public Administration Review*, 45, 3:403–10.

Flentje, H. 1981. The Governor as Manager. *State Government*, 54, 2: 76–81.

Fox, Douglas. 1974. *The Politics of City and State Bureaucracy*. Pacific Palisades, CA: Goodyear.

Hammond, Susan Webb. 1985. Legislature Staffs. In Gerhard Lowenberg, Samuel C. Patterson, and Malcolm E. Jewell, eds. *Handbook of Legislative Research*. Cambridge, MA: Harvard University Press.

Kee, James E. 1986. Scott Matheson's Eight Principles of Gubernatorial Excellence. *State Government*, 59, 2:64–69.

Lorch, Robert S. 1979. *Colorado's Government*, rev. ed. Boulder, CO: Colorado Associated University Press.

Lynn, Laurence E., Jr. 1988. *Managing Public Policy*. Boston: Little, Brown.

Management Resources Project. 1988. *Governing the Empire State*. Albany: State of New York.

Muchmore, Lynn R. 1983. The Governor as Manager. In Thad L. Beyle and Lynn R. Muchmore, eds. *Being Governor*. Durham, NC: Duke University Press.

_____. 1988. *Organization and Staffing Patterns in the Governor's Office*. Washington, DC: National Governors' Association.

National Governors' Association. 1978. *Governing the American States*. Washington, DC: National Governors' Association.

Osborne, David E. 1988. *Laboratories of Democracy*. Cambridge, MA: Harvard Business School Press.

Ransone, Coleman B., Jr. 1956. *The Office of Governor in the United States*. University, AL: University of Alabama Press.

Sabato, Larry. 1983. *Goodbye to Goodtime Charlie*, 2nd ed. Washington, DC: Congressional Quarterly Press.

Sanford, Terry. 1967. *Storm Over the States*. New York: McGraw-Hill.

Seidman, Harold. 1975. *Politics, Position, and Power*, 2nd ed. New York: Oxford Press.

Sharkansky, Ira. 1978. *The Maligned States*, 2nd ed. New York: McGraw-Hill.

Sherman, Sharon. 1985. Powersplit: When Legislature and Governors Are of Opposing Parties. In Thad L. Beyle, ed. *State Government 1985–1986*. Washington, DC: Congressional Quarterly.

Walter, Susan, and Pat Choate. 1984. *Thinking Strategically*. Washington, DC: Council of State Planning Agencies.

Weinberg, Martha W. 1977. *Managing The State*. Cambridge, MA: MIT Press.

Williams, Charles H. 1980. The Gatekeeper's Function on the Governor's Staff. *Western Political Quarterly*, 33, 1:87–93.

Wyner, Alan J. 1985. The Governor as Administrator. In Jack Rubin and Don Dodd, eds. *State and Local Administration*. New York: Marcel Dekker.

5 Executive-Legislative Relations: The Governor's Role as Chief Legislator

E. Lee Bernick and Charles W. Wiggins

No governor should be passive, that's a copout and the only time you're passive is when you are trying to straddle the fence. . . . The role of the governor as defined by the constitution in most of the states is to administer the laws. . . . Well, it is just not quite that clear. Yes, you have all of the administrative responsibilities but you have a definite moral responsibility and I think political responsibility to shape the role of the governor by proposing legislation, getting behind the program, and enacting it into law.
—Cecil D. Andrus, Governor of Idaho[1]

The governor is the major policy actor in state government. From the very genesis of the policy process when issues begin to reach the state policy agenda through the evaluation stage, no other individual has the potential to play as important a role. As such, governors are given the title of "change master," or policymaker (Durning, 1987). There is neither debate on the existence of the role nor on the fact that it continues to expand. Closely linked to a governor's role as policymaker is the job of "chief legislator."

Little doubt exists among numerous observers and participants in the state political process that being the chief legislator is a primary role for the governor. Media reporters, scholars, legislators, and even governors themselves frequently emphasize, directly or indirectly, the importance of this role. One need only peruse the print media to see numerous examples of governors being evaluated negatively because of their job performance during recently completed legislative sessions. In conjunction with a story about former Texas governor Dolph Briscoe, for example, the magazine *Texas Monthly* (Smith, 1976) presented a series of pictures with his image becoming increasingly faint until it completely vanished. The implication was that Briscoe was not acting in an appropriate gubernatorial manner, the main reason being his lack of legislative leadership. Furthermore, such negative assessments are not based just on a lack of involvement. The *Miami Herald* (1967), for example, observed in one of its end-of-year evaluations of a 1960s legislative session that: "It was the longest, most political, and least productive session in modern memory . . . demonstrating that . . . a Republican Governor and a Democratic legislature go together like oil and water . . . Governor Kirk's . . . cavalier use of the veto and his broken promises which frustrated legislative compromise add up to a highly erratic leadership."

According to Thad Beyle (1983: 206), the governor is the "chief legislator" and "a governor's relationship with and success in dealing with the legislature often determines the success of his administration." Other research (Bernick and Wiggins, 1981) has revealed that state legislators generally accept the governor's involvement in the legislative process; and if there is concern, it has more to do with the extent to which the governor is actually playing the part and not his or her right to do so. Indeed, governors themselves view their legislative role as an important aspect of their jobs. As former Florida governor Reuben Askew has commented, "I can see the role of [the] governor to furnish leadership for a recommendation in areas and then to try to pursue this program in the legislature." Another study found that working with the legislature was one of the four most important roles perceived by governors (Ransone, 1982). In fact, Herzik and Dodson (1984, and updated in this volume) found that governors believed it to be essential to work with legislators—even during the transition period. Although generally attributed much salience, the governor's chief legislator role has been the focus of only limited systematic research and inquiry (Jewell, 1972; Rosenthal, 1990). Not only is this deficiency problematic because of the overall importance of executive-legislative relations to an adequate understanding of state politics, it is also perplexing because it need not be so. There is little question that governors, singularly or as a collective group, do not receive as much attention as the president. Likewise, we cannot determine with the same clarity as we do the president the legislative programs and issue positions of state governors. However, the fact that there are fifty sitting governors, as well as many living former governors, makes systematic comparative research readily possible. Moreover, governors and their staffs are more accessible than the president and his staff. In an attempt to promote further research on this vital policymaking role, this chapter will be devoted to reviewing past research, analyzing conceptual issues, and suggesting areas of potentially fruitful research on the governor's role as chief legislator.

SOURCES OF ROLE

The role of chief legislator has developed by mandate and, willingly or unwillingly, been accepted by most governors. This mandate is both de facto and de jure in origins. A governor's de facto mandate comes from the public. Since governors are commonly the most visible state official, the public focuses its attention on them, holding them accountable for policies and programs having an impact on their quality of life. While all governors must assume a legislative role, some are more enthusiastic participants than others. A governor's personal proclivity to participate becomes important in determining the type of "chief legislator" he or she will be.

Much of the existing research on the governor as legislative policymaker has focused on the de jure sources of the role. By assigning certain tasks or responsibilities to the chief executive, provisions in state constitutions and statutes frequently require governors to play a legislative role, and are often critically linked to his or her success in this capacity. Thus, gubernatorial responsibility to present a state-of-the-state message and to propose a budget for state government have served as key vehicles through which researchers can analyze a governor's legislative policymaking role. In addition, the formal prerogative granted in all states (except North Carolina) for the governor to veto legislation is another potentially salient source of his or her legislative role, as is the power to call special legislative sessions and, at least in a significant minority of states, specify their agendas. What insights has research on governors as policymakers using these four de jure powers provided us?

In the policy process, elected officials play the dominant role in the agenda setting stage. In state government, no other elected official plays as an important a role as the governor in setting the policy agenda. High visibility for governors means that the issues highlighted by them draw the attention of the media and consequently the public. While the range and number of issues may be quite variable, almost every governor has a small number of issues or policy initiatives that define his or her term of office. While there may have been a long list of campaign promises offered by gubernatorial aspirants, usually no more than five or six key issues are subsequently pushed each legislative session by successful candidates (Christensen, 1987).

Although numerous opportunities are available for a governor to set the agenda, there is one occasion that is distinguished by its formal requirement for gubernatorial incursion into the legislative arena. Thus, the state-of-the-state message serves as the springboard for the chief executive to enter into the legislative policymaking process. As former North Dakota governor William Guy observed: "The governor has to lay out with broad strokes the picture of state needs at the beginning of legislative session . . . he has to be clear enough in outlining the state's needs and what he thinks must be done to solve the problems of the state so that the legislature has a course of action to follow."

Herzik (1983) has analyzed this gubernatorial function and concluded that three types of issues are usually presented by governors to the legislature: perennial, cyclical, and transitory. Perennial issues are found on the agenda every session, while the importance of cyclical issues for the legislative agenda follows a pattern of ebb and flow. Transitory issues come to the scene unexpectedly, but only with a short shelf life—quickly off the agenda. Governors do not uniformly lead or act as policy initiators in all three areas. Herzik concludes that on some issues governors merely reflect the prevailing public opinion, while on other issues they truly lead. For some issues, the governor attempts to pull loose ends together and capture the sense of the community. For others, especially transitory issues, the governor is a captive of the event and is merely trying to stay afloat.

If governors set the agenda for the legislature with their state-of-the-state messages, then understanding agenda setting is not a function of whether a governor's bill, per se, is passed. What is important to our understanding of agenda setting is whether gubernatorial initiatives result in legislative responses. Thus, governors should be evaluated as agenda setters by evaluating the types of issues they raise and the legislature's response. For example, North Carolina's Governor Jim Martin (Republican) proposed major tax cuts for businesses in his first term. While the legislature rejected his specific proposals, Martin forced the issues onto the agenda and they became the major items under consideration during the legislative session (Christensen, 1987).

In almost every state, this scenario has been evident for many years. Thus, more in-depth analyses are needed in order to understand how a governor's identification of an issue leads to a legislative response. Regardless of how anecdotal the data, the information available today permits us to conclude that the governor in any state is the major force in setting the issue agenda. Obviously, there are exceptions, but that is precisely the point—they are exceptions.

On the other hand, if the goal is to understand how successful governors are in formulating policy, then research that links specific gubernatorial proposals to specific legislative enactments is necessary. Unfortunately, this is not easily accomplished (Gross, 1989). In only a very few states can we readily determine the link between gubernatorial initiatives and legislative enactments. One problem researchers normally face is their inability to identify legislation sponsored by given governors. Very few states maintain records that are clear and definitive. Another problem is that some governors claim popular legislation that passed as theirs, while unpopular legislation becomes an orphan. Early policy formulation activities in the chief executive's office may also at times be tempered by the governor's need to compromise with key solons and other legislative influence agents if bills are eventually to pass. Thus, once an issue is on the agenda, a governor proposes alternatives for the legislature to enact, but analyzing the complex linkage between the language of a proposal and that of the eventual legislation is not easily done.

There is one policy area in which a governor does propose a specific legislative program—the budget. The budget is the single most important document in determining the policy initiatives and goals of government. The governor proposes a budget and the legislature must pass both appropriation and revenue measures in response to it. Unlike the state-of-the-state message, gubernatorially recommended spending guidelines are specific and easily discernable. Two different lines of research have developed dealing with the governor's budget power. The first seeks to determine the role played by the governor in the actual budget process. This research has, for example, analyzed different budget techniques employed by governors and the legislature's response. It also has sought to determine how and why governors influence legislators. For example, Lauth (1990) found that bicameral conflict in the Georgia legislature usually results in the senate winning over the house, with the senate's "victory" closely linked to its stronger ties to the governor. However, it has also been observed that a growing national struggle between state governors and legislatures has emerged over budget issues and that governors overall are in a somewhat weakened position of influence (Abney and Lauth, 1987). This weakening of the governor's role has occurred especially in states where lawmakers have greater access to independent budget information. By implication, it can be conjectured that the adoption of more and more sophisticated management information systems will spell even more trouble for governors in the budgetary process.

The other type of research on budgetmaking examines appropriation and/or revenue outcomes as a method of determining the chief executive's budgetary role. Thus, an early landmark study by Sharkansky (1968) concluded that the governor is preeminent in this area because what he or she recommends is the best predictor of what is approved. Subsequent studies confirm this budget prominence, but caution that it is no longer absolute (Clynch, 1989; Thompson, 1987). Thompson (1987) also concludes that the legislature takes a more affirmative role for agencies in an expansionist mode, while the governor is stronger where agencies receive major amounts of federal or earmarked funds. In sum, the budget provides a governor an important formal tool to influence policymaking in the legislature.

Perhaps no single power epitomizes gubernatorial strength in the legislative domain as does the veto. Its Latin origin means "to forbid" and, in a sense, says much about this tool. Of course, variations exist in the extent to which the veto power is provided governors. Some governors have a simple veto, while others have an item veto which, in most cases, applies to appropriations measures. Other governors (i.e., of Illinois, Massachusetts, New Jersey, and Montana) have the amendatory veto (Rosenthal, 1990: 9).

Traditionally, students of gubernatorial power delineate the formal power positions of governors by determining whether they possess the line item veto and the magnitude of the legislative majority required to override (Schlesinger, 1965; Beyle, 1983). Generally, stronger governors have the line item veto and face an unusual majority (usually three-fifths) on an override vote, while weaker governors have the line item veto and confront a legislature that must marshall only a simple majority to override. However, it should be emphasized that, given the circumstances, even the weakest veto may still be a powerful weapon in the governor's arsenal.

The veto's importance is the result of two factors. First, all governors have the veto power (except in North Carolina) and, as such, it grants them "a right" to act in the policy process. No conflict exists over whether the governor should be meddling in the legislative process—it is a fact of life. Second, the veto is seldom overturned and this fact makes it an important weapon for a governor. Although finding that governors during the mid-1970s were having their vetoes overridden somewhat more than in previous periods, Wiggins (1980) concluded that the preponderance of vetoes (over 94 percent) were sustained. As a result, the threat of the veto is often enough to change legislative behavior toward given gubernatorial policy objectives.

On the other hand, some observers (Rosenthal, 1990: 12) suggest that the use of the veto may actually be indicative of gubernatorial weakness and not strength, pointing out that no legislation would have to be vetoed if a governor were effectively exercising power (unless there were technical errors in a measure). As former governor Hathaway of Wyoming observed after noting that he had to veto only three bills during a legislative session, "I was able to see that the portions (of legislation) I objected to were stricken or I would just say 'I can't buy this concept' and it would end up in committee and not see the light of day."

In spite of its importance, our understanding of the use of the veto is still rather incomplete. In fact, research on the amendatory veto is almost nonexistent. This is unfortunate since we could learn much about the governor as policymaker by studying how this special veto has been used. Former Illinois governor James Thompson reportedly used the amendatory veto beyond the scope of merely making technical corrections, employing it instead to make significant policy changes in legislation (Sevener, 1985). For example, he abolished a tax multiplier and taxes levied on corporations with this power. He so frustrated lawmakers in the process that they complained of a breakdown of the traditional separation of powers. With an amendatory veto, so argues one Illinois state senator, "the chief executive transcends the traditional separation of powers and becomes a direct participant in the legislative process. While technically an outsider to the legislature, the executive, by strategically using the amendatory veto, can become the most influential of legislators" (quoted by Sevener, 1985: 16). Such observations certainly should provide impetus for systematic studies of this unique form of veto.

The main argument against research enterprises on the amendatory veto is that it is too unique and thus does not permit generalizations applicable to other states. This line of reasoning is weak and does not reflect the fact that the most recent and comprehensive analysis of the veto concluded that much of the behavior in the use of the veto tends to be "state specific." When overrides during the 1970s were examined, the researchers found that "no variable had any consistent or substantive relationship" in explaining a legislature's propensity to override a gubernatorial veto (Herzik and Wiggins, 1989). In sum, much still needs to be done on governors' use of the veto as an effective vehicle in the legislative policymaking process.

Another formal power possessed by governors is that of calling special legislative sessions. All governors have this power, although it is shared with the legislative branch in some fashion in a majority of states. This power permits governors to focus public attention on policy questions that are important to them, bringing some degree of pressure on the legislative branch (Jewell, 1969: 66). In a significant minority (or around twenty) of the states, chief executives have the exclusive power to determine policy agendas for special sessions. At times, governors with this power have skillfully used it in the bargaining process with lawmakers who have somewhat different policy goals or priorities (Kraemer, et al., 1975: 287). Systematic research on the actual roles of governors in calling special sessions and establishing their agendas is virtually nonexistent in the literature, but could add much to our understanding of gubernatorial power since it would be conducted in settings where chief executive involvement is focused and usually well publicized.

Our discussion so far has examined the formal and direct powers of governors in the legislative process. However, more indirect formal powers or duties are also available to governors and are often used in their interactions with legislators to obtain support for their policy initiatives. Appointments (or even the promise of such) are potentially useful tools for a governor in trying to garner lawmaker support. Although patronage in the traditional sense has diminished, most governors have at least 100 or so appointments to make to boards or commissions. Some of these appointments are more ceremonial than substantive; however, for a legislator who seeks to reward a friend (or demonstrate his or her influence), the appointment is often as coveted as an appointment to the state supreme court. Governors understand this and are not above doing a little horse trading with legislators. Thus, an appointment becomes the quid pro quo for a legislator's support and involves what Beyle (1983: 196) calls "coin spent for support" on legislation.

Another form of patronage is the awarding of contracts. More than the issue of who receives a contract are the questions of when and where should government construction projects be located. For example, some roads can be built sooner than originally planned, a decision that may be primarily a function of in whose legislative district they are located. Such an indirect formal power skillfully used by a governor can influence legislators on a particular issue (Beyle, 1983: Jewell and Patterson, 1977; Morehouse, 1981). Formal powers, direct or indirect, are not necessarily in themselves sufficient for gubernatorial involvement. For many governors, certain informal powers may be equal to or more important than formal authority in their pursuit of policy objectives. Potentially salient informal powers include such factors as the governor's party leadership, prestige of the office, personal bargaining skills, as well as key contacts and use of mass media. The importance of these powers may vary from state to state and at least partially compensate for deficiencies in the governor's formal powers (Bernick, 1979).

Sigelman and Dometrius (1988) conceptualize informal power as political clout that emanates from a governor having a significant electoral mandate and a substantial legislative margin—the governor's party controls a substantial number of seats. This thesis coincides with earlier work by Morehouse (1981: 251) who contends that a governor's party leadership (successful coalition building as indicated by primary success) generates party discipline within the legislature and, thus, gubernatorial success in policy development. While this is one method of operationalizing informal power, it does not capture the individual's ability to influence the policy process by the "power to persuade." Although a governor's power of persuasion is partially a function of party clout, the latter is not its only ingredient.

A related important component of persuasion is the prestige of the office itself and how it is used by a governor. Sprengel (1966) argues, for example, that legislators may defer to the governor out of a power syndrome that causes some to have a strong sense of respect and awe "for the governor personally, for his office generally, and for his power specifically." Governors normally understand the need to deal with legislators personally and to use the trappings of their office to help win support. As a result, during legislative sessions, most governors' doors are always open to any solon. As one governor has commented, "I have a rule at the front desk that no matter what my schedule is during a legislative session, if there's a legislator from either party that wants to see me—everybody else waits while I see him." Moreover, the adroit governor understands the importance of image for the legislator back home and how that can eventually lead to future legislative support for a program. Thus, Idaho governor Andrus has noted that frequent meetings with legislators permit them to go back to the local media and say "I met with the Governor last week and we decided. . . . " In sum, governors can garner considerable support for policy initiatives by "working" the legislators. This comes as much from the style of governors as it does from the formal powers of their office.

A variety of key personal contacts and public appeals through the mass media are other important informal tools at a governor's disposal. While such powers are not easily measured, their importance is recognized by both legislators and governors.

PERSONAL PROCLIVITY

The problem with any discussion of power, either formal or informal, is the underlying assumption that it will actually be used by governors with the same proclivity and adroitness—neither is true. The degree of personal acceptance and commitment to the role of chief legislator will determine how and when a governor will use power. Acceptance of the role is contingent upon the interplay of five factors: the governor's political experience, electoral ambitions, policy goals, sense of history, and personal style.

The prior experience of governors, political and otherwise, has been the topic of careful and painstaking systematic research (Schlesinger, 1957; Sabato, 1983). Few studies, however, have attempted to link such experiences to variations in the emphasis given by governors to particular roles, including legislative roles. At least one scholar (Rosenthal, 1990: 20) has suggested that a governor's prior service in the legislature, as a leader or rank and file member, may have a supportive bearing on his or her pursuit of the chief legislator role, although an unknown conversion rate must be applied to it. The length of time that a governor has served in the chief executive's position may also have an impact, with longer tenures permitting governors to build relationships with lawmakers and better predict how the legislature as a body will respond to gubernatorial intrusion.

Some governors are eager to enter the legislative arena in an attempt to build a record either for reelection purposes or a future campaign bid for what is perceived to be a higher office. Thus, one would expect a politically ambitious incumbent attempting to demonstrate political strength to seek approval for several significant policy initiatives. Some ambitious governors shy away from the legislative fray, however, because they have determined that a quiet tenure in office is the best strategy for future electoral success. For such governors, being a chief legislator is a role either to avoid or become involved in only on a very restricted and necessary basis. An ambitious governor's involvement in legislative policymaking may also be shaped by a desire to leave a legacy. Policies and action in the legislature serve as means to a much broader goal: to be remembered. Thus, a governor might initiate programs in education to be remembered later as the "education governor." The governor who wants to be remembered understands the need to be involved in the legislative process.

In the cynical world of today's politics, the media tend to stress the perspective that all gubernatorial actions stem from either political ambition or personal ego. Thus, few, if any, governors are considered to have strong and well-thought-out policy goals. This is neither a fair nor an accurate assessment of today's governor, however. Many are very desirous of shaping the role of government within their states (Sabato, 1983). One should not underestimate a governor's desire to have a meaningful and constructive impact on the policy process as a determinant of one's decision to enter the legislative arena. For some governors, good public policy is also good politics. Moreover, the marriage of political ambition and policy development makes for an even stronger and more active policymaker.

Probably the most important force, however, in determining a governor's legislative role proclivity is his or her personal perception of a proper level of involvement in the legislative process. This takes us back to a rather old but useful concept—role theory (Wahlke, et al., 1962). The governor's delineation of a proper level of activity is shaped by the rights, privileges, and duties associated with the office as he or she perceives it. The expectations are normative beliefs about what to do in the legislative process and how to do it. In other words, the role as defined by the governor shapes his or her actual behavior (Sarbine and Allen, 1968).

Not all governors define the job in the same way. Conceptually, one can develop the role definition by establishing a dimension called "assertiveness." Thus, at one end of the continuum is a governor who narrowly defines his or her role in the legislative process and, as a consequence, is a passive actor—only becoming involved when it is demanded. One justification made by some governors for their lack of involvement rests on a their state's constitutional demand for separation of powers between the two branches. Accordingly, former Oklahoma governor David G. Hall observed in 1974 that: "First of all, the Constitution requires the governor to be Chief Executive and to be separate and apart from the legislative process . . . that division is clear. One of the tragedies of most administrations has been the failure of the Chief Executive to recognize that separation."

At the other end of the continuum is the governor who clearly sees the need to be active and to define broadly the role of chief legislator. As former governor Thomas Salmon of Vermont observed: "My style is activist. Obviously, if I don't get excited about the legislation that my administration produces, others aren't likely to get very excited about it." The result for an active governor is the view that, if it's necessary to mix it up, a governor can hardly avoid getting into the fray.

Overall, opportunities abound for participation and it is the personal definition of the proper role that determines whether gubernatorial power is a mere crutch to keep one upright or a bludgeon to help secure a policy program. Governors who retreat from the use of power will render enormous resources useless while those who embrace it will find a deep reservoir.

ENVIRONMENTAL CONTEXT

The environmental contexts within which governors operate are a final factor that shapes their role in the legislative process. Environmental factors serve to expand or constrain a governor's perception of the proper role and use of formal and informal powers. Thus, social, economic, and political conditions may impel a governor to be either active or passive in pursuing public policies. Where no great issue demands are being made by the citizenry and a healthy economy prevails, governors predisposed to passive roles enjoy the freedom to avoid acting. In contrast under such conditions, activist-oriented governors are permitted broad latitude in interpreting their role and given added impetus toward action through resource abundance. On the other hand, suddenly faced with significant revenue shortfalls, passive-inclined governors may be forced to act. For example, former Texas governor Price Daniel spent most of his entire tenure of office resisting the establishment of a state sales tax only to conclude toward the end of his second term that he would (very reluctantly) have to introduce such a measure as a means of addressing his state's financial woes (Anderson, et al., 1989: 179–82). In conclusion, governors are either permitted the opportunity to define their role as they would be naturally predisposed, or they are faced with conditions that force them to act in a manner adverse to their personal proclivities.

CHIEF LEGISLATOR: A MODEL

We have reviewed the research on the role of the governor as chief legislator, filling in some gaps where needed with what we hope was reasoned speculation. Our review began with an analysis of formal powers, followed by a short review of potentially important informal tools. The analysis indicated that neither formal nor informal tools as distributed evenly among the governors or uniformly used by governors (even within a state). Moreover, it is our contention that the primary reason for differences in use of powers centers on gubernatorial inter-pretation. Thus, governors expand and contract their powers as the result of their own personal proclivities to use them. Finally, we briefly examined the effect of the environment in shaping gubernatorial behavior relative to the legislature. In summary, four dimensions (formal powers, informal powers, personal proclivity, and environment) serve to shape how governors define their jobs as chief legislator.

A graphic representation of the proposed relationships among the four dimensions which define a governor's role in lawmaking is shown in figure 5.1. A cube has been employed to portray the interaction of the four dimensions, with four sides representing each of the four dimensions. The two ends of the cube represent the governor's role defined at the extremes. The result of the four dimensions interacting is a particular role definition and can be visualized as a slice of the cube. There are actually numerous possible slices, with each linked to the angle of the cut. Therefore, two or more governors can define their role at the same level, but do so for significantly different reasons. For example, governors with "weak" formal powers may offset their poor formal position by using informal tools, while "strong" governors have less of a need for using the informal tools. Not withstanding these differences, the interaction of the factors results in the same role definition. In figure 5.1, the far and near ends of the cube represent the most extreme definitions of the governor's involvement in the legislative process. The far end depicts a governor with very limited formal and informal powers and who is free to be passive, while the near end represents one who is inclined to be assertive and has the resources and environmental stimuli to play such a role.

In the real world, the symmetry of cubes can obviously vary. As previously emphasized, a dimension is not made up of one element alone, but instead is a composite of several elements. Thus, a simple continuum for any of the dimensions does not fully capture its complexity. A plane more accurately represents the nuances of each element that shapes a dimension. For example, the governor's formal powers are typically presented as running from strong to weak, while treating the various powers as additive. However, we know that this is not certain. Some loss in one power cannot be offset by enlargement of another. It is inaccurate to say that a governor's ability to issue a state-of-the-state message is equal to a governor's veto capacity. Thus, particular attention must be given to the exact shapes of the cubes within which governors define their roles.

A word of caution must be added about the use of the cube. The model is still at a rather crude stage of development and we do not presume to be able to make exact placements of governors within the cube. Obvi-

Figure 5.1
Model of Governor's Chief Legislator Role Definition

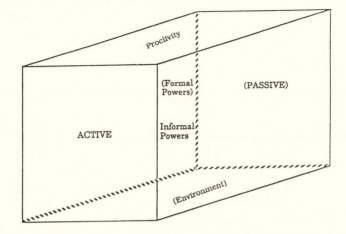

ously, the interaction of the four dimensions is complex and could lead to interminable points (or slices) of the cube. Our attempt is to depict graphically the four dimensions that shape gubernatorial definitions of the legislative role. Additional empirical research is required to examine the interaction effects of the four dimensions and develop a mechanism for locating given governors within the policy cube. A systematic set of interviews with former and sitting governors that seeks to determine the importance of each dimension should facilitate the development of a "function" that permits a parsimonious placement of governors within the cube.

GUBERNATORIAL ROLE AND SUCCESS: A FINAL MODEL

Given our analysis to this point, it is still not enough for a comprehensive portrait of the governor as chief legislator. We must move beyond the bias or view that considers government as totally executive-centered. Much of the research on the governor as chief lawmaker centers only on gubernatorial behavior, with other potentially salient participants treated as passive. Such a perspective assumes that all of the action emanates from one source and flows in one direction—from the governor to the legislature. Nothing, of course, can be farther from the truth! Any action taken by a governor is received by legislators who tend to guard their own powers and rights with the utmost of care. Legislators believe, correctly or incorrectly, that they are the true representatives of the citizenry. With the First Branch "protecting" the interests of the people, any significant action taken by a governor will likely elicit a response by solons. Moreover, legislators are not reticent to initiate actions to counter gubernatorial policy initiatives. Any model of the governor as chief legislator that does not recognize the interactive nature of executive-legislative relations fails to capture the reality of political life.

In figure 5.2, we present a model to assist in the understanding of the governor's overall role and success as chief legislator. It is a model that takes into account a governor's role definition, the legislature's response, and the context of the interaction. While designed to explain and predict behavior, the model's most important purpose is to focus future research efforts on executive-legislative policymaking.

Generally, the model posits that a governor's behavior has a direct effect on the legislature and consequently on how it reacts to the policy initiatives of the governor. The legislature's response, in turn, has a direct and primary impact upon the governor's success as chief legislator. Mediating the relationship between governor and legislature are a set of contextual factors. A governor's behavior toward the legislature is primarily a consequence of the role definition established by him or her. Gubernatorial action will normally conform to expectation concerning proper behavior. However, a chief executive's own role definition is not the only factor that shapes his or her behavior. It is also probably affected in many ways by the legislature's behavior, as well as the broader context within which it occurs.

The legislature's response to a governor is a function of several factors. Among those worthy of note are the lawmakers' perceptions of the appropriateness of the governor's behavior and certain contextual factors. The actual behavior of the governor, relative to the legislature's expectations, affects the legislators' perceptions. Overall, the extent to which lawmakers view the governor's role behavior as congruent with their perceptions of proper gubernatorial behavior will determine their response to the governor. Congruence should enhance gubernatorial success as chief legislator, while incongruence will result in greater failure. Specifically, legislators who feel that the governor has usurped their authority will resist the intrusion and respond negatively to gubernatorial initiatives.

Legislators' attitudes toward the governor and their reaction to gubernatorial involvement are also hypothesized to be affected by contextual factors. The first and probably most important factor is party. If a governor's party controls the legislature, this will have a positive effect

Figure 5.2
Model of Gubernatorial Role and Success in Lawmaking

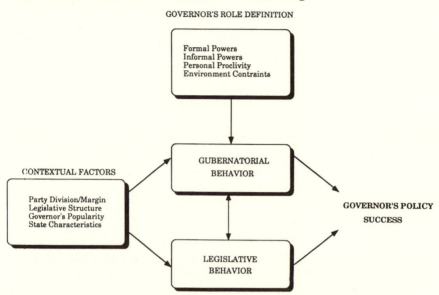

GOVERNOR'S ROLE DEFINITION

Formal Powers
Informal Powers
Personal Proclivity
Environment Contraints

CONTEXTUAL FACTORS

Party Division/Margin
Legislative Structure
Governor's Popularity
State Characteristics

GUBERNATORIAL
BEHAVIOR

GOVERNOR'S POLICY
SUCCESS

LEGISLATIVE
BEHAVIOR

on legislative behavior, while partisan division between the two branches serves as a constraint on gubernatorial success. Previous research (Wiggins, 1980) has generally demonstrated support for this notion, in that divided control of the two branches was found to result in enhanced conflict between them. This is especially important today since partisan interbranch division is more typical than atypical.

Besides party, the structure of the legislature plays an important role in fashioning a legislative response to a governor's policy initiatives. Specifically, a high level of independence and professionalism in a legislature will have a direct and negative effect on executive-legislative relations. The more independent and professional the legislature, the harder it is for a governor to dominate it on policy matters. In states where legislatures meet infrequently and only for short periods of time, have little staff support, and are technologically underdeveloped, the governor has an easier time in attempting to press policy initiatives. Conversely, more professional legislatures possess the powers and resources that permit them to be more independent in their dealings with the executive branch.

Two other types of contextual factors are hypothesized to shape the interaction of governor and legislature in our final model. One involves gubernatorial popularity and posits that governors who are popular among the mass public will probably enjoy a leg up compared to their less popular counterparts in attempting to influence legislative behavior on policy initiatives. The other type involves the broader state context. For example, we would suggest that larger and more diverse states have both more aggressive governors and stronger legislatures. As a result, conflict between the two branches will be greater in larger states than in smaller states.

CONCLUSION

In this chapter, we have attempted to outline several factors that, theoretically at least, impact upon a key role played by state chief executives in the policymaking process: chief legislator. Based on useful, but limited, previous research on this important phenomenon, we generally hypothesized that the governors' definition of their chief legislator role is primarily a function of the interplay of four dimensions: formal powers, informal powers, personal proclivity, and environmental conditions. Variations in the salience of each dimension assist in the explication of variations among governors, even those who have served in the same state, in definitions of their chief legislator role.

Governors do not define their roles and act in a vacuum, however. Mere role definition by itself is inadequate for explaining gubernatorial behavior and success. Consideration must be given to other factors, including the behavior of lawmakers, as well as their perceptions of the appropriate gubernatorial role. Another potentially salient factor is the context within which executive-legislative relations occur, and includes the strength of the governor's party, key characteristics of the legislative institution, the popularity of the governor in the public's eyes, and major social, economic, and demographic features of the state.

Future research on the impact of governors in the lawmaking process, comparative in nature, should focus not only on how chief executives define their roles, but the interactive effects of forces external to their offices. A systematic examination of governors should yield significant and meaningful explanations for variations in gubernatorial involvement and influence in the state lawmaking process.

NOTE

1. Unless otherwise cited, the quotations of governors presented in the text were obtained via personal interviews conducted by Bernick during the 1974 to 1976 period.

REFERENCES

Abney, G., and T. P. Lauth. 1987. Perceptions of the Impact of Governors and Legislatures in the State Appropriations Process. *The Western Political Quarterly*, 40, 3:335–42.

Anderson, J. E., R. W. Murray, and E. L. Farley. 1989. *Texas Politics: An Introduction.* New York: Harper and Row.

Beyle, T. L. 1983. Governors. In V. Gray, H. Jacob, and K. N. Vines, eds. *Politics in the American States: A Comparative Analysis*, 4th ed. Boston: Little, Brown.

Bernick, E. L. 1979. Gubernatorial Tools: Formal vs. Informal. *The Journal of Politics*, 41, 2: 656–64.

Bernick, E. L. and C. W. Wiggins. 1981. Executive-Legislative Power Relations: Perspectives of State Lawmakers. *American Politics Quarterly*, 9, 4:467–76.

Christensen, R. 1987. Well-liked Martin Packs Little Punch. *Raleigh News and Observer.* September 20:A-1.

Clynch, E. J. 1989. Gubernatorial and Legislative Influence Over Budget Decisions: Diversity Across the American States. Paper presented at the Annual Meeting of the Southern Political Science Association, Memphis, Tenn.

Durning, D. 1987. Change Masters for States. *State Government*, 60, 3:145–49.

Gross, D. A. 1989. Governors and Policymaking: Theoretical Concerns and Analytic Approaches. *Policies Studies Journal*, 17, 4:764–87.

Herzik, E. 1983. Governors and Issues: A Typology of Concerns. *State Government.* 56, 3:58–64.

Herzik, E., and M. Dodson. 1984. Developing Executive Roles: Gubernatorial Concerns in the Transition Period. Paper presented at the Annual Meeting of the Midwest Political Science Association, Chicago.

Herzik, E., and C. W. Wiggins. 1989. Governors vs. Legislatures: Vetoes, Overrides, and Policymaking in the American States. *Policy Studies Journal*, 17, 4:841–62.

Jewell, M. E. 1969. *The State Legislature: Politics and Practices.* 2nd ed. New York: Random House.

———. 1972. The Governor as a Legislative Leader. In T. Beyle and J. O. Williams, eds. *The American Governor in Behavioral Perspective.* New York: Harper and Row.

Jewell, M. E., and S. A. Patterson. 1977. *The Legislative Process in the United States*, 3rd ed. New York: Random House.

Kraemer, R. H., E. Crain, and W. E. Maxwell. 1975. *Understanding Texas Politics.* St. Paul: West Publishing.

Lauth, T. P. 1990. The Governor and the Conference Committee in Georgia. *Legislative Studies Quarterly*, 15, 3:441–53.

Miami Herald, 1967. July 16:6A.

Morehouse, S. M. 1981. *State Politics, Parties, and Policy.* New York: Holt, Rinehart, and Winston.

Ransone, C. B., Jr. 1982. *The American Governorship.* Westport, Conn.: Greenwood Press.

Rosenthal, A. 1990. *Governors and Legislatures: Contending Powers.* Washington, DC: CQ Press.

Sabato, L. 1983. *Goodbye to Goodtime Charlie*, 2nd ed. Washington, DC: CQ Press.

Sarbine, T. R, and V. L. Allen. 1968. Role Theory. In G. Lindzey and E. Aronson, eds. *Handbook of Social Psychology.* 2nd ed. Reading, Mass.: Addison-Wesley.

Schlesinger, J. A. 1957. *How They Became Governor.* East Lansing, Mich. Governmental Research Bureau, Michigan State University.

_____. 1965. The Politics of the Executive. In H. Jacob and K. N. Vines, eds *Politics in the American States: A Comparative Analysis.* Boston: Little, Brown.

Sevener, D. 1985. The Amendatory Veto: To Be or Not To Be So Powerful? *Illinois Issues,* February: 14–17.

Sharkansky, I. 1968. Agency Requests, Gubernatorial Support, and Budget Success in State Legislatures. *The American Political Science Review,* 62, 4:1220–31.

Sigelman, L., and N. Dometrius. 1988. Governors as Chief Administrators: The Linkage Between Formal Powers and Informal Influence. *American Politics Quarterly,* 16, 2:157–70.

Smith, G., Jr. 1976. Why Does Dolph Briscoe Want to Be Governor? *Texas Monthly,* 4:80–105.

Sprengel, D. P. 1966. *Legislative Perception of Gubernatorial Power in North Carolina.* Unpublished Ph. D. Dissertation, University of North Carolina, Chapel Hill.

Thompson, J. 1987. Agency Requests, Gubernatorial Support, and Budget Success in State Legislatures Reconsidered. *The Journal of Politics,* 49, 3:756–79.

Wahlke, J. C., H. Eulau, W. Buchanan, and L. C. Ferguson. 1962. *The Legislative System.* New York: John Wiley.

Wiggins, C. W. 1980. Executive Vetoes and Legislative Overrides in the American States. *The Journal of Politics,* 42, 4:1110–17.

6 The Power of the (Empty) Purse

Nelson C. Dometrius

Shortly after the turn of this century, the reform movement pushed for an executive-developed budget at all levels of government. The movement's goal was to reduce the waste and duplication inherent when government agencies submitted separate budget requests to legislative bodies. They presumed that a coherent budget developed by the chief executive stood a better chance of ferreting out overlapping activities and unnecessary expenditures. The executive budget is now a fact of life in American government, existing at the federal level in forty-seven of the fifty states, and in the vast majority of local governments that follow some variant of the strong mayor or city manager government structure.

Whatever its original purpose, the executive budget is seen to enhance substantially the office of governor in state government (Abney & Lauth 1989) and is included whenever scholars seek to measure gubernatorial power (Schlesinger, 1965; Dometrius, 1979; 1987; Beyle, 1968). The contention of this chapter is that gubernatorial budget authority waxes and wanes in potency and currently may well be in a waning state. To the extent this is true, it calls into question both our general discussions of budget authority and how that authority is measured.

Sigelman and Dometrius (1988) recently demonstrated what gubernatorial scholars long felt but had not presented empirically, that formal and informal gubernatorial powers interact. A governor with a strong personal power base can make far better use of the formal powers of the office than can one besieged by political problems. A recent study by Gross (1989) confirmed this interaction through looking at gubernatorial proposals passing a legislature as jointly influenced by a governor's formal legislative power and informal legislative support.

Beyond a governor's personal support and political skill, however, there are also environmental conditions that have an impact on the utility of the office's formal powers. In part, this statement is obvious for each governor differs from his or her historical and contemporary peers, and each state differs from its neighbors. I am not speaking here, however, of the legion of idiosyncratic factors continually raised whenever an interesting generalization is posited. Rather, I contend that economic resources vary across states, and probably cyclically across time, and these resources systematically affect the ability of governors to translate formal budget authority into policy impact. The net result is that the utility of formal budget authority is sometimes amplified and at other times muted by the interaction of formal powers, informal powers, and environmental conditions.

I will not attempt to provide a definitive test of this contention. Instead, I will support the claim that this conclusion is reasonable on three legs: first, showing how available economic resources are a necessary component of the reasoning typically used to connect budget authority with gubernatorial power; second, exploring the implications of this for our measures of gubernatorial power; and, finally, reviewing some contemporary evidence that provides an admittedly spotty, but still reasonably persuasive, case that the current condition of state budgets precludes the full exercise of gubernatorial budget authority.

BUDGET AUTHORITY AND EXECUTIVE POWER

To the first point: Why is budget authority viewed as a tool of gubernatorial influence? The reasoning is that budgets translate into policies, and thus, gubernatorial manipulation of the budget amounts to a governor's changing the policy priorities of the state. That the reasoning has merit even the most casual observer of recent national politics can attest. The Reagan administration was a friend of defense and foe of many social problems, but its attack on the latter was more back-door financial terrorism than a frontal political assault. After obtaining a substantial military increase for programmatic reasons, and a sizable tax cut for financial/political reasons, the rest of the battle was made politically feasible. Rather than having to attack social programs directly (many of which still enjoyed considerable popular support) administration chieftains could shift the rhetoric to financial terms, resignedly sighing, "Gee, they are nice little programs but we just can't afford them." After contouring the budget to their liking, government programs had to conform.

For this, or similar tactics, to be successful, however, at least three conditions must be met. First, executives need to know the policy impact of a specific set of dollars. Many budget reforms we have seen in recent decades have been designed to achieve exactly this end. Traditional line item agency budgets have a certain amount of protection against chief executive interference. It is difficult for those outside an agency's inner circle to know what the consequences will be of reducing or eliminating lines for clerical staff, vehicle maintenance, or computer purchases. Chief executives pondering obtuse line item agency budgets are the fullest illustration of Weber's political dilettante impotently wrangling with highly informed career bureaucrats.

The history of budgeting in America includes attempts to make expenditures understandable to nonexperts. Program Planning Budgeting (PPB) and Zero Based Budgeting (ZBB) are but two well-known attempts to require the translation of expenditure items into what program objectives they will achieve. Though originally justified, like the executive budget itself, as controls on duplication and waste, when budgets are made programmatically understandable, they are also made manipulable by nonexperts like generalist chief executives.

PPB and ZBB, after brief spurts of popularity, are now in decline, though each has left its mark on the budget scene. Accomplishing similar ends, and of considerably greater staying power, is the executive budget agency. Regardless of its location (executive office or separate department) or leadership (political appointee or careerist) the executive budget agency is a natural ally of the governor. Budget agencies compare expenditure proposals to some yardstick of state priorities and that yardstick is typically the governor's program. No governor, no yardstick, no reason to exist. For their part, governors can call on the budget agency's team of experts to interpret the numbers as program activities. The symbiosis is clear and compelling.

Forty-nine states have central budget agencies in either the executive office of the governor or an executive branch department (Abney & Lauth, 1989). On balance, then, governors can be said to have met the first requirement of using budget authority to influence state policy. With the assistance available to them, they can project the policy impact of financial maneuvering.

The second requirement for a viable budget—power connection—is that governors must be able to protect their budget choices from serious distortion by others. To a substantial part, this is provided by the authority most governors possess of being the sole source of a unified budget proposal presented to the legislature. This allows the governor to set the stage for legislative debate, a potent prerogative. This power of stage-managing policy debate through singular control of the budget is most vividly shown when absent. For example, the Texas governor submits a budget to the legislature but it is quickly dismissed as debate focuses around the competing proposal of the Texas Legislative Budget Board.

In addition to agenda setting, budget preparation involves making hundreds of expenditure (policy) choices, most of which are never changed. Legislators have particularized and competing interests (Herzik & Wiggins, 1989). They tend to focus only on selected budget issues where enough votes exist to make a difference. This leaves many gubernatorial budget choices unchallenged during the deliberative process.

The growing size of legislative committee staffs, as well as innovations like the Congressional Budget Office at the federal level, may allow legislators to more comprehensively evaluate executive budgets and make greater inroads into them (Abney & Lauth, 1987). Nevertheless, when legislatures go too far astray from executive wishes, nearly all governors can threaten or use the veto. Vetoes, item or otherwise, are seldom overridden by legislatures. Herzik and Wiggins (1989) observed that veto overrides are becoming more common with successful overrides rising from 1.2 percent in 1947 to 8.6 percent in 1980. Still, over 90 percent of all gubernatorial vetoes are not overridden, providing executives with a potent club to wield.

Budget adoption is but one step in the direction of policy through dollars. A second is overseeing the implementation of the budget when spent by state agencies. The fungibility of dollars allows clever administrators to manipulate budgetary resources in order to protect programs governors had planned to starve. There are limits to this strategy, however, for governors can cut further during the next budget cycle thereby reducing the slack in an agency's budget. No matter how clever, an administrator cannot spend money that is not there.

Equally common is the obverse situation, loyal bureaucratic troops carrying out executive policies with only a passing regard to legislative intent in budget appropriations. Again, numerous examples are easily recallable from the highly visible Reagan years—declaring ketchup to be a vegetable in meeting school lunch nutritional standards, manipulating defense budgets to pay for programs Congress thought it was cutting, and turning HUD into a subsidizer of wealthy contractors instead of a housing agency for the poor.

Two conclusions can be drawn about protection of the gubernatorial budget. First, budget control needs to be viewed interactively, as a conflux of the governor's budget authority, veto authority, political support in the legislature, and ability to influence the choices made by bureaucratic implementers. Former governor Evan Mecham of Arizona had high formal authority, but a decaying political base led to little success with his programmatic objectives (Herzik, Brown, & Mushkatel, 1989). In contrast, the Texas governor Anne Richards, has an exceptionally potent veto that makes her a key player in the budget process despite little real budget authority.

The second conclusion is that most governors appear to have sufficient budgetary clout to shape a considerable amount of state policy. The ability to appoint administrators varies considerably across the states and many governors face opposition control of the legislature, but most are able to combine formal budget authority and an effective veto threat to play a heavy hand in the budgetary process.

The final requirement for translating budgetary influence into policy is where I think the power of the purse is currently in a waning state. Executives can understand the policy impact of financial choices and protect their choices, but they also must have choices to make in the first place. The more, or more significant the choices, the greater a governor's ability to manipulate policy with dollars. Choices occur when a state has more revenues than are needed for vital expenditures, or when a state is facing substantial expenditure cutbacks.

In times of budget slack, where state revenues are growing faster than program demands, the governor will be allowed to target pet proposals for creation or revenue increases. Slack can also occur where resources can be moved from one agency to another without severely crimping the first agency's ability to carry out its programs (and, concomitantly, inviting a political backlash against the governor). Budget control during times of slack allows governors to play distributive politics—instituting policy preferences and gaining acclaim from supporters of the program while incurring little wrath among supporters of other programs that have not been severely gouged in the process.

Exercising budget authority for cutback management, however, is a risky proposition. If governors seek to minimize political dangers by cutting programs across the board, budget authority is not being used to implement gubernatorial priorities on state spending. If budget cutbacks are selective, governors can set priorities but they must also play redistributive politics at its most stark and visible. Someone's ox will be gored and the goree may both remember and vote commensurately in the next election. Facing such a prospect in a recent battle over equalizing public school funding, former Texas governor William Clements tried to avoid political liability by telling the legislature to adopt any proposal they wished as long as it did not call for tax increases—he just gave the legislature a dollar figure and then went fishing.

Both financial slack and budget cutbacks provide the potential at least for governors to heavily influence state policy priorities, though some governors may bypass opportunities provided by cutbacks. The middle point, a budget neatly balanced between political or legally mandated expenditures and available revenues, produces the lowest level of the dollars to policy connection for governors. The political support is not there for substantial cutbacks and slack resources that can be moved from one function to another are unavailable. In short, there are few choices facing the governor, and without choice, budget authority becomes irrelevant.

MEASURING BUDGET POWER

To the extent that this perspective on the interaction between budget authority and budget choices is accurate, it calls into question the way most models have attempted to quantify the budget authority–policy influence connection. Budget authority has typically been used (including by this author) as though it had a linear or monotonic relationship with power, somewhat like figure 6.1. Different levels of formal budget authority are identified, ranging from a low where the state budget plan is prepared by someone other than the governor to a high where the governor is the sole source of the budget proposal to the legislature. Each increase in formal budget authority is assumed to yield a higher level of gubernatorial influence over state policy.

The argument just presented, however, implies that the budget authority–policy influence connection, affected by the state's economic situation, is more likely a series of parabolas, akin to figure 6.2. With little budget authority, there is no policy influence. Even with higher levels of budget authority, policy influence remains low where demands and revenues are near balance. As we move away from the balance point in either direction, the potential for policy influence increases with the size of the increase (slope of the curve) depending on both the distance from the midpoint and the governor's influence over the budget.

Of course, the curves in figure 6.2 represent the potential impact of budget authority only. To the extent governors decline to use their authority during times of cutbacks—an empirical question to be explored by others—the curves on the left hand side of the graph may all fall at or near the horizontal axis. In either situation, the interaction of budget

Figure 6.1
Linear Relationship of Budget Authority and Gubernatorial Policy Influence

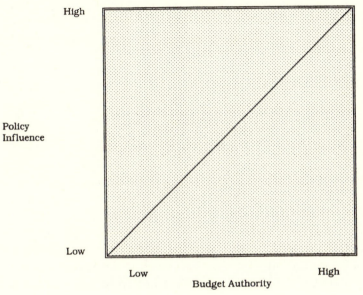

High

Policy
Influence

Low

Low   High
Budget Authority

Figure 6.2
Parabolic Relationship of Budget Authority and Gubernatorial Policy Influence

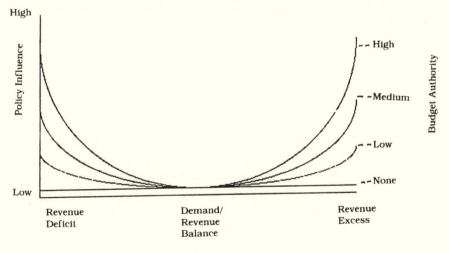

High

Policy Influence

- - High

- - Medium

- - Low

- - None

Low

Budget Authority

Revenue   Demand/   Revenue
Deficit   Revenue   Excess
                 Balance

authority with a state's economic condition raises questions about common quantitative models that include budget authority as a predictor variable. Most such models assume that a variable's coefficient is a constant in the population, instead, as suggested in figure 6.2, of being itself a variable. Consequently, prior estimates of the role budget authority plays in gubernatorial activities may be woefully off the mark.

THE STATE OF THE STATES

The problem with this revisionist view of gubernatorial budget influence is that it may be essentially correct but often unusable. Like the notorious Laffler Curve, there are often no clear criteria for determining when budget demands and available resources are in balance. The extremes may be identifiable, severe cutbacks or surpluses retained in reserve, but there is a broad middle where drawing distinctions is difficult. When is a financially balanced budget taut or flabby and full of slack? I can offer no magical way out of this quandary, but do feel that the evidence suggests many states are currently at the balance point—or at least far closer to it than they have been in the past.

The economic health of the states moves through the peaks and troughs of cycles. Many states entered the 1980s with healthy surpluses. A number of them moved through periods of severe cutbacks during the early 1980s and have since slowly moved back to normality. With a few exceptions, such as Massachusetts's current crisis, the recent history of the states seems to be one of battles at the margins, trimming programs here and there to make them fit within current revenues.

Whether state ledgers are in balance is only part of the picture. The long-recognized bane of gubernatorial budget leadership is the existence of earmarked funds—revenues collected which are constitutionally or statutorily required to be spent for specific purposes. We should broaden our perspective, however, and look beyond explicitly earmarked funds to mandatory allotments; expenditures that must be made even if not connected to an "earmarked" revenue source. Anyone who has ever made a budget comes quickly to the sad realization that the amount of discretionary funds in the budget is minimal. Just as the family must pay mortgages and utility bills, the state "must deal with the 'perennial' issues concerning the delivery of traditional state services—education, highways, correction, health and welfare" (Herzik, Brown, & Mushkatel, 1989:929).

The question we face, then, is what proportion of most state budgets is absorbed through mandatory expenditures and what proportion remains for gubernatorial discretion? The discretionary amount is a function of both the economic health of the states, which leads to higher government revenues, and the amount of mandatory expenditures each state faces. Both items seem to be currently moving to put a squeeze on discretionary funds.

At the same time that state revenues are looking less than robust, mandatory expenditures appear on the increase. Over the past two to three decades the courts have become more active in requiring some states to modify (usually meaning increase in practical political terms) their expenditures in areas such as prisons and schools. The federal government is also in the mandating business when, for example, it requires the states to develop their own environmental superfunds and share in the cost of hazardous waste cleanup (Medler, 1989).

Beyond legal mandating, there are also mandated expenditures required by political pressure. The scaling back of domestic programs at the federal level did not decrease either the need or the public support for the programs. The states were often pressured to fill the vacuum left by federal retrenchment. Simultaneously, the antitax brushfires at the beginning of the 1980s were fanned into raging infernos by politicians who knew a winning issue when they saw one. Consequently, states were often forced into making additional expenditures largely through use of any surpluses or other sources of financial slack in state budgets.

The result of all these forms of mandates is many executives with broad expanses of budget authority but few real choices where that authority can be exercised. This is readily seen at the federal level during the early years of the Bush administration where the self-designated education president was reduced to exhorting the states and localities to do better. President Bush is, in comparison with the governors, in a good position, for vital expenditures, like salvaging savings and loans or deterring Iraqi aggression, can always be made through expanding the federal deficit. With state constitutions requiring balanced budgets, governors have no such avenues of escape.

From the mid-1980s on, the states have been more willing to propose tax increases than the federal government (at least proposals actually called "tax increases" rather than some more palatable euphemism). Acquiescence to tax increases among state citizens, however, is not unqualified. Poll after poll shows that the public, by about a two-thirds majority, feels taxes are too high and state spending should be cut. When convinced that a dire situation exists, the public is "willing to *earmark* new taxes to deal with it" (Rothenberg, 1990:1, emphasis added). In Massachusetts, earmarked revenue "seems to be the only palatable way for the legislature to raise money for popular programs in education, the environment, human services, and infrastructure repair" (Chervinsky, 1990:6). Speaking of the South, Darden (1990:9) concludes, "It's tough to sell a general tax increase [though] ones earmarked for specific purposes are . . . much easier to get passed." In California, "the voters seemed to be saying that we will approve a tax increase if it truly will go for a manifest need and not in the general fund" (Field, 1990:12). Overall, says Rothenberg (1990:1), "the more general the specified use of the funds, the more likely voters are to reject tax hikes."

So the tax proposals we have been seeing recently, and the ones we are likely to see in the near future, produce revenues least influenced by gubernatorial budget authority. Even if the earmarking described by the pollsters previously mentioned is only a part of the sales pitch in favor of the tax, rather than legally binding, governors can later spend the money for other purposes only at the risk of providing a fat and juicy campaign issue to political opponents. The evidence is not definitive, but it is highly suggestive that governors of the present era may find formal budget authority to be of less value to them than it was to either their predecessors or successors.

DISCUSSION

Nothing in this chapter should be interpreted as claiming that governors are without policy influence. They have a formidable array of powers (formal and informal) they can exercise. Skillful governors can use the power of persuasion to bend the public's perception on an issue and thereby augment their policymaking influence. With respect to the budget, expenditures are as often required for political reasons as they are for legal or contractual ones. Thus, a chief executive who can convince the public that part or all of the budget for a specific program is unnecessary can create budgetary slack where none existed before.

We have been questioning here only the utility of one power and only within selected circumstances. When seeking to guide the states, governors use everything at their disposal and are not inclined to muse deeply over which tool was the straw breaking the camel-like back of the opposition. Ask any executive if he or she wants more power and the answer will probably be a resounding yes, regardless of the new power being offered. Even if it has no immediate utility, chief executives, like pentagon planners, are prone to build war chests against almost any conceivable future possibility. Indeed, studies indicate that governors have garnered to themselves about all the formal budget authority that is available (Beyle, 1968; Morgan, 1983).

It is the scholar's job to stand above the fray and dissect the reality taking place below—to evaluate whether the value of a particular tool is real or merely perceptual. Budgetary authority is both, for, among all the formal powers governors exercise, it is the most dependent on a host of other conditions. In statistical terms, it is the most interactive. Reelection potential (tenure), appointment authority, and use of the veto are not absolute, but, I would argue, they are far less trammeled by other conditions than is authority over the budget. Whether describing an individual governor or modeling the behavior of all governors, the interactive character of budgetary influence needs to be explicitly recognized and blended into our analyses. This is often accomplished in specific case studies, but incorporating the complexity of budget authority in broader comparative studies still remains elusive.

NOTE

There is a history to this essay. Eric Herzik called with a request late one summer. He was editing a book on governors and the budget chapter author had pulled out at the last minute. Would I save his bacon? I begged off, pleading too many time demands, having just taken over as department chair. Besides, (though I politely refrained from saying so) Eric, whom I had known for years, had the audacity to develop a book on governors without originally including me—a mortal sin if ever I saw one. After substantial groveling on Eric's part, I agreed to try.

Now, a rush job has definite advantages. No one can reasonably expect a thorough treatment of the literature, a rigorous methodology, or even a completely thorough analysis. Sensitive readers recognize the author is doing the best possible under severe time constraints. So, if you find something you like in these pages it is undoubtedly due to my diligence and amazing insight. If you find any weaknesses, gaps, or outright errors, it's Eric's fault.

REFERENCES

Abney, Glenn, and Thomas P. Lauth. 1989. The Executive Budget in the States: Normative Idea and Empirical Observation. *Policy Studies Journal*, 17:829–40.

_____. 1987. Perceptions of the Impact of Governors and Legislatures in the State Appropriations Process. *The Western Political Quarterly*, 40:335–42.

Beyle, Thad. 1968. The Governor's Formal Powers: A View from the Governor's Chair. *Public Administration Review*, 28:540–45.

Chervinsky, Gerry. 1990. Massachusetts. *The Public Perspective*, 1, 5 (July/August).

Darden, Claibourne. 1990. A Different Look from the South. *The Public Perspective*, 1, 5 (July/August).

Dometrius, Nelson. 1979. Measuring Gubernatorial Power. *The Journal of Politics*, 41:589–610.

_____. 1987. Changing Gubernatorial Power: The Measure vs. Reality. *The Western Political Quarterly*, 40:319–28.

Field, Mervin. 1990. California. *The Public Perspective*, 1, 5 (July/August).

Gross, Donald A. 1989. Governors and Policymaking: Theoretical Concerns and Analytic Approaches. *Policy Studies Journal*, 17:764–87.

Herzik, Eric B., Brent W. Brown, and Alvin H. Mushkatel. 1989. State Policymaking under Duress: The Governorship of Evan Mecham. *Policy Studies Journal*, 17:927–40.

Herzik, Eric B., and Charles W. Wiggins. 1989. Governors vs. Legislatures: Vetoes, Overrides, and Policymaking in the American States. *Policy Studies Journal*, 17:841–62.

Medler, Jerry F. 1989. Governors and Environmental Policy. *Policy Studies Journal*, 17:895–908.

Morgan, David R. 1983. Assessing Changes in Gubernatorial Power. *International Journal of Public Administration*, 5:419–33.

Rothenberg, Stuart. 1990. Tax Politics, 1990. *The Public Perspective*, 1, 5 (July/August).

Schlesinger, Joseph A. 1965. The Politics of the Executive. In Herbert Jacob and Kenneth Vines, eds. *Politics in the American States: A Comparative Analysis*. Boston, MA: Little, Brown.

Sigelman, Lee, and Nelson Dometrius. 1988. Governors as Chief Administrators. *American Politics Quarterly*, 16:157–70.

7 Managing the State Economy: The Governor's Role in Policymaking

Dennis Grady

Washington has a way of dealing with yesterday's issues. If you are a U.S. senator, you can give an ideological response to a serious problem and probably never be held accountable for it. Whereas the governors are dealing with the real world—they have to run things, to make them work.
—Governor James Blanchard

In 1936, Governor Hugh White of Mississippi unveiled his Balance Agriculture with Industry (BAWI) program in an effort to stimulate his moribund, Depression-wracked economy, and, in so doing, began the process of institutionalizing state government responsibility for proactive involvement in private sector decisionmaking. The elements of the BAWI program, while innovative at the time, are common features in current state economic development programming. First, he called for the establishment of a single state agency responsible for collecting information about the Mississippi economy and for recruiting out-of-state manufacturing firms into the state. Second, to address the problem of the lack of investment capital in his state, he proposed that local governments be given the authority to float bonds (IDBs) for the expressed purpose of acquiring land and constructing buildings as an inducement to out-of-state firms. Within four years, 14 percent of all industrial employment and 24 percent of all industrial payrolls in Mississippi were generated through the BAWI program (Eichner, 1970).

In 1959, Governor Luther Hodges of North Carolina (soon to be secretary of commerce in the Kennedy administration) led a state delegation composed of state officials and business leaders to Europe to attract foreign investment to his state. By the mid-1970s, North Carolina claimed national leadership in reverse foreign investment with 110 European firms having branch offices or manufacturing facilities in the state. In 1978, Governor George Busbee of Georgia formalized the international trade role of governors by establishing within the National Governors' Association (NGA) a standing committee on International Trade and Foreign Relations, which he chaired until being elevated to the chair of the NGA in 1982. In 1979, thirty-three governors led eighty-four trade missions overseas and forty states had established sixty-six trade offices around the world (Kincaid, 1984).

In 1979, the states spent collectively over $25 million for foreign investment activities, which equalled the foreign investment expenditure of the federal Department of Commerce for that same year (Berry and Mussen, 1980). By 1986, spending for international trade activities had increased by 56 percent ($39 million) and overall spending for state economic development activities approached $1 billion (NASDA, 1986). In their 1988 state-of-the-state addresses, thirty-three of forty-six governors giving an address mentioned economic development as one of their top three priorities following only education as a top concern among the states' chief executives (Penkalski, 1988).

While there is no question that governors consider economic development policymaking an important part of their executive responsibility (Grady, 1988), their actual role as "manager of the state's economy" is somewhat ambiguous. This ambiguity comes from two sources. First, there is a current debate regarding whether or not states should even be involved in molding internal market forces. While there are debates regarding other areas of state policy activity, no one questions whether or not states should be involved in education, transportation, criminal justice, or human services. In the economic development policy area, however the state's role, and therefore the governor's, is not so universally accepted. Second, how much influence does the governor possess over the policy area? As students of state administration have observed, the relative influence of the governor, the legislature, and interest groups over state agencies varies considerably across states and policy areas (Brudney and Hebert, 1987). Whether or not the governor is truly "manager of the state's economy" or just one actor in a more pluralistic policy process remains an open question.

The analysis in this chapter attempts to untangle the ambiguous nature of the governor's role as manager of the state's economy by focusing on three aspects of the policy area. First, the debate on the role of state government in fostering economic growth is outlined. By presenting both the pros and cons of the state involvement issue, we gain an appreciation of the cross-pressures confronting the governor in carrying out this role. Next, an examination of current economic development initiatives promoted by governors is presented. By analyzing the policy approaches being pursued by sitting governors, we gain a more detailed account of what governors actually do in promoting growth and diversification within the state economy. Finally, the formal power and informal influence of the governor over the policy area is examined by relying, in part, on survey data from the administrators of the states' economic development agencies.

THE DEBATE ON STATE ECONOMIC DEVELOPMENT POLICYMAKING

While states have always provided the basic infrastructure for private sector activities, the encouragement of private sector investment through the use of incentives and inducements has raised some question among analysts of state politics. Whether or not states have much influence over their economic health remains an open question. Further, unlike the president who possesses formal responsibility for certain aspects of macroeconomic policymaking, the governor's statutory responsibility for encouraging growth and investment within his or her economy is less formalized and varies among the states.

Opponents of state involvement in the economy raise three arguments to support their position. The first is that state development policies simply do not work based upon econometric evidence. What causes state economies to grow or contract has confounded empirical analysis. In Brace and Baumann's pooled-crossectional analysis of economic growth among forty-eight states over the period 1965–1980, they conclude that "attempts to develop a 'general' model of state political-economic performance may be futile, at least in the short run" (1986: 20). Hansen found, after examining the effects of various state incentive programs on unemployment rates and job growth that "these results certainly do not give much encouragement to those concerned about providing jobs through state industrial policies" (1984: 10). And, in a similar vein, Ambrosius concluded after examining the effect of various incentives on job growth, "The foregoing analysis supports the hypothesis that the economic development policies adopted by states will have no positive impact on measures of state economic health" (1986: 23).

The second argument is that attempts to lure industry through development incentives are an unhealthy zero-sum game, where success by one state means a loss for another thereby fostering detrimental competition (Peretz, 1985). Two bad outcomes result. Inefficiencies are created in markets because nonmarket considerations become important in the plant location decisions. And, in a federal system such as ours, cooperation among states, rather than irrational competition, should be fostered.

The third argument in opposition rests on ideological grounds—both from the right and the left. On the right end of the ideological spectrum, opponents argue that state intervention in markets is inherently bad. Any state intervention disrupts the Smithian "hidden hand," thereby disrupting the normal and healthy functioning of the marketplace (CED, 1986). Opponents on the left argue that development incentives simply redistribute wealth from the poor to the rich since the beneficiaries of the incentives are the wealthy stockholders of the corporations, while the costs are absorbed by middle income taxpayers and the poor who see their services reduced (Harrison and Kanter, 1978; Jacobs, 1979).

Proponents of state development policymaking raise four equally compelling points. First, to the extent precedent is an important principle in our society, states have always been actively involved in encouraging economic growth and expansion within their borders (Eichner, 1970). Newer efforts by states to encourage particular types of growth are simple extensions of the states' historical responsibility to provide the basic infrastructure for growth and development in our mixed economy. To prevent states from providing economic incentives would further diminish the autonomy of states within our federal system.

The second argument in favor of state activism in the economic arena is that the national government has failed to produce a national industrial policy (unlike most developed capitalistic democracies) and, therefore, the states have been compelled to fill the void (Dubnick, 1984). Since states exist in an international economic system, they cannot sit passively by while other international economic players aggressively pursue particular strategies to enhance their economic futures. To ignore economic development planning and programming would be irresponsible from this perspective.

The economic argument in favor of incentives is that, despite the inability of analysts to perceive their effect using blunt measures such as unemployment rates, the incentives do work at the margin. That is, all other factors being equal, differentials in taxation and incentives do have the impact of tipping the scales in favor of the jurisdiction with the best incentive package (Kale, 1984). It is therefore prudent, if not economically rational, for states to know what incentives are being offered by regional competitors so that they can compete effectively for new expansions. This rationale has been suggested as the reason why states have continued to increase incentives despite the econometric evidence to the contrary (Peretz, 1986; Grady, 1987).

The final point in favor of economic development policymaking is that it is good politics for the governor to be seen aggressively engaged in fostering growth. In Kenney's analysis of the affect of unemployment rates and inflation on the vote for governor over the period 1946 to 1980, he found absolutely no relationship between poor economic conditions and electoral retribution. "Economic conditions simply do not appear to mold voter response in gubernatorial elections" (1983: 157). To explain this counterintuitive finding, Kenney offered that voters do not see governors as the managers of the economy and, therefore, do not hold them accountable. However, research by the author (Grady, 1988) found that poor economic conditions were related to greater efforts by governors to recruit corporations into their states. The conclusion drawn from this paradox is that governors engage in symbolic efforts to ensure the citizenry that the economic problems of the state are being dealt with by state leaders. Whether governors are actually effective in their recruitment efforts is secondary to the voters' perception that the governor is making the effort.

The result of this uncertainty regarding the appropriate role of the state in fostering growth is that governors are given little guidance regarding how far a state should go in encouraging economic growth and how effective any particular program might be in achieving that end. There are no identifiable approaches embraced by either party nor are there identifiable ideological approaches in fostering growth. Essentially, it is up to each governor to strike a pragmatic middle ground between these competing camps. To do nothing holds the potential for the governor to be labeled as an enemy of growth and business. To overextend the state in offering tax and financial incentives holds the potential for the governor to be perceived as forsaking the public interest for the interests of the business community. How current governors are attempting to achieve this middle ground is the focus of the next section.

SETTING THE ECONOMIC DEVELOPMENT AGENDA

Examining the governors' 1988 state-of-the-state messages provides a recent snapshot of the concerns and approaches being addressed by the states' chief executives. The analysis is based upon the summarized version of forty-six gubernatorial messages to their legislatures provided by *State Government News* (1988) and follows the general procedures outlined by Herzik (1983) in his analysis of gubernatorial concerns over time.

Each summary was coded on four criteria: whether economic development was identified as one of the governor's top three concerns; the level of specificity of the governor's proposal; the structural area (labor force improvement, capital availability, tax reform, infrastructure improvement) of the proposal(s); and, for those mentioning specific legislation, what economic sector each proposal addressed.[1]

In the forty-six addresses examined, thirty-three (72%) governors identified economic development as one of their top three priorities for 1988. Republican governors placed more emphasis on the issue in that nineteen of twenty-two (86%) Republicans, as opposed to only fourteen of twenty-four Democrats (58%), placed major emphasis on the issue. There is a discernable regional bias for those governors who did not place emphasis on the issue in that nine of the thirteen governors in that category were in either New England or southern states. This perhaps reflects the uneven geographic economic recovery experienced in the nation during the latter 1980s.

Of the thirty-three governors emphasizing economic development, eighteen identified specific policy proposals while fifteen were more general in their agenda.[2] Examples of generalized proposals were Governor Bellmon's (Oklahoma) call to "create the nation's friendliest business climate" and Governor Sinner's (North Dakota) promise "to expand North Dakota's economy." Table 7.1 breaks down the specific economic development proposals mentioned by eighteen governors and divides the proposals into structural and sectoral subheadings. Structural proposals relate to broad aspects of the states' economies and affect the long-term ability of the states to adjust to changing international economic forces. Sectoral proposals relate to specific actors in the states' economies and reflect an area of either comparative strength or weakness requiring attention.

Table 7.1 indicates that the governors were equally concerned with structural and sectoral policy initiatives in that both received seventeen mentions. The emphasis on improving the labor force reflects the states' efforts to restructure their training and education systems to prepare workers for a post-industrial economy predicated on the rapidly expanding technology and information industries. The emphasis on infrastructure improvements illustrates the emerging awareness among students of economic development that one of the primary engines of growth in a state's economy is the quality of its transportation and public services. Interestingly, tax reform received only three mentions. On balance, in

Table 7.1
Gubernatorial Initiatives in Economic Development (1988 State-of-the-State Message)

INITIATIVE	NO. OF MENTIONS
Structural Reform	
Labor force upgrading	7
Infrastructure upgrading	4
Capital availability	3
Tax reform	3
	17
Sectoral Emphasis	
Export promotion	5
High technology	3
Rural development	3
Small business	2
Tourism promotion	2
Administrative reform	2
	17

Source: Council of State Governments, *State Government News*, February 1988, pp. 8–29.

examining the structural proposals, it appears that governors are willing to devote more resources to improving the potential for growth and few are taking the expedient and politically popular approach of lowering taxes to improve superficially the state's business climate. Since the processes for improving the labor force and enhancing infrastructure require years, if not decades, to come to fruition, it does not appear that governors are offering these initiatives for immediate political advantage.

The seventeen sectoral initiatives are concentrated in export promotion, high technology, and rural development proposals. In the face of decreasing competitiveness in the international economic arena, governors are attempting to facilitate export promotion and emphasize high technology industrial growth. The focus on rural development recognizes the uneven economic growth within states with much of the new activity gravitating toward urban centers, leaving rural residents little of the benefits of an expanding state economy but a longer commute to their new jobs.

As this snapshot indicates, governors are actively engaged in wrestling with the fundamental problems confronting our national economy. As our economy has become increasingly internationalized and technologically dependent, governors have staked their energy and political capital on specific initiatives to reallocate state resources to meet these challenges. This lends support to Dubnick's research (1984; 1985) on the role of state policy as part of a national development policymaking process and illustrates the role of the governor in setting the agenda of that process.

THE RELATIVE INFLUENCE OF THE GOVERNOR OVER ECONOMIC DEVELOPMENT

One of the major questions addressed by students of state administration in recent years has been the influence that various groups possess over state agencies (Abney and Lauth, 1983; Brudney and Hebert, 1987; Miller, 1987). The approach employed in determining who has influence over a particular agency has been to survey administrators of those agencies and ask them through various questions to rate the influence of external actors. Their responses are then used to derive a measure of relative influence over agency operations. This methodology is employed in determining the relative influence of the governor over the state economic development agency.

During the summer of 1987 the author mailed a thirty-item survey to the directors of the fifty state development agencies. Forty useable surveys were returned comprising the sample for the ensuing analysis.[3] Among the items in the survey, three focused specifically on the influence of nonagency actors. The directors were asked to rate on a seven-point scale how knowledgeable various groups were of agency policies and programs; and, on the same scale, they were asked to rate how influential various groups were for the initiatives of the agency during the past two years. Additionally, the directors were asked to rate how frequently the agency interacted with various groups. Since influence is a relative concept and since we are concerned with those external actors with legal authority over agency operations, the governor's influence relative to the legislature's is measured and employed as the indicator of the governor's control over the state economic development process.

Calculating the governor's relative power over the policy area followed the formula:

G–LPOW = (GGINFO–LINFO) + (GINIT–LINIT) + (GFRE–LFRE)

Where   G–LPOW = governor versus legislature influence
            GINFO   = rating of governor's knowledge
            LINFO   = rating of legislature's knowledge

GINIT = rating of governor as an initiator of programs

LINIT = rating of legislature as an initiator of programs

GFRE = rating of governor's frequency of contact

LFRE = rating of legislature frequency of contact

Table 7.2 displays the resulting measure of the governor's relative influence over the state development agency as indicated by respondents.

The table indicates that, in general, the governor is the lead actor in molding agency decisionmaking. Only three states reported the legislature to be more influential and eight states rated the governor and legislature to be equal in influence. Otherwise, in the remaining twenty-nine states, the governor is perceived to be the lead actor and capable of implementing his or her development agenda through the state development agency. (For an analysis of the factors associated with enhanced influence, see Grady, 1989.)

THE GOVERNOR'S FORMAL ECONOMIC DEVELOPMENT POWER

Beginning with Schlesinger's (1965) seminal work on measuring gubernatorial power, analysts of state politics have found the concept of formal power a useful indicator in explaining differences among state political systems. While the original measure has been refined over time (Beyle, 1983; Dometrius, 1988), the fundamental utility of the concept has remained important. In this section, the formal power of the governor over the economic development policy area is measured for the forty states responding to the state economic development agency survey.

While state policy analysts continue to debate the relative merits of the components of a governor's formal power (Dometrius, 1988), there is a consensus that, generally, the ability of the governor to mold specific policy areas depends largely on the governor's ability to appoint the administrator(s) responsible for implementing the governor's program. Following this logic, the governor's formal economic development power is constructed by examining how involved the governor is in appointing the leaders of those agencies involved in managing some aspect of the state's economy.

The measure is developed following the procedures outlined by Beyle (1983) as applied to the appointment power of the governor for ten functional areas of state government. These functional areas are: Commerce, Economic Development, Finance, Higher Education, Transportation, Labor, Utilities, Revenue, Tourism, and Budget. For each

Table 7.2
The Governor's Relative Influence Over the State Economic Development Agency

State	Influence Score
New Jersey	-2.0
Montana	-1.0
Kansas	-1.0
Florida	0.0
New Hampshire	0.0
Vermont	0.0
Oklahoma	0.0
Rhode Island	0.0
Louisiana	0.0
Minnesota	0.0
Tennessee	0.0
South Dakota	1.0
Delaware	1.0
Ohio	1.0
California	1.0
Mississippi	2.0
North Dakota	2.0
North Carolina	2.0
Alaska	2.0
Oregon	2.0
Utah	2.0
Idaho	2.0
Arkansas	2.0
Kentucky	2.0
Wisconsin	3.0
South Carolina	3.0
Nevada	3.0
New Mexico	3.0
New York	3.0
Pennsylvania	3.0
Nebraska	4.0
Maine	4.0
West Virginia	4.0
Iowa	4.0
Wyoming	4.0
Colorado	5.0
Indiana	5.0
Illinois	6.0
Georgia	7.0
Michigan	8.0

Source: 1987 State Development Agency Survey, University of Northern Iowa, Center for Social and Behavioral Research.

function, the index is scaled according to the governor's powers of appointment using the following formula:

$$\text{Index} = \frac{\text{Values of P}_1 + \text{P}_2 + \ldots + \text{P}_{10}}{\text{Max. values of P}_1 + \text{P}_2 + \ldots + \text{P}_{10}}$$

Where: P =   5 if governor appoints,

4 if governor appoints and one legislative chamber must confirm,

3 if governor appoints and both chambers must confirm,

2 if appointed by a council or administrator with governor's approval,

1 if appointed by an administrator or board without governor's approval,

0 if position is elected.

The procedure results in a percentage with higher values representing more formal power over those agencies involved in promoting and maintaining the economic health of the state. Table 7.3 displays the forty states used in the ensuing analysis ranked from lowest to highest.

Table 7.3 indicates a large variation across the states in terms of the governor's ability to control those agencies directly involved in economic development activities. Georgia's governor is weakest in that regard in that he possesses only one-third of the appointment power theoretically possible. Essentially, the Georgia governor shares formal power with other elected leaders, boards, and the legislature over the economic development policy area. The governor of Kentucky, on the other hand, is unrivaled in his or her state in terms of the economic development policy area. If we look at the states where governors possess less than half of their potential power, we notice a concentration of southeastern states (5 of 11) and no industrial states. If we examine the states where the governors' formal power exceeds 70 percent, we notice a clustering of industrial and larger states as well as the border states of Kentucky, Tennessee, and Arkansas.

THE INTERACTION OF FORMAL POWER AND ADMINISTRATIVE INFLUENCE

A perusal of tables 7.2 and 7.3 indicates that governors with considerable formal powers are not necessarily those with the most perceived influence in the policy area. In fact, the simple correlation between the two measures is −.1070, indicating that the two attributes are essentially independent from each other. It would seem that if a governor were truly

Table 7.3
Governors' Formal Economic Development Power

State	Index
Georgia	.31
Mississippi	.33
Florida	.40
Nebraska	.42
New Hampshire	.42
North Dakota	.43
Colorado	.46
North Carolina	.46
Wisconsin	.46
South Carolina	.49
Alaska	.50
Oregon	.52
South Dakota	.56
Utah	.60
Vermont	.60
Montana	.62
Maine	.63
Delaware	.64
Michigan	.66
Nevada	.66
New Jersey	.66
New Mexico	.66
Oklahoma	.67
Rhode Island	.67
Ohio	.68
Kansas	.69
Louisiana	.69
West Virginia	.69
California	.70
Minnesota	.70
Indiana	.74
New York	.74
Pennsylvania	.77
Idaho	.78
Illinois	.78
Iowa	.78
Wyoming	.78
Arkansas	.80
Tennessee	.80
Kentucky	.86

Source: Council of State Governments, *Book of the States*, 1986–87.

manager of the state economy, he or she would need both the formal authority to offer an agenda and the perceived influence to push that agenda through the administrative apparatus. We can assess which of the forty governors in our sample have these attributes by using the mean values of our two indicators as dividing points and displaying the governors on the resulting two dimensional axis. Table 7.4 presents the information.

The governors in Cell 1 have lower than average formal authority for economic development but are perceived by the state development agency to have more than average influence over agency programs. The governors in Cell 2 possess the ideal combination of formal authority and administrative influence. If any governor can be considered manager of the state economy it is these governors. Interestingly, the more industrial states of New York, Illinois, Michigan, and Pennsylvania fall into this category. The Cell 3 states are the opposite of the Cell 2 states in that their governors possess low formal power and relatively low administrative influence. It is the Cell 3 state governors who operate in a more pluralistic economic development policy process where the governor's voice is merely one of a number of institutional actors. Recalling the earlier review of the governors' state-of-the-state addresses where only thirteen of forty-six governors did not mention economic development as a top priority, six of those thirteen governors are in Cell 3 states. Perhaps their low priority on economic development policy reflects their realistic inability to implement an economic agenda without formal and informal power attributes. The governors in Cell 4 possess the formal authority over the policy area but are rivaled for administrative influence with an activist legislature. While these governors have the formal authority to propose an aggressive economic development program, their ability to implement that agenda is predicated on their bargaining ability with legislative leaders.

DISCUSSION

How much influence a governor actually has over the economic potential of a state remains an open question. As the review of the literature has indicated, the actual direct effect of specific state development policies is unclear. Therefore, it is much easier to defend state development policies from a political perspective than from an economic perspective. An aggressive economic development program may or may not work, but doing nothing to foster growth has the potential of sending the wrong message to the corporate community, which, fundamentally, controls the investment capital necessary for improving the quality of life for state citizens. Since the role of state development policies on the

Table 7.4
Interaction of Formal Power and Administrative Influence in the Economic Development Policy Area

Formal Power

	Low	High
High	CO GA NB WI SC	IA IL IN ME MI NM NV NY PA WV WY
	Cell 1	Cell 2
Low	AK FL MS NC NH ND OR SD UT VT	AR CA DE ID KA KY LA OH OK MN MT NJ TN RI
	Cell 3	Cell 4

economy is uncertain, the governor's role in molding the economy is equally uncertain.

Irrespective of whether or not states possess much influence over their economic futures, governors are actively engaged in offering development proposals. As the review of the initiatives mentioned by governors in their recent addresses to the legislatures indicates, governors are focusing on both structural and sectoral initiatives to position their states for a twenty-first-century economy. Their emphases on expanding exports, retraining their workforces, and promoting high technology enterprises indicate that governors are looking to the long term and are not using their position as manager of the state economy for short-term political advantage.

From a comparative perspective, it was noticeable how the governors' formal power and administrative influence varied across the sample of forty states. As in most aspects of the institution, some governors possessed the requisite authority to propose and implement a development agenda while others operated in more of a bargaining position with other state policy leaders. All in all, however, the governor is the most important economic development actor from the perspective of state development agency leaders, and the vast majority possess the authority to appoint most of the leaders of the state agencies involved in improving the state economy. If states have the independent ability to improve their economic futures, it is the governor who is charting the course and, in most cases, steering the state in that direction.

NOTES

1. The rationale for the coding scheme is provided in Marianne Clarke's, *Revitalizing State Economies: A Review of State Economic Development Policies and Programs*. Washington: National Governors' Association. 1986.

2. Five governors' summaries were simple lists of priorities without text or analysis since their addresses had not been delivered at the time of publication of the source used. These lists were provided to the Council of State Governments by those governors' offices.

3. States not in the sample are Alabama, Arizona, Connecticut, Hawaii, Maryland, Massachusetts, Missouri, Texas, Virginia, and Washington.

REFERENCES

Abney, G., and T. P. Lauth. 1983. The Governor as a Chief Administrator. *Public Administration Review*, 43:40–49.

Ambrosius, Margery M. 1986. Effect of State Economic Development Policies on the Health of State Economics: A Time-Series Regression Analysis. Presented at the Annual Meeting of the Midwest Political Science Association, Chicago, IL.

Berry, William M., and William A. Mussen. 1980. *Export Development and Foreign Investment: The Role of the States and its Linkage to Federal Action*. Washington DC: National Governors' Association Press.

Beyle, Thad L. 1983. Governors. In V. Gray et al., eds. *Politics in the American States*, 4th ed. Boston, MA: Little, Brown.

Brace, Paul, and Philip Baumann. 1986. Markets versus the Polity: The Politics of State Economic Growth. Presented at the annual meeting of the Midwest Political Science Association, Chicago, IL.

Brudney, J. L., and F.T. Hebert. 1987. State Agencies and Their Environments: Examining the Influence of Important External Actors. *Journal of Politics*, 49:186–206.

Clarke, M. K. 1986. *Revitalizing State Economies: A Review of State Economic Development Policies and Programs*. Washington, DC: National Governors' Association Press.

Committee for Economic Development. 1986. *Leadership for Dynamic State Economies*. New York: CED Press.

Dometrius, N.C. 1988. Changing Gubernatorial Power: The Measure vs. Reality. *Western Political Quarterly*, 40:319–28.

Dubnick, M. 1984. American States in the Industrial Policy Debate. *Policy Studies Review*, 4:22–27.

Dubnick M., and Lynne Holt. 1985. Industrial Policy and the States. *Publius: The Journal of Federalism*, 15:113–29.

Eichner, A. S. 1970. *State Development Agencies and Employment Expansion*. Ann Arbor, MI: University of Michigan Press.

Grady, Dennis O. 1987. State Economic Development Incentives: Why Do States Compete? *State and Local Government Review*, 19:86–94.

_____. 1988. Governors and Markets: Corporate Recruitment from the Gubernatorial Perspective. In Richard C. Hula, ed. *Market-Based Public Policy*. London, England: Macmillan Press.

————. 1989. Governors and Economic Development Policy: The Perception of Their Role and the Reality of Their Influence. *Policy Studies Journal*, 17:879–94.

Hansen, Susan B. 1984. The Effects of State Industrial Policies on Economic Growth. Presented at the annual meeting of the American Political Science Association, Washington, DC.

Harrison, Bennett, and Sandra Kanter. 1978. The Political Economy of States' Job-Creation Business Incentives. *AIP Journal*, (October):424–35.

Herzik, Eric B. 1983. Governors and Issues: A Typology of Concerns. *State Government*, 56:58–64.

Jacobs, Jerry. 1979. *Bidding for Business: Corporate Auctions and the 50 Disunited States*. Washington, DC: Public Interest Research Group.

Kale, Steven R. 1984. U.S. Industrial Development Incentives and Manufacturing Growth During the 1970's. *Growth and Change*, (January):26–34.

Kenney, Patrick J. 1983. The Effect of State Economic Conditions on the Vote for Governor. *Social Science Quarterly*, 64:154–61.

Kincaid, John. 1984. The American Governors in International Affairs. *Publius: The Journal of Federalism*, 14:95–114.

Miller, Cheryl M. 1987. State Administrator Perceptions of the Policy Influence of Other Actors: Is Less Better? *Public Administration Review*, (May/June):239–45.

National Association of State Development Agencies. 1986. *State Development Agency Expenditure and Salary Survey*. Washington, DC: NASDA.

Penkalski, Janice. 1988. Governors' Priorities: Education is . . . #1. *State Government News*, (February):8–19.

Peretz, Paul. 1985. The Market for Industry: Where Angels Fear to Tread. *Policy Studies Review*, 5:624–33.

Schlesinger, J. A. 1965. The Politics of the Executive. In H. Jacob and K. N. Vines, eds. *Politics in the American States*. Boston, MA: Little, Brown.

8 Education Reform in Arkansas: The Governor's Role in Policymaking

Dan Durning

This chapter presents a case study of an education reform adopted in late 1983 by the Arkansas legislature and uses the case to examine the policymaking roles played by Governor Bill Clinton. Specifically, I use this case study to identify how one governor used formal and informal powers to convince the state legislature to enact major reform legislation.

To complete this task, I briefly discuss previous research on the roles of governors in policymaking. Then I set out the case study of Arkansas' education reform, paying special attention to the governor's involvement. Finally, I present my conclusions about how the governor successfully influenced state policymaking.

GOVERNORS AS POLICYMAKERS

Research on governors stresses the many and diverse roles that they play in the political system. Ransone (1956) found that governors in the 1950s had three chief roles: (1) policy formation, (2) public relations, and (3) management. When he revisited governors in the 1970s, he discovered they were still carrying out these three roles and concluded again that "policy formation was the most significant and public relations the most time-consuming" role (Ransone, 1982:xv). Other scholars have different lists of gubernatorial roles; included on various lists are manager of intergovernmental relations, chief of staff, judicial officer, head of political party, and chief crisis manager (Beyle, 1983; Blair, 1988). However, whatever other roles are on these lists, scholars agree that a governor is the state's chief legislator—a leader in policymaking.

As the chief legislator, a governor initiates policy proposals and mobilizes resources to influence legislators to support or oppose proposed legislation. Governors propose highly visible legislative programs and exert tremendous personal and organizational energy to get the program passed.

In this role as chief legislator, governors rely upon both formal and informal powers. Formal powers come with the office and are a standard element in assessing gubernatorial politics and policymaking. The standard index of formal powers focuses on the relative strength of a governor's veto, appointment, budget, and tenure powers (Schlesinger, 1966). More recently, the power to reorganize government has joined this index (Beyle, 1983). Other researchers have identified additional formal powers such as staff resources, the right to deliver legislative messages, patronage, and the ability to call special legislative sessions (Kearney, 1987a; Bernick, 1979; Ransone, 1982).

Informal powers flow from the characteristics of the office (such as access to the media and prestige of the position) and of the incumbent (such as popular support, negotiation skills, party influence, energy, political skill, judgment, zeal) (Bernick, 1979). Within each state, informal powers vary from governor to governor and may even vary during a governor's administration from year to year.

The relative importance of formal and informal powers as tools of influence has not been thoroughly investigated, though anecdotal evidence has indicated that informal powers are more potent tools than formal powers. This anecdotal evidence has been disputed by Bernick (1979). In his research, he surveyed state senators in fourteen states and found that governors influenced legislators with formal powers as much as with informal powers, but he also found that informal powers were a more important source of influence in the weak-governor states than in strong-governor states. Of the formal and informal tools available to governors with weak formal powers, Bernick discovered that "popular support" (an informal tool) was the most important, and the governor's role in budget making (a formal tool) was the second most important.

Sigelman and Dometrius (1988) maintain that arguments about the relative importance of formal and informal powers are misguided. They write that the two types of power cannot exist apart from each other: formal powers create a "foundation upon which a governor can build his or her political influence," but a governor must have informal political resources to transform the potential influence available through formal powers into actual influence.

The conclusions of Sigelman and Dometrius are echoed by Kearney (1987b). Analyzing educational reform in South Carolina, Kearney found that "an outstanding individual can exercise strong leadership in a weak governor state." He concluded that Governor Richard Riley of South Carolina expertly used *both* his formal and informal powers to influence the state legislature to enact his proposed education reforms. The two important formal powers Governor Riley drew upon were his staff resources and his status as a second-term governor. As a governor serving his second term, he was experienced in working with the legislature and had appointed people to many key state government positions. Kearney also concluded that Riley had mastered the use of several informal powers, including negotiation skills, public relations, and the art of political strategy.

Like South Carolina, Arkansas has had a governor with weak formal powers (Schlesinger, 1965; Johnston and Durning, 1981; Beyle 1983) but, nevertheless, the governor has usually been a dominating force in the legislative process. According to Blair (1988:139), "Executive policy formation is especially likely in a state such as Arkansas, where the legislature, despite some dramatic improvements, remains a part-time and unprofessional institution." If Blair is right, education reform policymaking should result largely from executive leadership. Thus, success will be dependent upon the governor's effective utilization of both formal (especially the full-time nature of the job and staff resources) and informal (primarily negotiation, public relations, and political strategy) powers.

THE CONTEXT OF ARKANSAS' EDUCATION REFORM

In 1983, it was no secret that Arkansas' education system was substandard. The system's problems had been widely reported in a study of Arkansas' public schools completed in 1978. The so-called Alexander Report (named for the principal study investigator) concluded that "children of the state are not being offered the same opportunity to develop their individual capacities as children of other states. . . . from an educational standpoint the average child in Arkansas would be much better off attending the public schools of almost any other state in the country" (Arkansas *Gazette*, 1978).

The Alexander Report targeted inadequate spending as a primary cause of Arkansas' educational system woes. Inadequate spending on education was evident in some statistics. In 1959, Arkansas had ranked last in teachers' salaries; twenty years later, the state was still last. And in 1979, the average amount spent on each student in Arkansas schools was slightly half the national average.

In the 1960s and 1970s, concern about the state public education system had not been lacking. Beginning in 1966, Arkansas had elected a string of progressive governors who favored an improved education system. Governor Winthrop Rockefeller had tried in 1969 to almost double state tax collections to pay for improved education and other services (Ward, 1978). Following Rockefeller, Dale Bumpers had appointed an education task force to examine the problems of schools. Both Bumpers and David Pryor, his successor, had squeezed additional money from the state budget for increased teachers' pay.

Yet even with these progressive governors, Arkansas' schools continued to compare poorly to the schools of other states for at least two chief reasons: (1) Arkansas is a poor state ranking 48th in per capita income; and (2) It has a large number of school districts that adds to the administrative expenses of the schools.

Despite the state's relative poverty, many education advocates had asserted that Arkansas could do more with the resources it had. They accused the state of taxing itself too little, pointing out that in 1980 the per pupil expenditure (based on daily average attendance) was 64.5 percent of state per capita income; nationally, the ratio was 91.2 percent (Blair, 1988:258).

In 1978, the year the Alexander Report was issued, Bill Clinton was elected governor. While running for office, he stressed the importance of education for "addressing many of the state's economic ills" (Johnston, 1982:13). During his first term, he supported a large increase in funds for public schools, and the appropriations for public elementary and secondary education increased 40.5 percent (Johnston, 1982:14).

After serving one term, Clinton was upset in the 1980 general election by Frank White, a conservative Republican businessman. His surprising defeat was attributed, in part, to Clinton-backed legislation that increased the cost of car licenses from about $15 to $30.

In 1982, Clinton ran again for governor. He was not endorsed in the Democratic primary by the Arkansas Education Association (AEA), which was angry at Clinton because he had opposed an AEA-initiated act in 1980 that would have set stricter education standards for all school districts.[1] Nevertheless, Clinton won the primary, then trounced the incumbent. The AEA did support Clinton in the general election.

One of Clinton's campaign themes in the 1982 election was the need for better schools. During the campaign, he told the Arkansas *Gazette* editorial board that he was running for governor because he wanted to improve education in the state. He said that if he were elected, he intended to work to increase the state sales tax by two cents and use the new tax revenues for better schools (interview with Ernest Dumas). He sent a different message to voters, however: He said he would not raise taxes.

The key to Clinton's tax plans was a coming state supreme court decision that he thought would declare unconstitutional the formula for the distribution of state school aid. Knowledgeable observers believed the existing formula was unconstitutional because aid was distributed not only to pay for the education of the 430,000 students in the state, but also to pay for the education of several thousand "phantom" students. These phantom students were nonexistent students created through legislative tricks to increase state aid to small schools and to schools with declining enrollments. Clinton knew that if the Supreme Court declared the formula unconstitutional, the state legislature would be forced to change it.

SETTING THE STAGE FOR REFORM IN 1983

Despite the urging of the *Gazette*, the AEA, and others, Clinton did not propose major education reform during the regular session of the Arkansas General Assembly that began in January, 1983. Instead, he supported a $600-a-year increase in teachers' salaries that could be financed with existing revenues and higher "sin taxes."

In that session, the governor had wanted to avoid the controversial issue of whether small school districts should be consolidated. However, this issue was raised by Senator Max Howell of Little Rock and other legislators representing urban areas. Howell introduced legislation that would allow only one school district in each of the state's seventy-five counties.

Howell's proposal was fiercely opposed by anticonsolidationists, mostly legislators from rural areas; however, they were concerned enough about the growing pro-consolidation sentiment that they supported a compromise measure they thought would end the fight over school consolidation. The compromise legislation would set up a committee to recommend new education standards to the Department of Education; then the Department would be required to adopt new standards in 1984. Any school district that did not comply with the education standards by June 1987 would be forced to consolidate. Backed by both pro and anticonsolidationist groups, the proposal was enacted into law.

The new Education Standards Committee was to be chaired by the governor or his designatee. Clinton appointed his wife, Hillary Rodham Clinton, a Yale-educated lawyer, to chair the committee. Without doubt, Clinton's appointment increased his control of the committee, reducing the risk that it would run amuck and create political problems for him (Dumas interview). However, this appointment also raised the committee's visibility and the political stakes of its recommendations: Governor Clinton could not keep its recommendations at arm's length if they were too controversial.

By late summer 1983, several events clearly made education reform more likely:

- Arkansas had begun recovering from a severe recession.
- The National Commission on Excellence in Education produced a widely publicized report, *A Nation At Risk*, warning of the sad condition of American schools.
- Arkansas fell to a distant 50th in teacher's salaries and per student spending nationally.
- Reform of state educational systems as spreading throughout the nation with more than half of all states raising taxes to increase teacher salaries and pay for more rigorous school standards and curriculums (Kearney, 1987a; *Arkansas Gazette*, 1983a).
- Hillary Clinton's Education Standards Committee uncovered deep public concern about the quality of schools and incompetent teachers.

The move toward educational reform was pushed further on May 31, when the Arkansas Supreme Court ruled the state's formula for distributing education aid was unconstitutional because it did not provide equal educational opportunity for all children.

When the court decision came, Clinton could have responded by doing nothing, proposing to redistribute the available state revenue by taking state aid from about 150 school districts and giving it to the other 210, or supporting forced school consolidation that would reduce the funding inequity. All three alternatives presented difficulties. The first would be irresponsible (De Boer, 1986). The second and third were political dynamite: If Clinton proposed them, he could alienate voters living in rural areas.

Clinton also had a fourth, more attractive alternative. He could do what he told the *Gazette* editorial board during the election campaign: secure a tax increase for education. A tax increase could ensure that few districts would lose money under a new formula and that the districts getting too little aid would be given much more. According to Clinton's estimates, if a tax increase raised $100 million each year for education (increasing total state aid by over 20 percent), only twenty-nine districts would still lose aid under his proposed new formula.

The fourth alternative also carried risks for Clinton, however. After all, a much smaller tax increase had helped defeat him in 1980. If he really wanted a tax increase and education reform, however, the time was ripe for several reasons. Reportedly his polls showed that support for (or at least tolerance of) an increase in the state sales tax was growing as the state's education problems received more attention. He could blame the Arkansas Supreme Court for the tax increase. The new formula would also give him leverage over many state legislators: if they did not want the schools in their districts to lose state aid, they would have to vote for a tax increase.

PREPARING THE STATE FOR EDUCATION REFORM

Governor Clinton carefully set the stage for a special legislative session on the state's education problems through an extended "listening phase," during which time he formulated policy proposals, followed by an aggressive campaign to attract public support for his proposals. These steps mobilized public support for increased taxes and stricter school standards.

After the Arkansas Supreme Court decision in May, Clinton began his "listening phase." (He had promised during his 1982 gubernatorial campaign that he would spend more time listening to people, that he would not "lead without listening.") The listening phase lasted more than three months. During this time, Clinton conferred widely with interested and relevant groups. He talked to 133 of the 135 state legislators. And as the summer ended, he negotiated many days with various interest groups to formulate an acceptable compromise school aid formula.

The listening phase produced several results. It demonstrated to voters that he was keeping his promise to listen before leading. It permitted the governor to confer with diverse groups, giving them a stake in his proposals. It gave the governor and his staff time to determine what to include in his legislative reform package. It also gave time for the Education Standards Committee to complete its work and stirred curiosity, interest, and support among the public. While Clinton worked behind the scenes to formulate his program and hammer out needed compromises, his staff geared up for an all-out campaign to generate public support for a sales tax increase and education reform. The campaign would be conducted like a small-scale campaign for office. Governor

Clinton would lead the effort, kicking off the campaign with a televised address, then stumping across the state to sell his reforms.

At a press conference on September 12, Clinton announced that he would present his education reform plan during a telecast on September 19 and that he would call a special session of the state legislature to begin on October 4 that would be devoted entirely to education issues. His thirty-minute speech on September 19 was carried by every station in Arkansas. Clinton explained his education program and his reasons for it: "My fellow Arkansans, I want to talk to you tonight about the real problems we have in education. They are costing us jobs today and damaging our future. . . .To put it bluntly, we've got to raise taxes to increase your investment in education. Arkansas is dead last in spending per child. And the Arkansas Supreme Court has just ordered us to spend more money in poorer school districts to improve education there."

Governor Clinton explained that the higher tax he was proposing was not "just a tax increase. It's an investment in the future of our children and in the economic development of the state."

The primary elements of his reform proposals included:

- Changing the state aid formula.
- Enact as laws some of the standards proposed by the Education Standards Commission rather than making them Department of Education regulations. These proposed standards included increasing the length of the school year and school day; making kindergarten mandatory; extending the mandatory school age to seventeen; and requiring students to pass proficiency examinations in the eighth grade before being promoted to the ninth grade.
- Require practicing teachers and administrators to pass the National Teachers Examination by 1987.
- Experimenting with merit pay for teachers in twelve districts.
- Raising the sales tax by one cent and increasing some business taxes.
- Use money raised from the taxes to pay for the formula changes, implementation of standards, and higher teacher salaries (Arkansas *Gazette*, 1983b).

To promote the education reform effort, Clinton's office helped set up two citizen organizations: Arkansas Partners in Education (APE) and the Blue Ribbon Committee. The APE sponsored television, radio, and newspaper advertisements, and the Blue Ribbon Committee mailed about one hundred thousand brochures to ask Arkansans to show their support of Clinton's proposals by wearing blue ribbons. The theme of the advertisements and brochures was: "Let's put our kids in first place, support Blue Ribbon education in Arkansas" (Arkansas *Gazette*, 1983c). In all, the organizations backing education reform spent about $100,000 on their campaigns; the funds were raised from corporate and individual donations.

At the same time the paid advertisements were running, Clinton was touting his reform package at meetings and rallies throughout the state, and his reform proposals were publicly endorsed by an orchestrated parade of civic and professional groups.

This campaign was designed to whip up support for the sales tax increase, the most politically sensitive part of the legislative package, and to stir people to tell state legislators to vote for it (interview with Joan Watkins). The campaign evidently succeeded: When pollsters asked whether the person being interviewed wanted his or her state representative to vote for the proposed state sales tax increase, 63.4 percent of the respondents said yes (interview with Dale Enoch).

By the time the special legislative session began on October 4, educational reform was a highly visible issue. An Arkansas *Gazette* editorial observed, "Seldom if ever has a session of the Arkansas General Assembly been so heralded" (1983d).

THE SPECIAL SESSION

Governor Clinton opened the special session at 6 P.M. on Tuesday, October 4 with a speech that again laid out his program. He declared, "Our people are sick of excuses. They want action." He wore a blue ribbon on his lapel and the gallery was packed with people sporting blue ribbons (Arkansas *Gazette*, 1983d).

The session had three major phases that corresponded to the consideration of three major issues. The first phase was the fight over the new formula for distributing aid; this phase unexpectedly took up most of the session. The second phase was a short but bitter battle over teacher testing. The final phase was the struggle to get new taxes to pay for the new formula, new standards, and higher teacher salaries. As these three phases were occurring, other issues were being considered with less fanfare. Among the less visible issues, a few standards (including those requiring student testing, extending the mandatory school age to seventeen, and increasing the school day from five to five and one-half hours) were adopted. Other proposed standards (including lowering the mandatory school age to six, making kindergartens mandatory, and increasing the school year by five days) were defeated.

The formula proposal sparked what a participant called an "inside fight" (interview with Bobby Roberts). The proposal was so complex and detailed that the public paid little attention to it. However the issue was of vital concern to many interest groups; they engaged in a raw battle to get as much state aid as possible for themselves.

The second issue, teacher testing, produced a surprisingly brutal battle. This issue evoked in many—perhaps most—teachers an intense emotional response, likely a primal reaction to a threat to their status and self-esteem. The issue was highly symbolic, and thus teachers could not be persuaded by rational discussion or through deals to support—or even accept—the legislation.

The third issue was a proposal to take money from some people and give it to others. Three taxes were seriously considered by the legislature: a penny increase in the sales tax, a small increase in the state corporate income tax, and an increase in the severance tax on oil. While an increase in the sales tax was supported by a majority of the public, the two business taxes were opposed by some potent special interest groups. Thus, these corporate tax issues pitted powerful special interest groups against groups appealing for fairness in taxation.

The Formula Fight

The formula battle was purely a fight over the education budget pie. Clinton's challenge was to put together a coalition large enough to enact legislation that the Arkansas Supreme Court would not strike down as unconstitutional.

In 1983, the state provided local school districts with about $500 million. Of that, $347 million was distributed in the form of Minimum Foundation Aid (MFA) and the remainder was provided through categorical grant programs for such things as transportation and school lunches. Of the $347 million MFA aid, $223 million was distributed as "base aid" and $124 million was "equalizing aid." Of the equalizing aid, half was given to each school district as a simple grant per student and the other half was distributed to help poorer school districts. Thus, the real equalizing aid made up only 6.8 percent of the MFA.

Base aid was distributed according to the number of students attending school in a particular district, but it was adjusted for such things as programs for special education, vocational education, and gifted students. In addition, many districts received money for "phantom students." Aid going to districts with fewer than 360 students was not determined by the actual number of students; instead, these districts could pretend that they had 360 students. The small school districts claimed a total of five thousand phantom students, increasing their base aid by $3.5 million per year. This additional aid was justified on the basis that the per student administrative costs of small school districts are larger than costs in larger districts.

A different type of "phantom student" was created in other school districts. The base aid program, when originated in the Minimum School Budget Law of 1951, had guaranteed each district that it would not be given less aid in any year than it had received in the previous year. Thus, school districts could lose students without losing the aid that they received for those students. Because of these "hold-harmless" provisions of the base aid, districts in 1983 were receiving aid for forty thousand students that did not exist. The total annual cost of these phantom students was $30 million per year.[2]

The phantom students were the major reason why the formula was declared unconstitutional. With a fixed amount of state aid available, some districts were getting more than their share of money and others, mostly fast-growing districts, were getting less than their share.

The formula fight was over two main issues: (1) Should special assistance to 110 school districts with fewer than 360 students be ended? and, (2) Should the "hold-harmless" provisions of the base aid formula be eliminated? The former issue affected primarily rural districts while the latter would hurt mostly richer urban school districts if the "hold-harmless" provisions were eliminated. However, the issues did not cut across districts quite this clearly and several different camps, each fighting to maximize its share of the budget allocation, emerged.

Deliberation on the formula issue started smoothly enough; Clinton's formula to phase out aid for both types of phantom students over a five-year period quickly received "do pass" recommendations from the education committees in both the House and Senate. However, on October 12, the Senate rebelled. A coalition of legislators representing small and wealthy urban school districts, plus three legislators who were miffed at Governor Clinton, amended the formula to give more state aid to their school districts. The amendment continued aid for small-school phantom students and slowed the phase out of aid for schools with the other type of phantom students. By keeping the second type of phantom students longer, the twenty-nine wealthiest school districts in the state would benefit.

This amendment imperiled the entire reform package. If Clinton's proposed formula were amended, his whole package was likely to unravel. Dumas explained why the amendment threatened Clinton's tax proposals: "A number of urban legislators and others, whose support of the taxes is vital, are looking for a way to vote against the taxes because so little of the revenues are to be spent in city schools. Maintaining the status quo with the inefficient small schools would give them an alibi, if not a reason" (Arkansas *Gazette*, 1983e).

Clinton convinced the state House of Representatives to reject the Senate's formula amendment (the vote was twenty-two to seventy-two) and another amendment that would allow the small-school phantom students, but not the others, to exist (the vote was forty-three to forty-six). Finally, after eight days of work, Clinton crafted a compromise that pried enough senators away from the small school–rich school coalition. The compromise identified a couple of dozen "isolated schools" that would receive additional support outside of the school formula, but would phase out the aid to phantom students as originally proposed.

The legislature finally disposed of the formula issue on October 26, after it had been in session for more than three weeks. The approved formula contained no amendments opposed by Clinton, but his victory was a costly one. Enacting the formula had taken much more time than expected, causing Clinton's team to lose momentum. Also legislators, most of whom had full-time jobs elsewhere, were getting restless and irritable.

The Teacher-Testing Donnybrook

The formula fight was followed immediately by consideration of the teacher-testing legislation. Where the formula fight had been long and testy, the battle over testing was short and raucous.

Clinton had proposed teacher tests in his televised address on September 19. He had apparently added this proposal shortly before he made his address. When he briefed the AEA about his proposed reforms, he had *not* told them that he would include a teacher-testing requirement. Indeed, Clinton did not tell AEA leaders that he would advocate teacher testing until he called them an hour before his television address (interview with Bill Walker). On the Friday before his Tuesday television address, he had informed the *Gazette* editorial board that he would include either a teacher evaluation or teacher-testing bill in his program; he said he was leaning toward evaluation (interview with Dumas).

Teacher testing was immediately opposed by the AEA, representing about 17,000 of the 23,000 teachers in the state. Representatives of the organization said they opposed teacher testing for several reasons:

- The test was insulting and degrading.
- The test was racially motivated, intended to get black teachers out of the classrooms in eastern Arkansas, and it would be unfair to teachers who failed it.
- The test was politically motivated, using teachers as scapegoats to pass the tax increase.

The battle between Clinton and the AEA attracted widespread attention. The AEA was recognized as one of the most effective lobbying groups in the Arkansas state legislature. One study found the AEA the second most powerful interest group in Arkansas (ranking behind the state utilities), while another concluded that it was the most important interest group in the state (English and Carroll, 1986:32; Johnston, 1982:72).

The teacher-testing issue proved for Clinton to be both troublesome and a political bonanza. It was troublesome because of the ferocity of the AEA's opposition. It was a bonanza because teacher testing became *the* issue of the session. Since most of the public viscerally supported teacher testing, Clinton found himself on the popular side of an emotional issue. And, by standing up to the AEA on this issue, Clinton was seen as a strong, gutsy governor. The teacher-testing issue helped him gain immense political popularity as he advocated raising taxes by over $140 million a year (interview with Watkins, Dumas, and Enoch).

On October 27, as the formula legislation was being wrapped up, Clinton's teacher-testing proposal ran into trouble in the House Education Committee. It was defeated by a vote of seven to eight, with eleven votes needed to send it to the House floor. The next day, however, Clinton was able to get the needed eleven votes by playing political hardball. He threatened to stop any tax increase unless the teacher-testing bill was enacted and met with crucial legislators personally.

As soon as the bill was passed by the House Education Committee, it was enacted in the House. Since another version of the bill had previously been passed in the Senate, the final step to enactment of the bill was Senate passage of the House's version of the bill. However, on Friday, October 29, final approval of the teacher-testing bill was stopped when AEA supporters in the Senate filibustered. The apparent strategy of the teachers was to make an intense effort over the weekend to change the minds of as many legislators as possible.

In response to the AEA's tactics on "Bloody Friday," the governor's staff mobilized its own weekend telephone campaign (interview with Watkins). Its goal was to have, when legislators returned home for the weekend, the first four calls they received to be from supporters of teacher testing. Apparently, the Clinton blitz worked. One of the state senators targeted for phone calls, Senator Alvin Wiggins of Amity, who opposed teacher testing, complimented the governor's office "because his telephone rang every 15 minutes all weekend with callers urging a vote for the bill" (Arkansas *Gazette*, 1983f). When the legislature returned to work on Monday, the Clinton's teacher-testing bill was enacted as he proposed it.

The Final Battle: Taxes For Education

The final legislative battle was over taxes needed to pay for the new formula and standards. Clinton's main tax proposals were to (a) raise the sales tax from three to four cents, producing about $140 to $160 million in new revenue; (b) increase the severance tax on gas and oil, producing about $10 million in revenue; and (c) raise the corporate income tax for larger businesses from 6 to 7 percent, producing about $14 million in tax revenue.

Of these three taxes, Clinton had the best chance of convincing the legislature to increase the sales tax. Because of a quirk in the state constitution, the sales tax could be increased by a majority vote in both houses of the legislature, while other major taxes (including the severance tax and corporate income tax) required a vote of three-fourths of both houses. According to opinion polls, his proposal to raise the sales tax to help education was supported by a large majority of Arkansans (interview with Enoch).

On November 1, the House passed the sales tax with an emergency clause that would enable the tax to be collected immediately after the legislation was enacted. (Without an emergency clause, the tax increase would not go into effect for ninety days.) However, the House attached an amendment that would reduce the tax revenue. The amendment would allow low-income households in the state to receive a rebate of the sales tax paid on food. Clinton had backed the amendment, at least temporarily, because he needed the supporters of the amendment to get the two-thirds majority in the House needed for the emergency clause.

The Senate balked at the amendment and passed a bill that raised the sales tax without the rebate. And in subsequent days, it refused to add the rebate amendment to its tax bill. Despite originally supporting the food rebate amendment, Clinton worked to convince the House to remove the amendment from its version of the tax increase. After intense lobbying, the House gave in and on Friday, November 4, the sales tax was enacted with an emergency clause.

The two business tax increases were defeated, Clinton's major losses during the session. The severance tax increase was stoutly opposed by powerful poultry interests in Northwest Arkansas and some small gas producers. The corporate tax increase was opposed by the Arkansas Chamber of Commerce and several larger firms in the state. These business groups formed a coalition to oppose both taxes and used their lobbying muscle to stop them. While Clinton got both measures to the floor of the House, he could not get three-fourths of the House to vote for either tax.

Some people suspect that Governor Clinton was not too disappointed that the business taxes did not pass. According to Representative Jodie Mahoney, the floor leader for the tax bills, he (Mahoney) did not get the necessary support from the governor's office needed to pass the tax (interview with Jodie Mahoney). This view is echoed by other observers (interviews with Dumas and Walker) but is disputed by some participants (interview with Jim Pledger). According to both Dumas and Bobby Roberts, the business taxes could have been passed if they had been considered earlier in the session and if the session had not bogged down over the formula fight.

The Post-Mortem

The special session on education lasted thirty-eight days, the state's longest in the post–World War II era. Most of the legislation Governor Clinton had proposed was enacted. His handling of the session was viewed as "masterful" by both supporters and opponents. A columnist in the Arkansas *Democrat*, a paper usually unsympathetic to Clinton, marveled how he had "with a hand as firm as Faubus ever waved...rescued his education program from legislative limbo." Clinton himself judged that the session had "done a lot for Arkansas" (Arkansas *Democrat*, 1983).

Teachers had different views. Kai Erickson of the AEA said, "I'm afraid history is going to indicate this was a wasted opportunity" (Arkansas *Gazette*, 1983g). And, more ominously, Ermalee Boice declared that school teachers and Governor Bill Clinton were "at war." (Arkansas *Gazette*, 1983h).

UTILIZING GUBERNATORIAL POWERS TO ACHIEVE POLICY GOALS

Bill Clinton was the central character in the story of education reform in Arkansas. He and his office formulated the legislative reform package, sold it to the public, and led the fight to get it through the state legislature. To carry out these tasks, Clinton drew heavily from both the formal and informal arsenals of power. Without both, his reform proposals—especially the tax increase—would not have become law.

The success of Governor Clinton's education reform depended, above all, on his political skills, including his timing of the reform initiative, his judgment about what to include in his reform package, his masterful use of symbols, and his ability to mobilize public support for his proposals.

By presenting his education reforms to a special legislative session, he increased the chances of success. According to Blair (1988), special sessions in Arkansas are known as "governor's sessions." She notes, "With many legislators inconvenienced by this unplanned interruption in their income-producing occupations, governors usually find an assembly anxious to deal quickly with the gubernatorial agenda and return to their private pursuits." Thus, the formal power to call the special session augmented the more informal manipulation of the timing and strategy of the reform issue.

Clinton and his staff also used their access to the media—an informal power—expertly to generate public support for the education reform. They executed a first-rate issue campaign to raise public interest and then aggressively sell the proposed program. This issue campaign convinced many legislators that they could vote for taxes and survive politically.

Again, a formal power—to deliver legislative messages—aided the informal power by communicating through the media with the public. Clinton used this power when he opened the special session with a speech explaining and advocating his education reforms. This speech was fully covered by television and newspapers.

From all reports, Clinton's legislative strategy was excellent and his legislative tactics were skillfully executed. The ability to plan and implement a strategy is an important informal power. However, tactical actions use resources created by both formal and informal powers.

Several aspects of Clinton's legislative strategy paid off. For example, his media campaign was persuasive. His teacher-testing proposal became a symbol that caught the public's imagination. And by waiting until the new school formula was passed before moving to the rest of his legislative package, he would show legislators how much money schools in their legislative districts would gain if the sales tax were enacted or lose if it were not. Clinton also made the necessary deals to move his package along. He stopped potential opposition to education reform by higher education interests by giving them $40 million of the new revenues. He accepted the "isolated school districts" compromise to get the formula passed. He attracted key support for his sales tax with an exemption from the sales tax for contractors, appointments to boards and commissions, appointments to study commissions, and use of other currency in the Arkansas political pork barrel.

Clinton could make many of these deals because of his formal power to appoint the members of various boards, commissions, and other state advisory bodies. With his appointment powers, he had positions to trade for votes. Clinton used another formal power—the veto power—to back his threat to stop the tax increase unless the legislature passed his teacher-testing bill. This threat to stop the tax increase came at one of the decisive moments in the session. Clinton showed that, without doubt, he was serious about teacher testing and would not let legislators off the hook: they would either vote for teacher testing or some schools in their legislative district would be losing money in coming years. The threat of a veto was a major resource he had at his disposal to influence the legislature.

CONCLUSION: BEYOND FORMAL AND INFORMAL POWERS

This case study of Arkansas' education reform showed a governor filling the role of chief legislator, using a diverse range of formal and informal powers to gain enactment of a controversial legislative package. In this case, it was clear that a governor had to use both types of power to be successful. In fact, asking whether formal powers were more important tools of influence than informal powers seems like asking if lungs are more important for life than oxygen. Both pairs function together.

The Arkansas case shows that a governor who focuses his powers on a particular policy proposal is difficult to stop. A governor can bring tremendous resources to bear at any time on one or two policy battles. If the governor's resources are concentrated on one policy goal, rather than diffused to try to achieve several goals, he has the ability to overwhelm a legislature, especially a part-time legislature.

The Arkansas case also shows the importance of luck in policymaking. Several events beyond Clinton's control contributed to a social and political climate in which education reform was welcomed. For example, the Arkansas Supreme Court decision on the state's education formula, the state's recovery from its recession, and the *Nation at Risk* report all made Clinton's education reform more feasible.

Partly because of his adroit policy leadership and partly because of luck, the special legislative session was a success for Bill Clinton. Most of his proposed legislation was enacted, and equally important for him, he came out of the special session with greater political popularity and a better public image than ever before, despite being the author of the biggest tax increase in the state's history.

NOTES

1. The AEA's initiated act was a precursor to the standards adopted by law in 1983 and by the Arkansas Department of Education in 1984. The initiated act would have set minimum standards for all school districts on course offerings, graduation requirements, length of the school year, and student-teacher ratios. The AEA's initiative opened a rift between the organization and Governor Clinton. The AEA claimed that Clinton reneged on a promise that he would not oppose the measure. When he did, he displeased many members of the large interest group.

2. This provision creating these phantom students was altered in 1979 so that additional phantom students could not be created in the future, but the 1979 legislation did not eliminate the phantom students created from 1951 to 1979.

REFERENCES

Beyle, Thad. 1983. Governors. In Gray, Jacob, and Vines, eds. *Politics in the American States*, 4th ed. Boston: Little, Brown.

Arkansas *Democrat*. 1983. Oct. 20:5G.

Arkansas *Gazette*. 1978. Sept. 27: 1A.

_____. 1983a. Sept. 11: 1H.

_____. 1983b. Sept. 20: 1A.

_____. 1983c. Sept. 29: 1A.

_____. 1983d. Oct. 10: 20A.

_____. 1983e. Oct. 16: 1A.

_____. 1983f. Nov. 1: 1A.

_____. 1983g. Nov. 12: 3A.

_____. 1983h. Nov. 18: 1A.

_____. 1985. July 19.

Blair, Diane. 1988. *Arkansas Politics and Government*. Lincoln: University of Nebraska Press.

Bernick, E. Lee. 1979. Gubernatorial Tools: Formal vs. Informal. *Journal of Politics*, 41, May: 656–64.

De Boer, Marvin. 1986. Governor Clinton and Educational Reform in Arkansas: A Study in Communication. Paper presented to 1986 annual meeting of the Arkansas Political Science Association.

English, Art, and John Carroll. 1986. Interest Groups in Arkansas: The Politics of Modified Inequality. Paper prepared for delivery at the 1986 Annual Meeting of the Southern Political Science Association, Atlanta, Georgia.

Johnston, Robert, and Dan Durning. 1981. The Arkansas Governor's Role in the Policy Process, 1955–1979. *Arkansas Political Science Journal*, 2, 1:16-39.

Johnston, Phyllis. 1982. *Bill Clinton's Public Policy for Arkansas, 1979–1980*. Little Rock: August House.

Kearney, Richard. 1987. The 'Weak' Governor as Policy Maker: Dick Riley and the South Carolina Education Improvement Act. *Southeastern Political Review*, 15(2), Fall:99–119.

———. 1987a. How a 'Weak' Governor Can Be Strong: Dick Riley and Education Reform in South Carolina. *State Government*, 60, 4: 150–156.

Ransone, Coleman B., Jr. 1956. *The Office of Governor in the United States*. University: University of Alabama Press.

———. 1982. *The American Governorship*. Westport, CT: Greenwood Press.

Schlesinger, Joseph. 1965. Politics of the Executive. In Jacob and Vines, eds. *Politics in the American States*. Boston: Little, Brown.

Sigelman, Lee, and Nelson Dometrius. 1988. Governors as Chief Administrators. *American Politics Quarterly*, 16, 2.

Ward, John. 1978. *The Arkansas Rockefeller*. Baton Rouge: Louisiana State University Press.

Interviews with:

Ernest Dumas, editorial writer and columnist, Arkansas *Gazette*.

Dale Enoch, president of Precision Research, Inc., a Little Rock public opinion polling firm.

State Representative Jodie Mahoney, El Dorado.

Jim Pledger, Arkansas Department of Labor (Clinton's liaison to House of Representatives during the 1983 special session).

Bobby Roberts, University of Arkansas at Little Rock archives (Senate liaison during the 1983 special session).

Joan Watkins, former press secretary to Governor Bill Clinton.

Bill Walker, former chief lobbyist for the Arkansas Education Association.

9   Governors and Environmental Policies: A Comparative Analysis

Jerry Medler and Jeffery Berejikian

The United States has fifty governors and fifty environmental polices. In large part, the quality of life in America is determined by state and local decisions regarding the environment. Yet we know few of the details about these state leaders and policies. How do local voters respond to environmental problems and environmental policies? Do governors take visible stands on environmental issues? How do voters respond to governors when they do take a position? And, are there variations from state to state and time to time? These are some of the questions that will be addressed in this chapter.

The opening sections briefly describe the setting and political constraints for governors and state policymaking. Then questions of environmental policy and economic development are raised. The remainder of the chapter is devoted to a comparative analysis of environmental policymaking in Oregon and California through the mechanism of direct citizen participation in state initiatives and referenda. The role of governors is examined by a spatial analysis of voters' response to both governors and environmental policies.

GOVERNORS, STATE POLITICS, AND BUDGETS

It is tempting to seize on the parallel structure between state and national government and come to the conclusion that governors are the functional equivalents of presidents. That is, however, a misleading comparison as governors are considerably more constrained. In many states the executive functions are housed in separate sub-branches of state government under the control of independently elected statewide officials such as secretaries of state, state treasurers, and attorneys general. In this regard it is easy to see that a governor's authority is more severely limited than the president's.

Perhaps the most important distinction between state and national governments is the fact that the governors of the fifty states must operate with balanced budgets. In recent years state revenues have often been inadequate to meet state needs in traditional policy areas such as education, corrections, and highways. The device of a deficit budget cannot be used to meet competing demands or to build a political future as a visionary leader. Thus, governors are forced to build their careers and reputations within the straight and narrow confines of fiscal responsibility.

Governors then must pursue policies that are circumscribed by the ambitions of other statewide officials (not necessarily of the same party) while maintaining a balanced budget. The implications of these limitations can be stated as hypotheses: Governors will tend to limit their pursuit of environmental policies to policies that are not costly to the state treasury and not likely to infringe on other officials' political turf. Governors are most likely to embrace policies that minimize costs to the state and maximize their visibility as political leaders.

STATE AND FEDERAL POLICIES

Federalism, of course, plays a critical role in most contemporary policymaking. In some policy domains it is clear that the federal government has taken the lead in developing and implementing policy (e.g., the War on Poverty), while in other areas, states are recognized as initiators of policy with the federal government playing a reluctant or obstructing role (e.g., nuclear waste disposal). And in some policy matters the state and federal government can become embroiled in policy conflicts (such as offshore oil and gas development). Consequently the multilevel aspects of American federalism must be considered in any examination of factors that shape state policy.

The New Federalism is a recent development in the allocation of policymaking responsibility. Essentially, the New Federalism represents a devolution of policymaking responsibility from the federal government to the states (Van Horn, 1979). The political acceptability of the New Federalism has varied from state to state and from policy area to policy area. Perhaps most importantly, federal willingness to provide funding assistance for state policies has encouraged local acceptance of the New Federalism.

An excellent example of the New Federalism involving environmental policy is the Coastal Zone Management Act (1972) which explicitly called for locally devised management plans for each state's coastal resources. In the initial period following the establishment of the Coastal Zone Management Act, Congress provided substantial funds to underwrite the costs of local planning activities. Consequently, many coastal zone states found themselves involved with a new area of policy responsibility, creating a new state-level arena for the debate of environmental policy.

In other areas of environmental policy the federal government has taken the initiative and followed a more intrusive approach mandating that policies formulated at the national level must be adopted at the local level. For example, in the areas of clean air and water the national government has been more aggressive, setting standards and demanding that local entities meet national standards. This imposition of a national policy poses a sharp contrast to the local control provided under the New Federalism.

These two approaches to environmental policymaking create two distinct settings for gubernatorial action. While the New Federalism offers local control and a local arena for policymaking, national mandates leave little latitude for local action offering few opportunities for gubernatorial maneuvering. Consequently, governors may try to ignore the environmental problems targeted by federally imposed policies.

GUBERNATORIAL LEADERSHIP, THE ENVIRONMENT, AND ELECTIONS

The matrix of federal and state responsibilities in environmental policymaking defines the structure of political opportunities and risks associated with policymaking in this arena. Governors must assess the opportunities and risks of all policy arenas, not just environmental policy. Presumably governors assess environmental policymaking as an activity that may enhance their standing among the voters.

This is not to say that governors view environmental policy in only this utilitarian fashion. However, common sense and a considerable body of theory (e.g., Downs, 1957) suggest that governors are not insensitive to the political gains and losses to be won or suffered in the arena of environmental policymaking. It is reasonable to hypothesize that governors will enter the environmental policymaking arena in response to expected electoral gains and losses. If governors perceive that their involvement in the arena of environmental policymaking is likely to increase voter support, they will find ways to play an active and visible role in this arena. On the other hand, if governors feel that involvement with environmental policymaking will hurt their standing among voters, they will leave this arena to other actors such as legislators, judges, and bureaucrats.

This utilitarian view of gubernatorial activity in environmental policymaking suggests that under some circumstances governors can be expected to provide political leadership, staking their future (in part) on the popularity of specific policy positions. The environment, as a focus for political awareness, is generally speaking a "good" thing: motherhood, the flag, and the environment comprise "safe" topics for elected leaders. Almost everyone wants to save the whales. We can expect governors to be "for the environment" in the most general terms. The question of political leadership, however, implies a more intense involvement such as a governor taking the initiative on new policy issues for which there is no obvious preexisting body of support. Political resources need to be expended seeking specific policy outcomes before it would be reasonable to say a governor exercised political leadership. A more stringent approach would be to define political leadership in terms of an "effect." Specifically, we could argue that leadership is not effectively exercised until followers respond to the leader's proposals. In the context of gubernatorial actions this would mean that voters must recognize and respond to the governor's proposed environmental policies. If voters are unable to see the governor's initiatives or observe the governor's activities in the environmental policy arena, it would be hard to argue that the governor has offered effective leadership on environmental policy. Voter perceptions of governors is the topic of a later section where this question is addressed with empirical evidence.

GOVERNORS AND ECONOMIC DEVELOPMENT

Although there are few direct antagonists of environmental policy, the pursuit of specific environmental goals can conflict with established interests in society. At the state level, economic development is the most common source of policy conflicts that can involve governors. For example, the preservation of forest land as "wilderness" conflicts with the interests of traditional timber entrepreneurs who use forest lands to produce lumber. Similarly, the preservation of clean air conflicts with the interests of manufacturers who traditionally use the airshed to transport and dispose of waste products from their production sites.

When presented in this form it is obvious that environmental policy goals for preservation or enhancement of natural resources such as air and water can be challenged politically by characterizing these goals as "obstacles to economic development." From an economic perspective enhanced environmental values can reduce the efficiency of productive processes. The imposition of controls or regulations may or may not lead to the desired environmental outcome but, by definition, the cost of meeting these regulations will reduce the efficiency of production thereby lowering the overall level of material well-being that would otherwise flow from society's productive processes. It is possible, and perhaps reasonable, to accept reduced economic efficiency as the price of enhanced environmental values, but this "price" of clean air or water is extracted through higher product prices and, therefore, reduced sales. In the aggregate this leads to fewer jobs in productive processes.

This line of argument is well known and commonly used in fighting the apparently benign goals of enhanced environmental values. Rather than argue that clean air or water is not desirable, it is usually argued that cleaning up the air and water will deprive the community of jobs. Consequently, when governors consider championing widely embraced environmental values they must be prepared to face charges that they are threatening existing prosperity or placing unnecessary obstacles in the path of needed economic development.

Economic conditions, particularly demand for labor (that is, unemployment), in part define the political viability of environmental issues. If jobs are a pressing issue, governors are not likely to take the lead in providing enhanced environmental values. If the economy is expanding or unemployment is not seen as a pressing problem, governors are more likely to take a leadership role in environmental policymaking.

OREGON AND CALIFORNIA: THE EMPIRICAL CASES

The states of Oregon and California provide two cases where economic development and environmental policies have been debated by the public over the past two decades. Governors in these two states have had the opportunity to appraise environmental policy as well as economic development as vehicles for their political careers. Some governors have embraced environmental policies of conservation while other governors have pursued economic development. During this period these states have experienced economic downturns, especially in Oregon, adding salience to the calls for further development.

Both Oregon and California are blessed with plentiful natural resources. On the one hand, these resources have provided generations with livelihoods in agriculture, fishing, mining, and lumbering. On the other hand, these same natural resources are viewed by others as a heritage to be conserved for the benefit of future generations.

In this context, it is easy to see that environmental policymaking is likely to produce political conflict, particularly in those areas that have resource dependent economies (Medler and Mushkatel, 1979). The zero-sum nature of resource use and preservation is not always apparent. In times of economic growth the pinch of restricted resource use due to policies of preservation can be eased by expansion in other areas of economic activity. In Oregon, for example, during a relative boom period in the Oregon economy, a popular governor, Tom McCall, caught the public's attention with what he called the "Oregon Story," noting that the state could preserve its heritage of natural resources and still maintain prosperity. Essentially McCall argued that Oregon could have it both ways: a pristine environment with continuing prosperity. During this period (the early 1970s) both Oregon and California developed ambitious land use controls (Little, 1974; Medler and Mushkatel, 1980) aimed at preserving resources while shaping economic growth.

By the 1980s environmental policy underwent several changes. First, the environment simply slipped from the center of the political stage. President Reagan, at the national level, offered little leadership for the development of state-federal relations that had been initiated in the 1970s. Perhaps most importantly, the national economy stagnated. California's vast, diverse economy slowed while Oregon's timber dependent economy crashed. The emergence of economic hard times brought new force to arguments for greater development and less preservation of state re-sources (for a more detailed discussion see Medler, 1989).

The complex interplay between personalities, policies, and economics in these two states offers a rich historical base for an empirical analysis. Historically both Oregon and California have made extensive use of direct citizen participation in policymaking. This historical record of citizen participation in environmental policymaking is the basis for the analysis that follows.

THE DATA

For the purposes of this study, voting results on statewide environmen-tal ballot measures compiled by the secretaries of state of Oregon and California were employed to provide a county-by-county breakdown of election results. A broad definition of "environmental" measures was purposely used to empirically capture as much of the environmental policy domain as possible.

For Oregon, twenty ballot measures, from 1954 to 1986, were selected for analysis. Each of these measures was judged to have an environmentally relevant component. The Oregon measures included a wide range of topics such as fish and wildlife, billboards, waterways, land use, nuclear power, and nuclear wastes.

For California, forty-nine ballot measures, from 1948 to 1988, were selected. The substantive range of issues in California is extensive, including ballot measures dealing with wildlife habitat enhancement, hazardous substance cleanup, smoking restrictions, and tax exemptions for solar energy.

While the range of environmental issues presented to California voters was large, two categories are clearly dominant. Of the forty-nine ballot measures, sixteen were directly associated with water resources. Of the remainder, thirteen measures were in some way associated with land use. Additionally, almost half, twenty-four, required the issuance of state bonds to pay for whatever costs would be associated with the measures' provisions. Interestingly the "environmental decade" of the 1970s contained fewer environmental ballot measures (fifteen) than the 1980s (twenty-five). Part of this is explained by the recent emergence of water-related issues as a central concern. Of the twenty-five measures presented to voters in the 1980s, twelve were related to water.

The pro-environmental position was identified with reference to the content of each ballot measure. For example, a pro-environmental position might be a "yes" vote on a bond issue to fund clean drinking water or a "no" vote on the sale of tidelands for commercial development. Data on gubernatorial elections from 1958 to 1986 were also taken from the secretaries of state reports.

DIMENSIONS OF ENVIRONMENTAL VOTING

Each issue or ballot measure can be considered as a dimension in a policy space. (For a similar perspective applied to the study of legislative roll call voting see MacRae, 1970 or Poole and Rosenthal, 1985.) A geometric representation of policy positions on several environmental issues would require as many dimensions as there are issues. For example, if there were two issues, such as land use planning and nuclear power, two dimensions (a 2-space) would be required to represent policy positions in this policy space. Similarly, three issues would require a 3-space, and an extension to four or more environmental issues demands a 4-space or in general an n-space, where n can take any integer value. Although the concept of an n-space taxes our imagination, the notion of an n-space is indispensable in mapping policy positions when there are several (n) separate environmental issues before the public.

An important question within any dimensional analysis concerns the number of separate dimensions which are represented by identifiable issues. If two issues are substantively related then these two issues may not be independent. Therefore, it would not be necessary to use a separate geometric dimension to represent each issue. Rather, policy positions on n issues may be adequately represented by n–1 (or fewer) dimensions (Coombs, 1964). The reduction of dimensionality is an important consideration because it reduces the level of complexity and detail that must be maintained in the analysis. For example, Poole and Rosenthal (1987) report that historically, roll calls in the U.S. Senate can be considered as existing in a 2-space. The ultimate reduction in complexity would be a 1-space or a single dimension that could be used to represent policy positions on all issues.

The goal of a dimensional analysis is to locate issues and political entities in a joint space in which spatial proximity, closeness in space, represents similar policy positions. For example, if two environmental issues are closely located to one another this would mean that the two issues are substantively similar. Thus, if two issues concerning nuclear power occupied adjacent locations in a policy space, we would not be surprised—these issues are, at face value, quite similar.

The question that remains is the location of political leaders, such as governors, in the policy space. It is quite possible to consider policies and governors as occupying the same policy space. In fact, spatial theories of electoral competition assume that candidates can in fact stake out a policy position (a location in space) and communicate this position to voters. Presumably the position is one shared by the modal voter, which places the candidate in a location that is most attractive to the voters. If the candidate is accurate in picking the location of the modal voter and is successful in communicating this policy position to the voters, the candidate will benefit from the support of voters seeking their policy preferences (Downs, 1957).

GOVERNORS, MEASURES, AND FACTOR ANALYSIS

The location of a candidate can be derived in several ways. For example, factor analysis (Kim and Mueller, 1978a and 1978b) or multidimensional scaling (Kruskal and Wish, 1978) are two computational algorithms commonly used to locate positions in a joint space. With these methods, the data used to compute spatial locations are measures that lend themselves to a spatial (proximity) interpretation. The input data needed to map issues and leaders are thus indices of closeness. The most common indices used are any of several types of correlation coefficients (e.g., Pearson's r). In the context of a spatial analysis, correlation coefficients are interpreted as inverse measures of distance: $1 - r = $ distance. Thus the higher the value of r_{xy}, the closer the location of x and y. A perfect correlation ($r = 1.0$) represents zero (0) distance. The higher the correlation between issues or between issues and governors, the greater the proximity in policy space.

With these assumptions, it is a relatively easy matter to locate governors and issues in a joint policy space. All that is required is a set of correlation coefficients reflecting judgements about the relative similarity of issues and governors. Historically, the initiative and referendum provisions of the Oregon and California constitutions and the common practice of electing governors provide a database for locating governors among a set of environmental issues. Historical records of county-by-county election returns can be used to provide similarity (and therefore proximity) measures for an historical set of environmental issues and governors. In this sense, each county is asked to respond to a variety of issues (through initiative and referendum measures) and a variety of governors (as candidates in general elections). The similarity in the patterns of county responses to issues and governors can be used as assessments of distances between issues and governors that can be used to map locations in a joint space.

Principal components factor analysis is the computational algorithm used in this study (see Rummel, 1970). Factor analysis is used here to determine the number of dimensions needed to map the location of ballot measures and governors. The substantive identification of factors is by its nature a subjective exercise. The factors are an algebraic abstraction (obtained by Varimax rotation, Harmon, 1967) with no direct connection to substance or content. Consequently, the definition of factor content is entirely an inferential process based on a content analysis of items that are located at the extremes of each dimension.

RESULTS: THE STRUCTURE OF OREGON BALLOT MEASURES

Principal components factor analysis of the county-by-county election returns for twenty ballot measures (from 1954 to 1986) produced a simple two-dimensional solution. Land use planning and nuclear issues emerge as the two dominant foci of these twenty ballot measures. Simplification of the analysis by reduction of ballot measures with relatively low factor loadings produced results of remarkable clarity. Three measures designed to curtail radioactive material and three measures aimed at rescinding land use planning produced two separate clusters in the Varimax rotation as shown in figure 9.1. Thus, the environmental policy space revealed by factor analysis suggests that the debate over twenty ballot measures during the past three decades can be understood as two-dimensional.

The second step of the spatial analysis is to insert governors into this policy space to see where they are placed by the voters. Proximity or closeness indicates similarity of treatment by voters. Each ballot measure was coded to reflect the pro-environment vote. In the case of land use planning this is a vote "against" the initiative measure to rescind land use planning. In the case of nuclear issues this is the vote "for" the measure to prohibit nuclear development. Each governor was coded to reflect the vote in support of the winning gubernatorial candidate. If a governor lies close to a nuclear power measure it would indicate that voters responded to the governor and the ballot measure in a similar manner (voting for the environment and for the candidate). If a governor is distant from a ballot measure it would indicate that the voters responded differently to the governor and the ballot measure.

Analysis of figure 9.1 shows that, in general, Oregon's eight most recent governors are quite different from one another and they show a wide range of locations in the environmental policy space. Some governors are placed relatively close to the ballot measures while others are more distant. For example, Mark Hatfield (1958 and 1962) was a "pre-environmental" governor holding office in a period before the environment had become a clear national or state issue. Hatfield's locations are relatively distant from both the nuclear and land use measures and near the origin of the policy space, suggesting that voters did not see Hatfield closely related to environmental issues.

In sharp contrast, Tom McCall's positions (1966 and 1970) show greater proximity to the environmental issues, especially land use planning. This is not surprising as McCall was a strong advocate of land use planning and related issues. Interestingly, in McCall's second election the voters have placed him closer to the environmental issues. This suggests that over time McCall became increasingly perceived as associated with environmental issues.

In 1974 Oregon voters placed Robert Straub in a relatively central position indicating that Straub also was associated with environmental issues, but, it is noteworthy that Straub's position falls away from McCall's position on land use planning during the period when land use

Figure 9.1
Oregon Governors and Ballot Measures

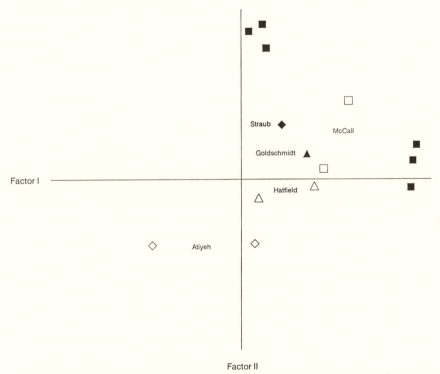

planning came under attack. Voter response suggests that Straub was perceived as less supportive of land use planning than McCall.

The most dramatic positions are held by Victor Atiyeh (1978 and 1982). Atiyeh's first election places him in the negative-negative quadrant of the factor space, suggesting that voters considered him the least similar to the pro-environmental ballot measures. At his second campaign (1982) Atiyeh moves closer to land use planning but remains distant from antinuclear power measures. Again, these locations are logically consistent with Atiyeh's actions as governor. As unemployment became more and more severe, Atiyeh sought to stimulate development, explicitly repudiating McCall's invitation to "visit but not stay," by repeatedly declaring that Oregon was "open for business." It appears that voters clearly perceived his policy leadership as not supportive of environmental issues.

In 1986 voters placed Neil Goldschmidt in a more central environmental position. Goldschmidt is not perceived as positively as McCall in his second term (1970) but he is clearly considered more proenvironment than his predecessor (Atiyeh) and the pre-environmental governorships of Hatfield. Goldschmidt's more central position suggests that voters see him as a moderate in his support of environmental polices.

RESULTS: THE STRUCTURE OF CALIFORNIA BALLOT MEASURES

Mapping the California ballot measures was accomplished by principal components factor analysis of the forty-five ballot measures decided between 1960 and 1988. Over one-third (sixteen) of these measures pertained to water issues such as safe drinking water, water quality, and water conservation. Moreover, twelve of these water-related measures were decided in the eight-year period from 1980 to 1988. In 1988 three water measures appeared in serial order (propositions 81, 82, and 83) on the ballot. Not surprisingly, these water measures were treated in a highly similar manner by California voters. The high inter-item correlations on these water measures overwhelmed the factor analytic technique producing a dominant dimension comprised of water measures. Historically, issues surrounding water have always been prominent in California politics. The results of this mapping clearly reconfirm this fact and suggest that this issue has become even more salient in recent years.

The analytic dominance of water issues, however, is, in part, an artifact of the factor analytic technique and in part due to the concentration of numerous water measures in recent elections. Related measures decided in a short period of time can be expected to produce high correlations between measures. Factor techniques are designed to focus analytic attention on items with high correlations. Consequently, the similarity and large number of water measures simply overwhelm the diversity of the other measures, reflecting little detail of voter response to these other issues. Stated differently, the dominance of water-related ballot measures obscures the considerable texture represented in the other twenty-nine ballot measures that cover a wide variety of topics such as smoking, beverage containers, open space preservation, nuclear weapons production, park acquisition, air and water pollution, and alternative energy sources.

In order to explore the domain of environmental issues with greater sensitivity, the dominance of water-related issues was reduced by removing most of the water-related measures. The most highly intercorrelated water measure (proposition 83 from November 1988, dealing with clean water and water reclamation) was retained to represent the location of water issues without allowing water issues to dominate the issue space. In the discussion that follows, the role of water issues in California ballot measure politics is purposely understated in order to reveal the relative location of other issues.

The factor analysis of this reduced set of ballot measures produced two interpretable factors (Varimax rotation) explaining approximately 75 percent of the variance in the items. The first factor had high loadings on ballot measures aimed at preserving open space, acquiring park lands, and establishing parks. Basically, this factor appears to be a land use dimension aimed at maintaining or expanding public access to land resources. The second factor is characterized by high loadings on ballot measures dealing with pollution, nuclear weapons, nuclear energy, and alternative energy. Substantively, this second dimension is comprised of measures involved in the tradeoff between economic development (energy and pollution) and halting further degradation of the environment (nuclear weapons production halt and alternative energy facilities). While recognizing it is an oversimplification, for the sake of convenience the first factor is considered the "land use" factor while the second is labeled the "pollution" factor.

To enhance the clarity of the mapping of this two-dimensional portrayal, those measures with factor loadings less than 0.80 were removed. Ten measures (including a water-related measure) were ultimately retained in the two-dimensional representation shown in figure 9.2. This simplified mapping greatly reduces the complexity and detail of the original forty-five measures. As a data reduction technique, factor analysis can be expected to provide great parsimony. In this case a forty-five dimension hyperspace was reduced to a two-dimensional space. Of course, to gain this level of simplification, much detail has been sacrificed to parsimony.

California governors were then inserted into this two-space by including them with the set of ballot measures. This joint mapping of politicians and ballot measures allows direct comparison of voter response to both persons and issues. The governors included in this analysis were all two-term governors: Edmund Brown (1958 and 1962), Ronald Reagan (1966 and 1970), Gerry Brown (1974 and 1978), and George Deukmejian (1982 and 1986). Consequently, it is possible to follow the trajectory of each governor from term to term as well as to compare governors to one another.

Eight gubernatorial contests with ten ballot measures produced a three-dimensional factor structure adding a party factor to the previously identified land use and pollution factors. Although it is reassuring that

Figure 9.2
California Governors and Ballot Measures

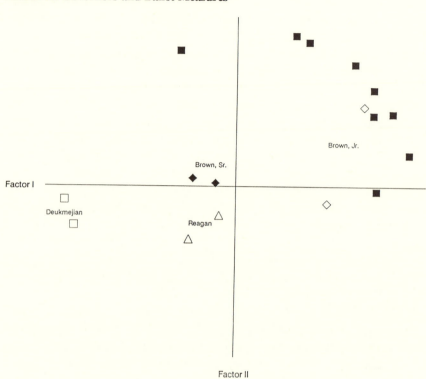

Factor II

voters distinguish the candidates of one party from another, the inclusion of a Democratic-Republican axis adds no new information to our understanding of this issue domain. For visual simplicity, this party factor is ignored in further analysis.

Taking the governors in chronological order, Edmund "Pat" Brown is located near the origin of the factor space of ballot measures. Both in 1958 and 1962 Brown, Sr., is not proximate to any environmental measures. Essentially voters treated Brown, Sr., as unrelated to environmental issues. Like Hatfield, Brown, Sr., can best be considered a "pre-environmental" governor.

Ronald Reagan is also located near the origin of the ballot measure space. Although Reagan's 1966 election is substantially in the negative-negative quadrant, his 1970 candidacy takes him nearer the origin of the space. This movement is small and perhaps does not merit extensive comment. However, it does suggest that even a staunch ideologue may be able to change voter perceptions of his position on environmental issues.

Edmund "Gerry" Brown offers a sharp contrast to his father and Reagan. In 1974 voters placed Brown, Jr., well along the "pollution" dimension but near the origin of the land use dimension. In this limited way, Brown, Jr., must be recognized as the first California governor to be recognized by voters as an environmental governor. This claim is even further buttressed by Brown's 1978 candidacy which places him quite centrally in the positive-positive quadrant. Voter response to Brown, Jr., the second time around suggests that Brown had made the environment his issue.

If Edmund Brown, Jr., can be considered California's environmental governor, George Deukmejian must be recognized as the anti-environmental governor. In 1982 the voters located Deukmejian the most distant of all governors from environmental measures. Moreover, in 1986 Deukmejian moved only slightly toward the zero point of the land use dimension, suggesting that Deukmejian did not significantly alter his position from term to term.

CONCLUSIONS: OREGON-CALIFORNIA COMPARISONS

A comparison of Oregon and California offers a study in contrasts. Oregon is a small state (roughly two million residents) while California is the largest state in the nation (over twenty million residents). Oregon has only one large city (Portland) while California has two megalopolises. Oregon is highly dependent on a single industry (timber) while the California economy is so large and diverse it is often compared to national economies. Oregon has a reputation for cranky conservationism and no-growth perspectives while California is often held up for emulation as a model of pro-development policies.

Given these differences one would expect that the politics of ballot measures in the two states would be quite different as well. Yet, the results reported earlier suggest this is not the case. The structure of the ballot measures displayed in figures 9.1 and 9.2 is strikingly similar. Setting aside the overwhelming importance of water to California politics, it is interesting to note that both the Oregon and California factor structures contain one factor concerned with land and another factor concerned with nuclear/energy facilities. This two-factor similarity suggests that environmental issues may have a universal structure that transcends the substantial differences between these two states. To be sure, two cases cannot be used to prove the existence of a general structure for environmental issues in American states. However, the rather large differences between Oregon and California suggest that this structure is apparently robust and deserves further study. This two-factor structure may serve to define a common political culture underlying environmental politics in American states.

The data used in this analysis cannot be used to explain this factor structure similarity between Oregon and California. Consequently, this finding raises additional questions. Specifically, why should two such different states have such a similar structure in their response to environmental problems? A preliminary answer to this question can be phrased in terms of the nature of the problems commonly confronted in the environment and the institutional processes in American political culture that are commonly used to address policy problems.

The common aspects of problems from state to state probably outweigh local differences in environmental problems. For example, urban sprawl encroaching on agricultural land is recognized as a land use problem in both San Jose and Portland. Thermal inversions and smog are threats to air quality in both Los Angeles and Eugene. The Oregon environmentalists' rallying cry of "don't Californicate Oregon" reflects the obviousness of the similarity in problems from one state to another.

Although there may be numerous potential solutions to these common problems, there is, in fact, a rather limited repertoire of environmental policies that have been brought forth to deal with problems such as sprawl and pollution. Although the American states are often considered to be fifty independent laboratories for the invention and testing of innovative policies, this is seldom the case. Rather, as Walker (1969) has shown, policy innovations in the states are often passed from one state to another with only minor changes to accommodate local conditions. That is to say, innovative policies which offer solutions to common problems may undergo a process of diffusion from one state to another.

Assuming diffusion of innovation is the case in environmental policy, then citizens in one state may be asked to implement the same policy as the citizens of other states. From this perspective environmental policies can be seen as a stimulus to which voters respond in local initiatives and referenda. To the extent that the set of stimuli (ballot measures) are similar from state to state, then we should expect a similar pattern of responses (factors) from state to state.

The trajectory of gubernatorial candidacies also gives evidence of similarities between Oregon and California. The candidacies of both Mark Hatfield and Edmund Brown, Sr., appear unrelated to environmental issues. This should not be surprising as environmental issues simply were not well recognized as such in the 1950s and early 1960s. Hatfield and Brown, Sr., share the role of pre-environmental governors.

In Oregon, Tom McCall's first candidacy (in 1966) was located in the positive-positive quadrant of the issue space suggesting a modest difference with Hatfield. However, McCall's second candidacy (1970) moves into a central position midway between the land use and nuclear measures. For Oregon voters, McCall's second candidacy was clearly seen as a pro-environment candidacy.

In California, both Ronald Reagan's candidacies (1966 and 1970) are located in the negative-negative quadrant indicating that Reagan may have been perceived by the voters as antipathetic to environmental issues. While Oregon moved into the "environmental decade" with strong environmental leadership from Tom McCall, California began the environmental decade without pro-environmental leadership from its governor.

However, one term later in California, Gerry Brown's candidacies (1974 and 1978) follow the direction taken in Oregon two terms earlier. While McCall staked out a pro-environmental position in 1966 and 1970, Brown, Jr., accomplished this feat for California in 1974 and 1978.

In Oregon, during his 1978 candidacy, Victor Atiyeh began a shift away from pro-environmental positions. Atiyeh moderated this position slightly in 1982, but in effect was not seen by Oregon voters as a pro-environment candidate. This position was ultimately reversed by Neil Goldschmidt in 1986, when his candidacy moved into the positive-positive quadrant. Although Goldschmidt's position is not as proenvironment as McCall's second term, Goldschmidt's candidacy suggests that the environment may be reemerging as an important electoral issue in Oregon.

This back-and-forth pattern displayed by Oregon governors is particularly interesting to compare with the historical pattern in California. In 1982 and 1986 California's George Deukmejian follows the same path taken earlier by Oregon's Victor Atiyeh, moving well into the negative-negative quadrant or an anti-environmental position in voter perceptions.

If California politics follow the path taken by Oregon, then Pete Wilson, the new governor elected in 1990, should move to the positive-positive quadrant as Goldschmidt did in Oregon in 1986. This "prediction" is based on the tenuous assumption that Oregon is an environmental bellwether state and that California will, in time, follow Oregon's lead by returning to a pro-environmental governor in the 1990s.

There is little reason to believe that Oregon serves as a bellwether for any state, much less California. However, there is considerable evidence that American voters have remained concerned with environmental issues throughout the 1980s. Growing voter impatience with the implementation of effective environmental policies does in fact suggest that attentive gubernatorial candidates may move to take visible, pro-environment positions in the 1990s. If Pete Wilson, the new governor of California, makes this move, no one should be surprised.

REFERENCES

Coombs, Clyde H. 1964. *A Theory of Data*. New York: John Wiley & Sons, Inc.

Downs, Anthony. 1957. *An Economic Theory of Democracy*. New York: Harper and Row.

Harmon, Harry H. 1967. *Modern Factor Analysis*. 2nd ed. Chicago and London: University of Chicago Press.

Kim, Jae-On, and Charles W. Mueller. 1978a. *Introduction to Factor Analysis: What It Is and How to Do It*. Sage University Paper series on Quantitative Applications in the Social Sciences, 07–013. Beverly Hills and London: Sage Publications.

_____. 1978b. *Factor Analysis: Statistical Methods and Practical Issues*. Sage University Paper series on Quantitative Applications in the Social Sciences, 07–014. Beverly Hills and London: Sage Publications.

Kruskal, Joseph B., and Myron Wish. 1978. *Multidimensional Scaling*. Sage University Paper series on Quantitative Applications in the Social Sciences, 07–011. Beverly Hills and London: Sage Publications.

Little, Charles. 1974. *The New Oregon Trail: An Account of the Development and Passage of State Land Use Legislation in Oregon*. Washington, DC: The Conservation Foundation.

MacRae, Duncan, Jr. 1970. *Issues and Parties in Legislative Voting: Methods of Statistical Analysis*. New York: Harper and Row.

Medler, Jerry F. 1989. Governors and Environmental Policy. *Policy Studies Journal*, 17, 4:895–908. Summer.

Medler, Jerry F., and Alvin Mushkatel. 1979. Urban-Rural Class Conflict in Oregon Land-Use Planning. *The Western Political Quarterly*, 32, 3:338–49.

_____. 1980. Support for Oregon Land Use Planning: A Multilevel Analysis. *Coastal Zone Management Journal*, 8, 1:63–83.

Poole, Keith T., and Howard Rosenthal. 1985. A Spatial Model for Legislative Role Call Analysis. *American Journal of Political Science*, 29:357–84.

_____. 1987. Roll Call Voting in Congress 1789–1985: Spatial Models and the Historical Record. In *Science at the John Van Neumann National Computing Center*. Annual Research Report, 111–16.

Rummel, R. J. 1970. *Applied Factor Analysis*. Evanston: Northwestern University Press.

Van Horn, Carl. 1979. *Policy Implementation in the Federal System*. Lexington, MA: Lexington Books.

Walker, Jack L. 1969. Diffusion of Innovations Among the American States. *American Political Science Review*, 63:880–99.

10 Governors and Health Care Policymaking: The Case of Medicaid

Saundra Schneider

State governors have become important actors in the American health care system. The rise in gubernatorial influence is one component of a broader trend in intergovernmental relations: the expanding role of state governments in the American policy process. Gubernatorial influence goes beyond this, however. Governors have become strong advocates for major health care programs and initiators of change in the health care field.

As the chief executives of their respective states, governors have a variety of formal ways of influencing policymaking. State constitutions and statutes give them the ability to affect the administration, financing, and regulation of many health care systems (Levine, 1984). Ironically, however, this is not where governors have the strongest impact. Instead, governors have used more informal powers to focus public attention on important health care issues (Schneider, 1989). In so doing, they have had a tremendous effect on policymaking within their states.

Interestingly, the role of governors has been virtually ignored in previous analyses of health care policy in the American states. As a result, our understanding of the American health system is incomplete. In order to address this problem, I will conduct an empirical analysis of the Medicaid program. For present purposes, the most important feature of this analysis is that gubernatorial influence will be explicitly examined. Equally important, the governor's role will be considered within the context of the other factors that exert a systematic impact on the Medicaid program. Although Medicaid is only one program, it is a particularly large and important one. As such, it is indicative of the broader health care system existing in the United States today.

INFLUENCES ON THE MEDICAID PROGRAM

The basic proposition of this study is very simple. Democratic governors are significantly more supportive of health care programs than are Republican governors. There is an enormous amount of anecdotal evidence to support this assertion. For example, former Democratic Governor Richard Riley of South Carolina pushed for major expansions in that state's Medicaid program to provide more comprehensive benefits for low-income pregnant women and infants. Similarly, Democratic Governor William Schaefer has played a leading role in focusing public attention on many pressing health care problems in his state of Maryland. On the other hand, the recent governor of California (George Deukmejian) and Wisconsin's James Thompson, both Republicans, have vetoed many significant health-related bills and have made concerted efforts to cut back on health care spending in their states.

Gubernatorial influence, however, can not be considered in isolation. There are simply too many other important factors that must be taken into account. To ignore them would lead to serious distortions in the assessment of gubernatorial impact.

For one thing, the Medicaid program has grown enormously over time. At the national level, the clearest manifestation of this has been the increase in total program expenditures (Weikel, 1980; Gornick, Greenberg, Eggers, and Dobson, 1985). During the first full year of the program's implementation (1967), Medicaid expenditures came to only $3 billion. By 1975 program costs were at $12.2 billion, by 1985 total Medicaid payments had reached more than $37 billion, and by 1987 Medicaid spending had climbed to $45 billion. This represents a fourteen-fold increase over the entire time period. Any effective analysis of the program must take this temporal variation into account (O'Toole and Montjoy, 1984).

Another characteristic which must be considered is the tremendous variation in program costs from one state to the next (GAO, 1987). This variation cannot be explained by the size of the state or by other demographic factors (Holahan and Cohen, 1986:16-18). For example, the populations of Texas and New York are roughly identical (both have over 16 million residents), but these states spend vastly different amounts on Medicaid (e.g., Texas spent $1.8 billion, while New York spent $8.8 billion on the program in 1987). Also, Wisconsin and Oklahoma have approximately the same number of individuals in poverty (395,000), but their Medicaid expenditures are quite different (Wisconsin spent $1 billion and Oklahoma only $502 million in 1987).

This variability across states seems to be largely due to three factors. First, states vary in the ways they implement the program. The federal government sets the broad parameters for general Medicaid policy, but the states retain discretionary responsibility for important aspects of program scope and structure (Hanson, 1984). Second, state economic environments may also affect Medicaid spending. As numerous studies have shown, some states simply have more money; thus, they are able to devote more resources to programs like Medicaid (Dye, 1966; Lewis-Beck, 1977; Savage, 1980; Tucker and Herzik, 1988). Third, cultural environments vary across the states. There are long-standing regional differences in the willingness to provide health care services, and even within regions, state policies are influenced by their political culture (Wright, Erikson, and McIver, 1987). All of these state-level influences must be considered in order to measure accurately gubernatorial influence.

Finally, the states are also affected by political changes at the national level. Obviously, policy initiatives from the national government aimed at health care problems will affect what the states do. This is particularly important given recent efforts, particularly by the Reagan administration, to broaden the states' responsibility for policymaking. As the top executives of their states, governors are affected by the broader political environment—especially by significant changes in the intergovernmental system—and this must be taken into account in analyzing their role in the health care process.

MODEL

It is clear that an effective analysis of gubernatorial influence on Medicaid spending must incorporate several features beyond the governor's party affiliation. It is also necessary to consider variability over time, differences across states, and national-level political and economic characteristics. These features are all combined in a model which is represented by the following equation:

$$\begin{aligned} \text{MED\$}_{ij} = {} & B_0 + B_1 \text{PGOV}_{ij} + B_2 \text{MED\$}_{i,j-1} + B_3 \text{REC}_{ij} + B_4 \text{INC}_{ij} \\ & + B_5 \text{LOCAL}_i + B_6 \text{NORTHEAST}_i + B_7 \text{SOUTH}_i + B_8 \text{WEST}_i \\ & + B_9 \text{CPI}_j + \text{error}_{ij} \end{aligned}$$

The dependent variable in the equation, $\text{MED\$}_{ij}$, is simply the total dollar amount spent on Medicaid in state i during year j.[1] Among the independent variables, PGOV_{ij} is the most critical for the present study.

It represents the political party affiliation of the governor. It is a dichotomy, coded 0 for Republican governors and 1 for Democrats. If Democratic state governors are more supportive of Medicaid spending than Republicans, this variable should have a significant, positive influence. This variable's effect is the central focus of the study. However, several other variables must also be incorporated into the model. These variables can be divided into two sets. First there are state-specific variables: $MED\$_{i,j-1}$, REC_{ij}, INC_{ij}, $LOCAL_i$, and $REGION_i$ (broken down into $NORTHEAST_i$, $SOUTH_i$, and $WEST_i$). The $MED\$_{i,j-1}$ term represents the influence of the previous year's expenditures $(j-1)$ on those of the current year (j). According to state officials, Medicaid policymaking is definitely affected by incrementalism: State legislators and administrators use the previous year's spending as a starting point for determining present and future year's spending levels.[2] If program expenditures are affected by past policy decisions, these lagged expenditures should exhibit a strong, positive impact on the dependent variable. $REC_{i,j}$ is the number of Medicaid recipients in state i for year j. This variable measures the demand for the program as well as the scope of coverage within each state. This is potentially an important factor because Medicaid, at least in principle, is an entitlement program. Therefore, the size of the recipient population should determine the amount of money needed to provide services (Davidson, 1980; Bovbjerg and Holahan, 1982:25–32).[3] State-level economic conditions are measured by the INC_{ij} variable. INC_{ij} represents the per capita income of state i for year j. This variable is typical of those used in the policy literature to measure state-specific economic conditions. [4] It has frequently been argued that such socioeconomic variables are the *best* predictors of policy efforts, particularly of program expenditures at the state level (Dye, 1966). Thus, we would expect this variable to have a strong, positive effect on Medicaid spending.

The fourth state-level variable, $LOCAL_i$, represents the level of government within a state that is responsible for program administration; it is a dichotomy, coded 0 for state control and 1 for local control.[5] The policy implementation literature (Pressman and Wildavsky, 1984; Bardach, 1977; Ingram, 1977; O'Toole and Montjoy, 1984), as well as specific analyses of Medicaid, make it clear that locally administered programs incur higher expenditures than systems administered at the state level. In addition, previous empirical research shows that local administration does have a strong, positive impact on state Medicaid spending (Schneider, 1988).

The final state-level variable, REGION$_i$, identifies the regional location of a state. In past research on Medicaid, regional differences have
been observed (Holahan and Cohen, 1986). The more liberal eastern
states spend the most on Medicaid, the "middle-of-the road," midwestern
states usually spend to close the national average, the states in the West
spend less, and the conservative, southern states spend the least. Accordingly, three dummy variables (instead of one single variable) are included
in the equation to test for these regional effects (NORTHEAST$_i$, SOUTH$_i$,
and WEST$_i$). The Midwest region has been omitted as the reference
category. The regional variable used in this analysis is based on the
breakdown employed by the U.S. Bureau of the Census.

There are two national-level variables in this analysis. The first, CPI$_j$,
is economic. CPI$_j$ represents the consumer price index for medical care
during year j. Thus, it measures the impact of increases (or decreases)
in medical costs on program expenditures. This variable should have a
positive impact on Medicaid payments.

The second national-level variable is the presence of the Reagan
administration. This variable does not appear in the equation itself.
Rather, it is incorporated indirectly by estimating the model's parameters
separately for the pre-Reagan years from 1975 to 1981 and then the
Reagan era, from 1982 to 1985.[6] The reason for incorporating the
Reagan administration in this indirect fashion is straightforward. The
Reagan administration did try to reduce the overall level of Medicaid
spending (Hill, 1984). However, it was not successful in this regard
(Holahan and Cohen, 1986). Therefore, it is not pictured as having a
significant, direct effect on the dependent variable. On the other hand,
the Reagan administration did succeed in altering the nature of health
care policymaking by returning more responsibility to the states (Holahan
and Cohen, 1986). This would be manifested as changes in the "mix"
of factors that impinge on Medicaid spending. Hence, the model's
coefficients are expected to vary significantly over the two time periods.[7]

The model does incorporate all the factors that are expected to affect
significantly Medicaid spending: gubernatorial partisanship, state-level
characteristics, and national political/economic conditions. It is also
important to note that the model takes temporal variability into account
as well.

ANALYSIS

The data for this analysis were compiled by the author from documents
obtained directly from the U.S. Bureau of the Census, the U.S. Bureau

of Economic Analysis, the U.S. Department of Labor, and the U.S. Department of Health and Human Services.[8] There are a total of 539 observations: forty-nine states for each of eleven years (1975 to 1985).[9]

The model's parameters are estimated using regression analysis. However, several features of the research design require special attention. First, the model incorporates both time-series and cross-sectional data. Although this could cause difficulties in the estimation of the coefficients, there do not appear to be severe problems in the present application.[10] Second, the model is dynamic in the sense that one of the independent variables contains lagged values of the dependent variable. Because of this, ordinary least squares estimation would produce misleading results, and two-stage least squares (2SLS) must be used to calculate the coefficients.[11]

As mentioned earlier, the model is estimated for two time periods. Table 10.1 shows the results for the pre-Reagan period, from 1975 to 1981. The table entries are 2SLS regression coefficients. The R^2 shows that 82 percent of the variance is accounted for by the independent variables.

In this time period, gubernatorial influence on Medicaid is virtually nonexistent. The coefficient for governor's partisanship does not achieve statistical significance. Although the point estimate seems fairly sizable (45.92), the large standard error (39.56) shows that this value is not reliably greater than zero. This, in turn, indicates that there are no real differences in the spending patterns of states led by Democratic versus Republican governors.

While governors alone do not have much impact, other state-level variables do have a significant influence on Medicaid spending. For example, the regional location of a state does make a difference. States in the northeast spend significantly more (+138.83) than states in the South, West, or the Midwest. It is often argued that Northeastern states are more generous when it comes to social welfare programs, while the South is more conservative and the West more "reserved" and more "individualistic" (Holahan and Cohen, 1986). Thus, these variables are probably tapping certain aspects of the political environment that are unique to these regions (Tucker and Herzik, 1988).

In addition, two state-level administrative factors really stand out during this time period: previous year's spending and local administration. Both have statistically significant, positive impacts on program costs. The regression coefficient for previous year's spending ($MED\$_{i,j-1}$) is +1.16, indicating that current year's expenditures are closely related to those from the previous year. Thus, Medicaid spending decisions prior

Table 10.1
Influences on Medicaid Program Expenditures: 1975–1981

INDEPENDENT VARIABLES	INFLUENCE	
	Estimate	Std. error
Governor's Party (PGOV$_{ij}$)	45.92	(39.56)
Previous Year's Expenditures (MED\$$_{i,j-1}$)	1.16	(.39)
Recipient Population (REC$_{ij}$)	-0.28	(.39)
Per Capita Income (INC$_{ij}$)	1.03	(.02)
Northeast Region (NORTHEAST$_i$)	138.83	(56.72)
South Region (SOUTH$_i$)	-25.48	(55.09)
West Region (WEST$_i$)	-91.74	(54.02)
Local Administration (LOCAL$_i$)	245.03	(61.21)
Price Index Medical Care (CPI$_j$)	1.47	(0.78)
Intercept	-636.24	
R^2 = .82		
N = 294		

*Table entries are unstandardized two-stage least squares regression coefficients. Standard errors are in parentheses.

to 1982 seem to follow the incrementalist theory of policymaking: Past Medicaid decisions do have a tremendous influence on subsequent program costs. The coefficient for LOCAL$_i$ shows that, as anticipated, states that administer Medicaid locally spend much more (over $245 million more) than states with centralized administration.

Two other state-level variables did not exhibit significant impacts. Expenditures in this early period were clearly not tied to recipient demand for services, represented by the REC$_{ij}$ term. The coefficient for REC$_{ij}$ is very small (-.28). This finding is quite reasonable given the incrementalist nature of the Medicaid policy process. In addition, the per capita income of a state (INC$_{ij}$) has no significant influence (+.03) on Medicaid spending. This finding is surprising because many other comparative state policy studies indicate that socioeconomic variables are good predictors of state welfare efforts. However, this is just not the case here. State Medicaid expenditures are not closely tied to state economic wealth in the 1975–1981 time period.

The national economic variable, CPI$_j$, does have a significant impact. For every percentage increase in the consumer price index for medical care, Medicaid expenditures increased by approximately $1.5 million. As anticipated, the general cost of medical care contributes noticeably to the cost of Medicaid in this pre-Reagan time period.

The Medicaid policy process changed in important ways during the Reagan years (table 10.2). From 1982 to 1985, the model's explanatory

Table 10.2
Influences on Medicaid Program Expenditures: 1982–1985

INDEPENDENT VARIABLES   INFLUENCE

	Estimate	Std. error
Governor's Party (PGOV$_{ij}$)	263.52	(82.89)
Previous Year's Expenditures (MED$\$_{i,j-1}$)	-1.41	(1.01)
Recipient Population (REC$_{ij}$)	2.80	(1.02)
Per Capita Income (INC$_{ij}$)	0.02	(.02)
Northeast Region (NORTHEAST$_i$)	409.55	(113.92)
South Region (SOUTH$_i$)	-28.26	(112.28)
West Region (WEST$_i$)	-120.98	(106.95)
Local Administration (LOCAL$_4$)	454.69	(128.91)
Price Index Medical Care (CPI$_j$)	0.91	(1.48)

Intercept   -713.43
R^2 = .80
N = 196

*Table entries are unstandardized two-stage least squares regression coefficients. Standard errors are in parentheses.

power(R^2) is slightly lower, but still quite respectable. However, the effects of the specific independent variables present a marked contrast to the earlier period.

During the Reagan era, politics is clearly more important than economics. The political party affiliation of the governor now has a very large and statistically significant effect. The coefficient for PGOV$_{ij}$ shows that states with Democratic governors spend an average of $263.52 million more on Medicaid than states with Republican governors. Surely it is not coincidence that political forces become more relevant after 1981. The Reagan administration pushed for the transfer of responsibility from the federal government to the states. It is precisely this "transfer" that has enabled state governors to play a more powerful role in Medicaid decisionmaking. And Democratic governors have taken the lead in actively and avidly pushing for changes to expand the scope and coverage of the program (Schneider, 1989).

The regional effects have also changed somewhat. The impact of the Northeast has jumped from +138.83 in 1975–1981 to +409.55 during 1982-1985. This change is probably, again, a result of the resurgence of the states in our federal system. States in the Northeast are often described as more liberal, more progressive, and "bigger" program spenders. It could very well be that greater state authority has given these states the room to pursue policies more in line with their own thinking. Apparently, however, the New Federalism movement of the 1980s was not handled the same way by states across the country: The coefficients for WEST$_i$ and SOUTH$_i$ are both nonsignificant. Thus, regional differences became less pronounced outside of the Northeast.

The influence of local administration (LOCAL$_i$) more than doubles over the first time period. During 1982–1985, states with locally administered programs spent over \$450 million more than those with centrally administered systems. Evidently, the onset of the Reagan presidency did accentuate the differences among states that implemented the program at different levels. The impact of previous year's spending (MED\$$_{i,j-1}$) is no longer significant (−1.41), while the effect of the recipient population (REC$_{ij}$) has increased dramatically up to +2.80. Thus, for each additional one thousand Medicaid recipients, program expenditures increased by \$2.8 million in the Reagan era. These results are exactly the reverse of the pattern found in the earlier period. Now policy demand, rather than previous year's spending, dominates the policy process. This represents an extremely important change in the determinants of Medicaid spending.

Even more than in the first time period, national-level economic variables (CPI$_j$) pale in comparison to the importance of state-level factors. Again, this emphasizes the states' role in Medicaid program developments, but it is important to remember that a national-level change is responsible for the differences between the two time periods. The Reagan administration did alter the *nature* of the policy process. Although unable to contain program costs, it did achieve one of its main objectives: increasing state and local power relative to the federal government. It is important to recognize that Democratic governors have benefited enormously from this shift in intergovernmental relations. They have become particularly effective in expanding the scope and nature of the program. And these expansions have led to higher Medicaid expenditures within their states.

DISCUSSION AND CONCLUSIONS

The empirical results presented in this study show that governors have become key actors in the Medicaid policy process. Part of the rise in gubernatorial influence is due to the generally increasing role of state governments in the health care field. A prominent theme of the late 1970s and early 1980s was to "turn back" many social programs, including health care programs, to the states (Stenberg, 1981). As a result of this, there has been a conscious effort to diminish federal control and to increase state discretion over many health care issues. This New Federalism movement has compelled state governments to assume a more commanding role over important health care issues.

The shift in intergovernmental policymaking does not tell the entire story, however. Even after other state influences are taken into account, the impact of Democratic governors still increases markedly during the time period covered in this analysis. This represents a significant change in the ways that governors influence public policy. In the past, governors used their traditional formal powers to affect the administration, regulation, and financing of health care programs (Schneider, 1989). However, gubernatorial impact in these three areas of state responsibility was more symbolic than real: It was largely indirect in nature and often shared with other public officials (i.e., legislators) and private entities (i.e., hospitals and nursing homes). Thus, governors were simply unable to have a significant impact of their own on major health care programs like Medicaid, regardless of their partisan affiliation. Recent events, however, have placed governors in a unique position to focus public and governmental attention on significant problems. In this way, Democratic governors are able to generate interest in and action on important health care concerns. In short, they have become prominent agenda-setters. As such, they have a profound impact on state policy responses.

The change in gubernatorial influence is clear-cut during the time period of this study. However, the implications for the future remain uncertain. On the one hand, Democratic governors may continue to take a distinctively active role in health care policymaking. Yet, it is also possible that partisan patterns may recede or disappear. Recently, Republican governors have become increasingly interested in health care problems. For example, John Sununu, the former governor of New Hampshire, pushed for state and federal support to expand that state's home health services so that the elderly could remain in their homes and still receive needed medical care. Similarly, former governor Bob Martinez played a major role in getting the state of Florida to adopt a drug prevention, education, treatment, and enforcement package. Apparently, health care concerns cut across ideological lines. To the extent this trend continues, partisan differences in gubernatorial influence will obviously disappear. It is also possible that the states' roles relative to the national government may move back to previous levels. With the end of the Reagan administration there may be less of an emphasis on changing the balance of power (between the national and state governments) in the American federal system. If this occurs, governors, along with state governments in general, may become less prominent actors in the policy process. In any event, it will be important to monitor closely gubernatorial influence on health care policy in the future.

NOTES

1. It is important to note that the dependent variable, MED$_U$, represents the *total* spending per state. There are several reasons for this. First, and foremost, this analysis seeks to explain how much each state spends on Medicaid and not the amount that each state spends on each individual recipient or on each person per capita. This is, in turn, justified for substantive reasons. Public and private discussion almost always focuses on the total amount of money spent on Medicaid, not on the amount spent per person. State legislators and bureaucrats use total expenditures to trace the program's development and to determine the content of the program within their respective states. Accordingly, a model that uses expenditures per recipient or per capita would be misleading, and it would severely misrepresent the nature of the policymaking process. Second, Medicaid does not operate like a cash assistance program. It reimburses the health professionals who provide care to recipients: Payments are *not* made directly to program beneficiaries. As a result, the costs per recipient or per capita reveal little about the real impact of the program (Davidson, 1980:95–108; Bovbjerg and Holahan, 1982:11–16). Third, individuals who receive Medicaid benefits have vastly different health care needs, and, thus, individual-level costs vary dramatically. One Medicaid recipient, e.g., a low birthweight infant born to a poor woman, for example, may rapidly incur tremendous medical bills (over $500,000 in a six-month period); while another recipient may never require treatment and thus may never have a medical expense. Once again, it would be misleading to use average expenditures per person to measure the program's content, output, or outcome.

2. In the summer of 1987, the Office of the Budget, Ohio Department of Human Services asked state Medicaid officials across the nation to identify how Medicaid policy decisions were made. Of those that responded to the survey, almost all (90 percent) indicated that previous year's expenditures played an extremely important role in program decisionmaking. This is consistent with the incrementalist theory of policymaking.

3. Several other aspects of the Medicaid recipient population were examined: the existence of a medically needy program and the establishment of state-imposed eligibility criteria for the Supplemental Security Income (SSI) population. Although it was thought that these variables would have important impacts, they did not help to explain Medicaid costs at all. Consequently, they were not included in subsequent analyses.

4. Several other state-level socioeconomic variables—the percentage of the population living in statistical metropolitan areas and the percentage of the population with (or above) a high school education—were also analyzed. These variables did not exert significant influences on Medicaid spending and were removed from the model.

5. The eight states with local administration during the time period under examination are: California, Minnesota, Nebraska, New York, North Carolina, North Dakota, Ohio, and South Carolina.

6. These two time periods were selected because they represent the pre-Reagan era (1975 to 1981) and the years of Reagan's impact (1982 to 1985). Although Reagan was elected in 1980 and inaugurated in 1981, his impact on public policy was not felt

until the beginning of the 1982 federal fiscal reporting period (Bovbjerg and Holahan, 1982). His influence would have continued until the end of federal fiscal year 1985 (which runs from October 1, 1984 to September 30, 1985).

7. I did examine another theoretically-relevant national-level variable—the percentage of the population in poverty—in earlier stages of this research. However, this variable did not have a significant impact on state Medicaid expenditures. Thus, it was dropped from the model.

8. The Medicaid data were obtained from the annual statistical reports (referred to as the HCFA 2082) which all states are required to submit to the federal government. The information was then verified with each respective state agency and corrections/revisions made to the data.

9. Since Arizona did not establish a Medicaid program until 1982, and then only a "demonstration" program, it is not included in this analysis.

10. This analysis uses cross-sectional, time-series data which could potentially complicate the estimation procedure (see Johnston, 1983). Fortunately, however, the problems do not seem to be too severe in the present case. As James Stimson (1985) indicates, data sets that are "cross-sectional dominant" (more data points in the cross-section than in the time series) are amenable to analysis with least squares, dummy variable procedures.

11. The problem is that a lagged dependent variable is correlated with the disturbance term in the equation. To correct for this, the lagged variable must first be purged of this covariation. Hence, the first stage of the analysis involves regression MED\$$_{i,j-1}$ on the exogenous variables to obtain predicted values. The latter serve as the values of the purged variable, which is then included as an explanatory variable in the second stage of the analysis, predicting to current program expenditures, MED\$$_{ij}$ (see Johnston, 1983).

REFERENCES

Bardach, Eugene. 1977. *The Implementation Game.* Cambridge, MA: MIT Press.

Bovbjerg, Randall R., and John Holahan. 1982. *Medicaid in the Reagan Era: Federal Policy and State Choices.* Washington, DC: Urban Institute.

Davidson, Stephen M. 1980. *Medicaid Decisions: A Systematic Analysis of the Cost Problem.* Cambridge, MA: Ballinger Publishing Co.

Dye, Thomas. 1966. *Politics, Economics, and the Public: Policy Outcomes in the American States.* Chicago: Rand McNally.

General Accounting Office. 1987. *Medicaid: Interstate Variations in Benefits and Expenditures.* Washington, DC: General Accounting Office.

Gornick, Marian, Jay N. Greenberg, Paul W. Eggers, and Allen Dobson. 1985. Twenty Years of Medicare and Medicaid: Covered Populations, Use of Benefits, and Program Expenditures. *Health Care Financing Review,* Annual Supplement:13–59.

Hanson, Russell L. 1984. Medicaid and the Politics of Redistribution. *American Journal of Political Science,* 28:313–39.

Hill, Ian Todd. 1984. *Medicaid Eligibility: A Descriptive Report of OBRA, TEFRA, and DEFRA Provisions, and State Responses.* Washington, DC: U.S. Department of Health and Human Services, Health Care Financing Administration.

Holahan, John, and Joel Cohen. 1986. *Medicaid: The Trade-Off Between Cost Containment and Access to Care.* Washington, DC: Urban Institute.

Ingram, Helen. 1977. Policy Implementation Through Bargaining: The Case of Federal Grants-in-Aid. *Public Policy,* 25:499–516.

Johnston, J. 1983. *Econometric Methods.* New York: McGraw-Hill.

Levine, Peter B. 1984. An Overview of the State's Role in the United States. In Litman and Robins, eds. *Health Politics and Policy.* New York: Wiley and Sons.

Lewis-Beck, Michael. 1977. The Relative Importance of Socioeconomic and Political Variables for Public Policy. *American Political Science Review,* 71:559–68.

O'Toole, Laurence J., Jr., and Robert S. Montjoy. 1984. Intergovernmental Policy Implementation: A Theoretical Perspective. *Public Administration Review,* 44:491–503.

Pressman, Jeffrey L., and Aaron Wildavsky. 1984. *Implementation.* Berkeley: University of California Press.

Savage, Robert. 1980. *The Literature of Systematic Quantitative Comparison in American State Politics.* Philadelphia: Center for the Study of Federalism, Report No. 11, Temple University.

Schneider, Saundra K. 1988. Intergovernmental Influences on Medicaid Program Expenditures. *Public Administration Review,* 48:756–63.

_____. 1989. Governors and Health Care Policy. *Policy Studies Journal,* 17:809–26.

Stenberg, Carl. 1981. Beyond the Days of Wine and Roses: Intergovernmental Management in a Cutback Environment. *Public Administration Review,* 41:10–20.

Stimson, James A. 1985. Regression in Space and Time: A Statistical Essay. *American Journal of Political Science,* 29:914–47.

Tucker, Harvey, and Eric B. Herzik. 1988. The Persisting Problem of Region in American State Policy Research. *Social Science Quarterly,* 67, 1:84–97.

Weikel, M. K. 1980. *A Decade of Medicaid: Some State and Federal Perspectives on Medicaid.* Washington, DC: Health Care Financing Administration.

Wright, Gerald C., Robert S. Erikson, and John P. McIver. 1987. Public Opinion and Policy Liberalism in the American States. *American Journal of Political Science,* 31:980–1007.

11 Governors and Nuclear Waste: Showdown in the Rockies

Marilyn K. Dantico and Alvin H. Mushkatel

This chapter examines the efforts of western governors to intervene in the federal government's agenda for the disposal of radioactive waste at the Western Isolation Pilot Project (WIPP) in New Mexico. By analyzing the actions of three western governors regarding shipments of nuclear waste material we can gain insight into the role governors play in the policy process. Specifically, the case of the WIPP reveals strong policy efforts by governors in the area of problem definition, efforts to direct public opinion and secure resources, and to cooperate to attempt to make the federal government meet previously given commitments to these states. The case of WIPP, and the adversarial role these governors played regarding federal waste policy reveal the important and critical policy functions chief executives may have under some circumstances.

Many scholars have explored the ways governors shape and influence various factors of state politics (Schlesinger, 1965; Dometrius, 1979; Sigelman and Smith, 1981; Beyle, 1983; Herzik and Wiggins, 1989). Fewer analysts have focused on gubernatorial roles in state policymaking (Laderle, 1972; Medler, 1989; Florestano and Boyd, 1989). Indeed, only more recently have scholars started to examine chief executives' roles in a multistate policy context (Gross, 1989; Grady, 1989; Alford, 1975). A key element of this broader context for analyzing gubernatorial roles in policymaking includes examination of the division of responsibilities between the states and the federal government in the implementation of policy (Jones, 1976).

Gubernatorial involvement in the policy arena with the federal government is now generally viewed as inevitable. This involvement not only results from the intergovernmental nature of the policy process, but also from the need of governors to articulate and protect state interests (Beyle and Muchmore, 1983), to increase federal revenues to the states (Beyle, 1983), and for advancing their careers (Grady, 1987). Yet, on occasion it seems likely that the roles may conflict. The maximization of federal revenues to a state may come into conflict with the governor's role of protecting state interests. The literature to date provides little insight into what to expect from governors when such conflict occurs. The case study of the WIPP provides clear evidence that while governors are the coordinators of state-federal relations (Sabato, 1983), these relations may result in conflicting demands on chief executives.

Haider (1974) suggests that gubernatorial lobbying, multiple audiences, constituencies, and roles are built into the federal system. In the case of nuclear waste the assignment of primary responsibility appears quite easy. The federal government, through the Department of Energy (DOE), is responsible for the oversight of nuclear weapons production and the disposal of resulting waste. Governors are responsible for protecting the health and safety of state residents. These roles do not appear to be inherently conflictual. Yet, in this policy area the interpretation of their roles and responsibilities by some western governors resulted in state-federal conflict on one side, and gubernatorial cooperation on the other.

THE GOVERNORS

In this case study there are three important state chief executives; thus, a brief review of their past records and accomplishments is in order. Cecil Andrus served as governor of Idaho from 1971–1977, and 1987–present; and as secretary of interior from 1977–1981. He served in the state legislature for over seven years, and has close affiliations to numerous environmental organizations. His tenure as secretary of the interior was marked by decisions to protect 103 million acres of virgin land in Alaska for parks. He has held key leadership positions on the National Governors' Conference.

Roy Romer, the Democratic governor of Colorado, also plays a key role in the WIPP case. Romer's experience in government was largely confined to the state where he served in the legislature for eight years, rising to the post of assistant minority leader in the Senate. He had extensive experience in a previous Colorado governor's office, and was the state treasurer from 1977 to 1987.

Both Andrus and Romer campaigned heavily on issues of economic development and stimulating their state's economies. Both governors stressed quality of life issues, especially those related to the environment. Romer's approval of a controversial dam early in his term has been seen as a compromise reflecting the need to balance environmental concerns with economic development.

Finally, New Mexico's Republican governor elected in 1986, Garry Carruthers, was the first Republican elected to that office in sixteen years. His relevant federal experience is limited to three years service as an assistant secretary of interior, and his state experience is primarily related to his tenure as party chair from 1977 to 1979. Carruthers, as governor of one of the nation's poorest states, has stressed economic development and planning to improve education. His service in the Department of the Interior was during the controversial term of Secretary James Watt and resulted in charges of irregularities during his gubernatorial campaign.

All three governors are over the age of fifty, with Romer being the oldest and Carruthers the youngest. Yet, all three are past the age the literature defines as "ambitious"; under the age of forty-five who work the federal system because they are interested in moving to the Senate, cabinet, and other higher level positions (Grady, 1987). All three governors have placed major emphasis on the issue of economic development for their state, but all three have also indicated that the environment must not be sacrificed for such opportunity.

There is little in the background of these three governors to suggest that they would be able to cooperate if faced with political conflict with the federal government. Yet, if an adversarial relationship developed, we would expect Andrus to be placed in the lead because of his relative knowledge of federal agency workings and his lack of federal ambitions. In addition, Carruthers seems least likely to lead if a conflict with the federal government developed because of his party affiliation with the president and relative poverty of his state.

SETTING THE FEDERAL AGENDA

On October 19, 1988, Idaho governor Cecil Andrus wrote the DOE Secretary Herrington indicating that Idaho borders were *closed to new shipments of nuclear waste* (Andrus, 1988A). Andrus soon said that he would not hesitate to call out the national guard or the state police to maintain control of the borders (Butterfield, 1988A). The Department of Energy had been storing waste produced at the Rocky Flats, Colorado, weapons factory at the Idaho National Engineering Laboratory (INEL) on a temporary basis. At the time of Andrus's letter, the temporary storage time of the nuclear waste material was approaching two decades.

Andrus's action followed close on the heels of receipt of a letter from the chair of the Idaho House Environmental Affairs Committee, Emerson Smock. Smock wrote Andrus that the WIPP was as safe a storage facility as exists and the New Mexico congressional delegation was actively delaying its opening (Smock, 1988). Moreover, Smock's letter urged the governor "to take immediate measure(s)" to get the WIPP program underway. Smock's observations were consistent with Andrus's beliefs.

New Mexico's Governor Carruthers had been a proponent of WIPP and Senate Bill 1272 that provided for the withdrawal of public lands for the project. Just two years earlier, Carruthers had testified to that effect on behalf of the state before a senate subcommittee (Senate, 1987). In his testimony, Carruthers pointed out that he had become familiar with the project while he served as assistant secretary of the interior; that the project had scientific and economic consequences for the state, and would receive the full support of state officials. Carruthers did request that Congress change the name to the Delaware Basin National Laboratory, in keeping with the scientific and research natures of the endeavor; compensate the state for loss of revenues in an amount just under $5.5 million; and provide $190 million for roads and bypasses around major metropolitan areas.

The day Andrus penned his letter, United States senator Timothy E. Wirth, Democrat from Colorado, wrote Energy Secretary Herrington expressing concern that Idaho's ban on nuclear waste shipments would create problems for Colorado's Rocky Flats nuclear generating facility. Rocky Flats is a DOE facility, located sixteen miles from downtown Denver. It is the only plant that manufactures the plutonium triggers that are used to ignite nuclear warheads. Waste from Rocky Flats was routinely shipped to the INEL facility in Idaho for "interim" storage (Reid, 1989d). Wirth wrote that Rocky Flats was not equipped for long-term storage, and that requiring storage on site would be "inappropriate" (Wirth, 1988). Wirth had a history of opposition to the management of Rocky Flats (Butterfield, 1988a). Although the facility was operated under the auspices of DOE, management of the facility was contracted to Rockwell corporation as the facility was privatized.

Rocky Flats has had at best a spotty safety history. A 1970 study of plutonium contamination reported concentrations 400 to 1,500 times higher than normal. The concentrations of plutonium around Rocky Flats were the highest ever recorded near an urban area, including the city of Nagasaki. The plant had been repeatedly accused of poor and sloppy management. Nevertheless, the plant was one of Colorado's largest employers. For managing the facility in 1987, DOE had paid Rockwell a guaranteed $4.55 million and a performance bonus of $2.91 million (Butterfield, 1988a).

Andrus acknowledged that his ban on out-of-state nuclear waste could be challenged in court, but to the press he indicated that he could use the courts, too, and would until "you could step on my beard" (Butterfield, 1988b). At the same time, Andrus expressed confidence that DOE would not bring unwanted material into Idaho, and he accused the Department of Energy of reneging on two deadlines related to the opening of WIPP (*Idaho Statesman*, 1988). In response, Representative Bill Richardson, Democrat from New Mexico, claimed that the facility still did not meet all of the federal safety requirements. Richardson's charge was technically correct, as the facility had not yet met two critical regulations of a total of about 1600 regulations requested by DOE (Smock, 1988). Questions regarding the suitability of the WIPP site had been raised by scientists, but had seemingly been ignored by DOE (Begley and Miller, 1987; Crawford, 1988; Monastersky, 1988a, 1988b, 1988C; see also, Schneider, 1989; Reid, 1989a). By this time, DOE had spent nearly a billion dollars preparing the WIPP site for storage. In addition, Carruthers continued to insist that the DOE had not met many of its important commitments to New Mexico, especially those related to socioeconomic impacts from the project.

October 20, the day after Andrus announced his ban, presented a practical dilemma. A railcar carrying transuranic waste bound for storage at INEL sat in Pocatello. No one was willing to order it moved. The Energy Department said they wanted to avoid a confrontation, claiming that Andrus was a friend (Barker, 1988). Increasingly, Andrus's public posture was that Congress or the administration needed to act, that WIPP had to open, and that those responsible for generating waste needed to accept responsibility for solving the storage problem (Andrus, 1988b).

Three days after Andrus's ban on nuclear waste shipments into Idaho, amid speculation that DOE and Rockwell would seek to expand waste storage capacity at Rocky Flats, an aide to Colorado governor Romer told the press "We don't want longer term storage at Rocky Flats" (Butterfield, 1988a). Nonetheless, on October 25, when the boxcar that had been refused access to the INEL storage facility in Idaho was returned to Colorado, Romer agreed to let it return to Rocky Flats for temporary storage. The boxcar had been sitting for four days; Romer said that he agreed to let it return because he did not want it just "rolling around on the rails." In his statement at the time, Romer announced that he planned to call a meeting of western governors to see if they could work collectively to move DOE along on WIPP. Romer said that while he was permitting the single boxcar to return to Rocky Flats, he would not permit the facility to expand its storage facilities (*New York Times*, 1988).

On October 26, DOE closed part of Rocky Flats for safety reasons. A government accounting office report quoted a special DOE investigator as having found a series of "very serious" violations at Rocky Flats, violations that left no safety margins. In response to the announcement and events of the preceding weeks, citizens near Rocky Flats turned out in mass for a meeting called by the Rocky Flats Environmental Monitoring Council, a citizens group appointed by Governor Romer (Butterfield, 1988c).

The activities of state officials appear to have been coordinated, setting the stage for a concerted effort against the federal government. In effect, Andrus had organized a small number of strategically placed governors (and other officials) that was intent on moving the federal government to act. As a former interior secretary, he was able to anticipate—and in some cases script—federal responses. By November 1, DOE officials had scheduled a meeting with Andrus, Carruthers, and Romer. Andrus's press bulletin announcing the meeting reiterated his position that continued interim waste storage at INEL was not a solution (Andrus, 1988c).

STRIKING A BARGAIN

In his October 24 "View From the Capitol," Andrus raised the issue of a *cleanup* for waste buried near INEL (Andrus, 1988b). Andrus clearly had public opinion behind him, and that opinion motivated subsequent activities of the Idaho congressional delegation. Congressman Stallings, Democrat from Idaho, met with House colleagues from New Mexico and Colorado prior to the start of the 101st Congress; and the public record began to report the common interests of the states.

On December 17, the *New York Times* described the events of prior months as "an extraordinary confrontation between the states and the Federal Government" (Wald, 1988). The *Times* described the governors of Idaho, Colorado, and New Mexico as members of the "vanguard of a movement" by state officials to force DOE to make major changes.

The Department of Energy responded by emphasizing the importance of the weapons work to the governors; holding a classified briefing in a guarded, windowless room, replete with antibugging devices. The governors reportedly told federal officials at the meeting that they were no longer going to concede exclusive authority on this issue to the federal government (Wald, 1988). Within a month's time, the *Washington Post* characterized events in the western states as "plutonium poker" (Reid, 1989b).

In the meeting with the Energy Department, Romer indicated that he would not tolerate additional nuclear waste storage in the Denver metropolitan area (Wald, 1988). In fact, Romer threatened to order Rocky Flats to close as soon as it reached existing storage capacity. By this time, seven boxcars filled with nuclear waste were sitting outside Rocky Flats as a result of having been turned back by Idaho. The Energy Department promised Romer that they would stay within state imposed limits for waste storage at Rocky Flats (Peterson, 1988).

The Energy Department clearly had nowhere to put the waste that they had intended to store in Idaho. The department told the governors that they would do everything possible to facilitate the land transfer that would make it possible to open WIPP, but Carruthers told reporters, "Their (DOE) chances of opening (WIPP) in August are about as good as my flying on the next space shuttle" (Peterson, 1988).

As the stalemate between Idaho and DOE wore on, boxcars full of waste piled up in Colorado. A February 1, 1989 press release from Andrus's office reported that DOE had capitulated to his demand for an accelerated cleanup at the INEL plant (Andrus, 1989a). The press release indicated that DOE had agreed to spend "nearly half a billion dollars over the next five years on buried waste clean-up." Moreover, Andrus announced, Idaho would receive nearly a million in federal funds; $400,000 in fiscal year 1989–1990 and $500,000 in fiscal year 1990–1991. These funds were committed without strings, meaning that the state could use them to carry on oversight functions at INEL. The commitment to an expedited cleanup at INEL, coupled with an agreement to conduct an epidemiological study and initiate administrative land withdrawal action for WIPP meant that three of the four conditions Andrus had originally established for continuing operations in Idaho had been met. Andrus's press release indicated that he was willing to discuss the waste situation with DOE *when* a land withdrawal bill was introduced in Congress.

On February 23, Andrus announced that national security required that he modify Idaho's ban on importation of nuclear waste (Andrus, 1989b). The ban remained in effect for all shipping sites except Rocky Flats. His statement blamed DOE for creating the national security crisis. According to Andrus, the crisis had been created by DOE's failure to deal with the storage question. He noted further that the change in his ban on nuclear waste was temporary, subject to reevaluation, and contingent on a September 1, 1989 operational readiness date for WIPP.

Andrus also noted that he and Colorado governor Romer had bent over backwards to try to deal with the problem, but that the problem was neither Idaho's nor Colorado's—the problem was a national one and required a national solution.

When Andrus agreed to temporarily set aside his ban on waste shipments to INEL, Romer was able to agree not to shut down Rocky Flats (Reid, 1989c). The national press was now quoting Andrus and Romer as though they spoke with a single voice. Romer told the press, "We are communicating with the (Bush) administration in the loudest terms that they must come up with a permanent answer for this waste . . . or that plant [Rocky Flats] could close" (Reid, 1989c). Lifting the ban helped Romer out of a difficult situation; Romer would not have enjoyed closing the plant and putting 6,000 people out of work (Reid, 1989c). The average salary of Rocky Flats employees was $48,000 (Reid, 1989d). But, Romer was unable to simply watch lethal waste accumulate in boxcars in such proximity to Denver. Romer noted that the actions he, Andrus, and Carruthers had taken put the federal government in a difficult situation. But he also noted that as governors they were without options—only DOE had options (Reid, 1989e). At the time, estimates indicated that Andrus's temporary change would permit Rocky Flats to operate until December 1989.

On February 27, in another "View from the Capitol," Andrus indicated that Idaho would accept a dozen more shipments from Rocky Flats, but that after September 1 no more waste shipments would be permitted to enter the state (Andrus, 1989c). Andrus's message went on to note that the primary concern was not with the waste produced at Rocky Flats, but with the older waste that had been "indiscriminately buried at INEL before 1970." Indeed, he noted that it was this concern that had originally compelled him to act and that he was more committed than ever to ending the storage of nuclear waste in Idaho (Andrus, 1989c).

KEEPING THE PRESSURE ON

On May 5, 1989, Andrus's office announced that Andrus and eight other governors had sent a letter to Energy Secretary Watkins. That letter, cosigned by governors Gardner (Washington), Romer (Colorado), Miller (Nevada), McWherter (Tennessee), Celeste (Ohio), Goldschmidt (Oregon), Wilkinson (Kentucky), and Carruthers (New Mexico) noted that concern over health and environmental questions related to waste disposal was growing, and that they were all frustrated with the lack of progress in policy addressing their concerns. They noted that the problem was national in scope as the facilities in question were all DOE operations. The governors expressed their commitment to working constructively with the administration and the Congress to deal with cleanup, and attached a policy paper they claimed contained the elements essential to a credible, effective cleanup. By the end of May, the press was reporting that a bill that would provide for the release of public lands for WIPP was unlikely to secure congressional passage; this was the second consecutive year the bill would fail (Schneider, 1989).

On June 1, the acting comptroller general of the United States responded to an inquiry from Representative Mike Synar, chair of the House Environment, Energy, and Natural Resources Subcommittee (Committee on Government Operations) regarding the legality of Andrus's border closing. The response claimed that Andrus's action conflicted with the supremacy clause of the Constitution. The letter went on to indicate that informal discussions with both Andrus's staff and the Idaho attorney general's staff revealed that Governor Andrus's ban was based on his perception of violation of agreements made by federal officials, especially one in a letter from the then chair of the Atomic Energy Commission (AEC) in 1972. In his letter, the chair of the AEC indicated that the nuclear waste stored in Idaho would be removed by 1983. The comptroller's letter continues by noting that there is no formal memorandum of understanding or any other document memorializing the commitment (Comptroller, 1989). The letter concludes by noting that the information being transmitted to Synar was prepared for hearings on WIPP, and that the opinion would be available for public distribution in ten days. In a response for the state of Idaho, Attorney General Jim Jones wrote that the state could block transportation of waste to INEL until DOE could demonstrate that the facility complied with requirements in the National Environmental Policy Act (Jones, 1989). In his June 5, 1989 "View from the Capitol," Andrus reiterated his September 1, 1989 cutoff for additional waste shipments to INEL. This time, his document addressed questions related to the transportation of nuclear waste; he noted that highways in Idaho and elsewhere would be affected, and that federal funds for emergency response training, response capacity, and cleanup costs that might result from an accident were necessary (Andrus, 1989e).

On June 12, 1989, Romer raised the possibility that Colorado health officials might close Rocky Flats (Abas, 1989). Romer insisted that state inspectors be permitted to monitor air and liquid discharges from Rocky Flats, and that they be able to enter the plant without notice for environmental inspection. Romer's demand came a week after the U.S.

Justice Department and the Environmental Protection Agency (EPA) raided the plant. The Justice Department justified the raid, claiming that DOE knew of illegal environmental hazards at the plant for years but had lied in order to keep the plant operating. The FBI's affidavit also indicated that a spy plane that had flown over the plant in December found "illegal burning of toxic solids, and illegal dumping of tainted chemicals into streams" (Reid, 1989d). The criminal investigation that resulted was expected to go on for more than a year. Operation Desert Glow, as the investigation was dubbed, involved seventy-two FBI agents. In response to the charge that DOE and Rockwell may have "made false statements or concealed material facts . . . [and] criminally violated the Clean Water Act" (Wartzman, 1989a), residents of Broomfield, a Denver suburb near Rocky Flats, gathered to build a mile-long ditch to divert streams running through Rocky Flats away from the municipal reservoir (Abas, 1989; Reid, 1989d; Wartzman, 1989a).

Romer appealed to Energy Secretary Watkins to either clean up Rocky Flats or shut it down, but in either case to act quickly (Morain and Romaine, 1989). He went on to tell Watkins that the work would have to be independently verified. Watkins agreed to provide $700,000 for a health impact study, $730,000 for equipment to monitor Rocky Flats, and $1.8 million annually for improved inspections that would be led by Colorado health officials (Abas, 1989).

The DOE maintained that they were renewing their commitment to cooperate with the state in cleaning up the site (Abas, 1989). On June 26, the *Wall Street Journal* reported that DOE had withheld information in the past; but under Congressional pressure the department agreed to release statistics in a timely fashion. The announcement reversed a long standing DOE policy on secrecy, but it was insufficient to satisfy critics. That same day, a preliminary report on the investigation at Rocky Flats reported no evidence of illegally burned nuclear waste (Barnett and Gutfeld, 1989).

The week of June 27, 1989, Andrus met Energy Secretary Watkins in Carlsbad, New Mexico. The meeting, set to include the governors of Colorado and New Mexico, was one of recent monthly briefings on the status of WIPP. That same day, a press release commended Watkins for his willingness to confront DOE's persistent facility problems. The statement noted that Watkins shared Andrus's view that DOE's credibility with regard to oversight functions was poor, and closed with a reiteration that INEL would be closed to incoming waste effective September 1 despite the fact that WIPP would not be ready as an alternative (Andrus, 1989f).

On June 28, Andrus issued another statement regarding his meeting with Watkins. The statement commended Watkins's willingness to recognize that the safe storage of nuclear waste was as important as its generation. Watkins indicated that WIPP would not be ready on schedule and demurred when asked for a start-up date, but went on to indicate that he did not intend to ask or force Idaho to take additional waste (Andrus, 1989g).

That same day, amid admissions that DOE had serious problems with weapons plants, Secretary Watkins said he was surprised the department had ignored National Academy of Sciences' recommendations on WIPP. He indicated that the department would ask the academy to endorse plans to open the repository, noting that the facility would not open until 1990. The *New York Times* quoted Watkins saying, "It has been a nightmare . . . to try to unravel the background . . . to make some decision" (Wald, 1989). The week of July 3, Andrus's "View" reported on another visit to New Mexico, during which he learned of more delays in opening WIPP (Andrus, 1989h). By July 5, Secretary Watkins conceded that WIPP would not be open in the fall. In fact, he indicated that it would probably be mid-1990 before the facility opened (Reid, 1989e). Increasingly, it appeared that DOE had concealed difficulties that—once they were made known—indicated that WIPP would open way behind schedule, if ever, and that Rocky Flats had been a serious problem for some time (Reid, 1989a; Wartzman, 1989b).

EXPANDING THE SCOPE OF THE CONFLICT

Later that month, at the annual meeting of the Western Governors' Association, Andrus sponsored two resolutions dealing with water and hazardous waste. One resolution called on Congress to waive federal sovereign immunity in solid or hazardous waste, an effort to insure that waste facilities complied with provisions of both federal and state laws (Andrus, 1989i). This resolution also called for the expeditious opening of WIPP and for federal funds to support transportation, emergency response, and educational programs in connection with the transportation of waste to WIPP.

On July 20, 1989, Andrus announced his appointee to a newly created panel to advise the DOE on issues associated with WIPP (Andrus, 1989j). The oversight group was hailed as an indication of a new working relationship between the western states and the federal government. In addition, Andrus indicated that he would remain personally involved in DOE and INEL activities (Andrus, 1989k).

Three days later, the governor's office announced that Andrus was to head a national task force to improve environmental oversight at DOE facilities. The task force was established jointly by governors (National Governors' Association) and attorneys general (National Association of Attorneys General). In his press release, Andrus criticized federal sovereignty in energy issues saying, "Washington says it wants to tackle this problem, but it has obstructed efforts by the states—and by its own Environmental Protection Agency—to force federal agencies to clean up sites or enforce penalties" (Andrus, 1989l). The task force indicated that they planned to issue a report in the fall of 1989.

The involvement of the attorneys general and their association, and the NGA are important changes. Their involvement is a clear demarcation of an expanding conflict, one that involves states' rights and power. In addition, the involvement of the attorneys general—especially in Idaho— provides a specter of wide support. In Idaho, where the governor and attorney general were from different parties, it was widely suspected that Andrus would face the attorney general in the next election (*Idaho Statesman*, 1988). Hence, the support of the attorneys general organization for the NGA position, particularly in light of the fact that so few states are mandated to elect both officials from the same party, is indicative of wide support at the state level for Andrus's position. Indeed, it may indicate that he had been successful in changing the scope of the issue to focus primarily upon states' rights and the mandate to protect the health and safety of state citizens.

On August 1, Andrus wrote Energy Secretary Watkins, noting that the New Mexico congressional delegation had requested that Watkins rescind his support of an administrative land withdrawal, and that there appeared to be little chance of success for a legislative land withdrawal bill. Andrus called the move "totally unacceptable," indicating that it had been an integral part of the agreement that prompted him to renew acceptance of waste from Rocky Flats. Andrus challenged the "reliability" of New Mexico's officials, and noted that he had kept his part of the bargain and expected other participants to keep theirs (Andrus, 1989m). If the land withdrawal were accomplished administratively, rather than through congressional action, the state of New Mexico would have lost $240 million in federal funds that was included in the legislative package (Peterson, 1988). Thus, the reluctance of the New Mexico delegation is easily understood. Three weeks later, Andrus followed up with a letter informing Watkins that Idaho had met its commitment to accept twelve additional boxcars of waste from Rocky Flats, and that Idaho's borders were once again closed (Andrus, 1989n). Andrus repeated that message on August 28.

On August 5, 1989, Colorado governor Romer wrote President Bush encouraging a reduction in nuclear arms manufacturing, noting that the nuclear arsenal depleted resources needed to build a competitive domestic economy. The communication went on to suggest to the president that Colorado residents would be forming a human circle around the Rocky Flats Nuclear Weapons Plant on August 6, 1989. Romer explained that the act symbolized an interest in reducing the threat of nuclear war, and ensuring that the production of nuclear weapons does not endanger the citizens of Colorado. The letter asked for Bush's cooperation in making Rocky Flats operate cleanly and safely, pledged the governor's support in cooperating with the federal government, and encouraged multilateral agreements to limit the proliferation of nuclear weapons (Romer, 1989).

On September 1, the *Wall Street Journal* reported that Moody's Investigators Service was watching events to see if the Rockwell Corporation was going to be fully indemnified by DOE in the event that criminal financial sanctions were leveled in connection with the FBI's investigation of Rocky Flats (Morain and Romaine, 1989). Later that month, in an unprecedented move, DOE Secretary Watkins and Rockwell agreed to terminate Rockwell's Rocky Flats management contract early. The agreement between the secretary and Rockwell was announced a day after Rockwell brought suit against DOE claiming that the department had forced them to violate hazardous waste laws because of federal failure to provide permanent storage facilities for waste (Abas, 1989).

On February 7, 1990, the Federal Facilities Task Force Report, written by a joint committee of governors (for the NGA) and attorneys general (for the NAAG) was released. Task force cochairs Andrus and Ken Eikenberry (attorney general, State of Washington) were joined by Senate Majority Leader Mitchell and House Speaker Foley at a news conference to release the report. At the press conference where the report was released, Andrus said: "In America, the fundamental law is, 'If you make a mess, you clean it up.' We want to make that apply to the United States" (Teare, 1990). Andrus noted that the states are demanding participation in the cleanup of federal facilities, insisting that the work begin promptly, and that it be appropriately funded. In a similar vein the task force report called for better environmental compliance, improved oversight at federal facilities, a time frame for cleanup and compliance, funding for cleanup and compliance, and comprehensive waste management plans (Andrus, 1990).

Andrus, Romer, and Carruthers had managed to muster bipartisan support when they mobilized the National Governors' Association. Moreover, regardless of the reasons that the state attorneys general joined the governors, the support they provided increased the credibility of the governors' demands. The use of professional associations for such purposes is not new, and as questions regarding responsibility and authority continue to be raised in the federal context the roles of these associations in articulating demands on behalf of the states is likely to increase (Haider, 1974).

CONCLUSION

This case study clearly indicates that in certain circumstances governors can play effective roles in policy areas previously defined as the sole domain of the federal government. In this case, the federal experience of Governor Andrus seems to have played an important part in his ability not only to sense what federal actions might be, but also to mobilize actors that could influence federal policy. Gubernatorial cooperation can be an important factor in shaping federal policy. In this case, such cooperation seems to have thwarted certain federal initiatives, and it is unlikely that nuclear waste disposal will ever again be the sole domain of federal policy.

Our examination of gubernatorial policy involvement indicates that governors can mount impressive campaigns to oppose federal initiatives. State chief executives have demonstrated they are capable of cooperative efforts to oppose federal policy aimed at denying them a voice in programs that affect their states. Indeed, gubernatorial leadership in such policy areas may have been a neglected area of investigation resulting in underestimating the policy powers of these chief executives.

REFERENCES

Abas, Bryan. 1989. Rocky Flats: A Big Mistake from Day One. *The Bulletin of Atomic Scientists*, (December):19–24.

Alford, Robert. 1975. *Health Care Politics*. Chicago, IL: University of Chicago Press.

Andrus, Cecil D. 1988a. Letter from Office of the Governor, to U.S. Energy Secretary Herrington. Oct. 19.

_____. 1988b. A View from the Capitol, October 24.

_____. 1988c. Press Release, October 27.

_____. 1989a. Andrus Says DOE Agrees to Half-Billion Dollar INEL Clean-up. Press Release, February 1.

_____. 1989b. Press Release, Andrus Announces Modification of Waste Ban in Idaho. February 23.

_____. 1989c. A View from the Capitol, February 27.

_____. 1989d. Andrus, Eight Other Governors Endorse National Waste Clean-up Plan. Press Release, May 5.

_____. 1989e. A View from the Capitol, June 5.

_____. 1989f. Press Release, June 27.

_____. 1989g. Press Release, June 28.

_____. 1989h. A View from the Capitol, July 3.

_____. 1989i. Andrus Pushes Water, Waste Issues at Governors' Conference. Press Release, July 18.

_____. 1989j. Andrus Appoints Boise Attorney to WIPP Oversight Group. Press Release, July 20.

_____. 1989k. Governor Andrus Announces Staff Assignments on INEL Oversight by State of Idaho. Press Release, July 28.

_____. 1989l. Andrus Heads National Task Force to Improve Environmental Oversight Efforts at Federal Facilities. Press Release, July 31.

_____. 1989m. Letter to Admiral James D. Watkins, Secretary of the Department of Energy, August 1.

_____. 1989n. Letter to the Honorable James D. Watkins, Secretary of Energy, August 21.

_____. 1990. Governors, Attorneys General Release Report on Environmental Clean-up and Compliance at Federal Facilities. Press Release, February 7.

Barker, Rocky. 1988. DOE Hopes to Avoid Struggle Over Shipments. *Post-Register*, October 20.

Barnett, Paul M., and Rose Gutfeld. 1989. As FBI Investigates Rocky Flats Weapons Plant, Groups Accuse Energy Agency of More Cover-Ups. The *Wall Street Journal*, June 26: A10(E).

Begley, Sharon, and Mark Miller. 1987. A Nuclear Dump Springs a Leak. *Newsweek*, 110(26): 65.

Beyle, Thad. 1983. Governors. In Gray, Jacob, and Vines, eds. *Politics in The American States*, 4th ed. Boston: Little, Brown and Company.

Beyle, Thad, and Lynn Muchmore. 1983. *Being Governor: The View From the Office*. Durham, NC: Duke University Press.

Butterfield, Fox. 1988a. Dispute on Wastes Poses Threat to Operations at Weapons Plant. The *New York Times*, October 21: 1 (N) A1 (L).

_____. 1988b. Idaho Firm on Barring Atomic Waste. The *New York Times*, October 23: A 1(N), 32(L).

_____. 1988c. Report Finds Perils at Atom Plant Greater than Energy Dept. Said. The *New York Times* October 27: 1(N) A1(L).

Comptroller General of the United States (Acting). 1989. Correspondence to the Honorable Mike Synar, Chairman, Environment, Energy and Natural Resources Subcommittee, Committee on Governmental Relations, U.S. House of Representatives (June 1).

Crawford, Mark. 1988. DOE Challenged on WIPP Site. *Science*, 241:1590.

Dometrius, Nelson. 1979. Measuring Gubernatorial Power. *Journal of Politics*, 41, 2:589–610.

Florestano, P., and L. Boyd. 1989. Governors and Higher Education. *Policy Studies Journal*, 17, 4:863–79.

Grady, Dennis O. 1987. Gubernatorial Behavior in State-Federal Relations. *Western Politics Quarterly*, 40 2:305–18.

———. 1989. Governors and Economic Development Policy. *Policy Studies Journal*, 17, 4:879–94.

Gross, Donald A. 1989. Governors and Policymaking: Theoretical Concerns and Analytic Approaches. *Policy Studies Journal*, 17, 4:764–81.

Haider, Donald H. 1974. *When Governments Come to Washington*. New York: The Free Press.

Herzik, Eric, and Charles W. Wiggins. 1989. Governors vs. Legislatures. *Policy Studies Journal*, 17, 4:841–62.

Idaho Statesman. 1988. Andrus Bans Bringing N-Waste to Idaho. October 20:1, 6A.

Jones, Charles. 1976. Regulating the Environment. In Jacob and Vines, eds. *Politics in the American States*, 3rd. ed. Boston: Little, Brown.

Jones, J. 1989. Correspondence to the Honorable Mike Synar, Chair, Environment, Energy and Natural Resources Subcommittee of the Committee on Government Operations, U.S. House of Representatives, June 29.

Laderle, John W. 1972. Governors and Higher Education. In Beyle and Williams, eds. *The American Governor in Behavioral Perspective*. New York: Harper & Row.

Medler, Jerry F. 1989. Governors and Environmental Policy. *Policy Studies Journal*, 17, 4:895–908.

Monastersky, R. 1988a. Concern over leaks at Radwaste Site. *Science News*, 133 (Jan. 23):54.

Morain, Dan, and Lisa Romaine. 1988b. DOE to Limit Radwaste Operations. *Science News*, 133 (Mar. 19):188.

———. 1988c. Opening Delayed for Nuclear Waste Site. *Science News*, 134 (Sept. 24):199.

———. 1989. Clean or Close Nuclear Plant —Gov. Romer. The *Los Angeles Times*, June 13: 20, part 1.

New York Times. 1988. Waste Feud Resolved for Now. October 25: 8(N), A16(L).

Peterson, Cass. 1988. DOE 'Optimistic' on Waste Impasse. The *Washington Post*, December 17: A4.

Reid, T. R. 1989a. New Atomic Dump Poses Unprecedented Challenges. The *Washington Post*, July 5:A4.

———. 1989b. Rockies Crisis: Where to Put Nuclear Waste. The *Washington Post*, January 18: A3.

———. 1989c. Idaho Governor Lifting Ban on Plutonium Waste. The *Washington Post*, February 24:A3.

———. 1989d. Governor Demands Right to Monitor, Inspect Rocky Flats. The *Washington Post*, June 12:A19.

———. 1989e. U.S. Rebuffed On Storage of Nuclear Waste. The *Washington Post*, June 29:A3.

Romer, Roy. 1989. Letter to the Honorable George Bush, President of the United States, August 5.

Sabato, Larry. 1983. *Goodbye to Goodtime Charlie*. Washington, DC: Congressional Quarterly Press.

Schlesinger, Joseph. 1965. The Politics of the Executive. In Jacob and Vines, eds. *Politics in the American States*. Boston: Little, Brown.

Schneider, Keith. 1989. Nuclear Waste Dump Faces Potential Problem. The *New York Times*, June 3:6(N).

Senate, U.S. (1987). Hearing before the Subcommittee on Public Lands, National Parks and Forests of the Committee on Energy and Natural Resources, United States Senate, 100th Congress, 1st Session, on S.1272 to withdraw certain public lands in Eddy County, New Mexico. Carlsbad, NM, October, 12. Washington, DC: U.S. Government Printing Office.

Sigelman, Lee, and Roland Smith. 1981. Personal, Office, and State Characteristics as Predictors of Gubernatorial Performance. *Journal of Politics*, 43, 1:169–80.

Smock, Honorable Emerson. 1988. Chairman of the Environmental Affairs Committee, Idaho, Letter to Governor Cecil D. Andrus, October 11.

Teare, John. 1990. Andrus, Others ask U.S. for Waste-cleanup Powers, Funds. *Idaho Statesman*, February 8:1C.

Wald, Matthew L. 1988. 3 States Ask Waste Cleanup As Price of Atomic Operation. The *New York Times*, December 17:1(N), 1(L).

_____. 1989. Energy Chief Says Top Aides Lack Skills to Run U.S. Bomb Complex. The *New York Times*, June 28:A1(L), A16.

Wartzman, Rick. 1989a. Moody's Watching Probe of Rockwell's Weapons Factory. The *Wall Street Journal*, September 1:C15(E).

_____. 1989b. Rockwell Bomb Plant Is Repeatedly Accused of Poor Safety Record. The *Wall Street Journal*, August 30:A1, A2.

Wirth, Senator Timothy E. 1988. Letter to Energy Secretary Herrington, October 19, 1988.

Selected Bibliography

Before the 1960s governors generated very little interest among academics. The lack of attention given governors perhaps reflected the popular perception of the office. As described by Sabato (1983), governors were generally viewed as being merely elevated courthouse politicians, a group of "goodtime Charlies." The perception of governors also matched the perceived importance of state government. With the United States carving out an ever larger position in world affairs, the activities of state governments and their chiefs paled in comparison with the president and Congress.

Just prior to the decade of the 1960s, however, an influential segment of political scientists were discovering state politics and governors. V.O. Key's landmark *Southern Politics* had set up the discovery by noting the persistent importance of state governments and politics in the daily lives of citizens. Key followed with his text *State Politics*, launching, at least unintentionally, the comparative study of state and policy. Over the next two decades a variety of analysts examined the determinants, outputs, and outcomes of state policy in the leading journals of political science. With increasing methodological sophistication analysts realized that state governments provided a wealth of data on a wide range of political and policy issues.

Caught up in the general sweep of the comparative study of state politics was the office of governor. As the salient actor in state government, governors were both important variables influencing state policy outcomes and objects for study in their own right. Now, some thirty years after the emergence of comparative state politics analysis, a fairly extensive literature on governors is developing. Most of the literature on governors is covered by this book's authors, and a common core of works can be found in every chapter of the book. The following bibliography highlights a selected group of core studies that help define the literature on governors. We have grouped these studies by broad categories noting the analytic thrust of the work. This is done for convenient division of the literature and is not meant to be some deterministic cataloging of the field.

GENERAL WORKS

Beyle, Thad L. 1990. Governors. In Gray, Jacob, and Albritton, eds. *Politics in the American States*, 5th ed. Glenview, IL: Scott, Foresman.

———. 1983. Governors. In Gray, Jacob, and Vines, eds. *Politics in the American States*, 4th ed. Boston: Little, Brown and Company.

Beyle, Thad L., and Lynn Muchmore. 1983. *Being Governor: The View from the Office*. Durham, NC: Duke University Press.

Beyle, Thad, L., and J. Oliver Williams. 1972. *The American Governor in Behavioral Perspective*. New York: Harper & Row.

Center for Policy Research. 1987. *Reflections on Being Governor*. Washington, DC: National Governors' Association.

Durning, D. 1987. Change Masters for State. *State Government*, 60, 3:145–49.

Fairlie, John A. 1912. The State Governor. *Michigan Law Review*, 10, 5–6:370–83, 458–75.

Kallenbach, Joseph E. 1966. *The American Chief Executive: The Presidency and the Governorship*. New York: Harper & Row.

Lipson, Leslie. 1939. *The American State Governor: From Figurehead to Leader*. Chicago: University of Chicago Press.

Mathews, John M. 1912. The New Role of the Governor. *American Political Science Review*, 6, 2.

National Governors' Association. 1981. *Reflections on Being Governor*. Washington, DC: Center for Policy Research.

Ransone, Coleman B., Jr. 1956. *The Office of Governor in the United States*. University, AL: University of Alabama Press.

———. 1982. *The American Governorship*. Westport, CT: Greenwood Press.

Sabato, Larry. 1978. *Goodbye to Goodtime Charlie: The American Governor Transformed, 1950–1975*. Lexington, MA: Lexington Books.

———. 1983. *Goodbye to Goodtime Charlie: The American Governor Transformed, 1950–1975*, 2nd ed. Washington, DC: Congressional Quarterly Press.

Schlesinger, Joseph 1965. The Politics of the Executive. In Jacob and Vines, eds. *Politics in the American States*. Boston, MA: Little, Brown and Company.

Young, William. 1958. The Development of the Governorship. *State Government*, 31:178–83.

GUBERNATORIAL POWER

Abney, Glenn, and Thomas P. Lauth. 1989. The Executive Budget in the States: Normative Idea and Empirical Observation. *Policy Studies Journal*, 17, 4:829–40.

_____. 1987. Perceptions of the Impact of Governors and Legislatures in the State Appropriations Process. *The Western Political Quarterly*, 40, 3:335–42.

Bernick, E. Lee. 1979. Gubernatorial Tools: Formal vs. Informal. *Journal of Politics*, 41, 2:656–64.

Beyle, Thad. 1968. The Governor's Formal Powers: A View from the Governor's Chair. *Public Administration Review*, 28, 4:540–45.

Beyle, Thad, and Scott Mouw. 1989. Governors: The Power of Removal. *Policy Studies Journal*, 17, 4:804–28.

Dometrius, Nelson. 1979. Measuring Gubernatorial Power. *The Journal of Politics*, 41, 2:589–610.

_____. 1988. Changing Gubernatorial Power: Measure vs. Reality. *Western Political Quarterly*, 40: 319–28.

Dye, Thomas. 1969. Executive Power and Public Policy in the States. *Western Political Quarterly*. 27, 4:926–39.

Herzik, Eric B., and C. W. Wiggins. 1989. Governors vs. Legislatures: Vetoes, Overrides, and Policymaking in the American States. *Policy Studies Journal*, 17, 4: 841–62.

Lockard, Duane. 1976. The Strong Governorship: Status and Problems—New Jersey. *Public Administration Review*, 36, 1:95–98.

Meuller, K. 1985. Explaining Variation and Change in Gubernatorial Power, 1960–1982. *Western Political Quarterly*, 424–31.

National Governors' Association. 1987. *The Institutionalized Powers of the Governorship: 1965–1985*. Washington, DC: Office of State Services.

Prescott, Frank. 1950. The Executive Veto in American States. *Western Political Quarterly*, 3, 1:97–111.

Sigelman, L., and N. Dometrius. 1988. Governors as Chief Administrators: The Linkage Between Formal Powers and Informal Influence. *American Politics Quarterly*, 16, 2:157–70.

Wiggins, Charles. 1980. Executive Vetoes and Legislative Overrides in the American States. *The Journal of Politics*, 4:1110–17.

POLICY AND POLITICAL ROLES

Bernick, E. Lee, and C. W. Wiggins. 1981. Executive-Legislative Power Relation: Perspective of State Lawmakers. *American Politics Quarterly*, 9, 4:467–76.

Florestano, Patricia, and Laslo Boyd. 1989. Governors and Higher Education. *Policy Studies Journal*, 17, 4:863–78.

Grady, Dennis. 1987. Gubernatorial Behavior in State-Federal Relations. *Western Political Quarterly*, 40, 2:305–18.

Gross, Donald A. 1989. Governors and Policymaking: Theoretical Concerns and Analytic Approaches. *Policies Studies Journal*, 17, 4:764–87.

Herzik, Eric B. 1983. Governors and Issues: A Typology of Concerns. *State Government*, 56, 2: 58–64.

Morehouse, Sarah McCally. 1966. The Governor and His Legislative Party. *American Political Science Review*, 60, 4: 923–42.

_____. 1976. The Governor as Political Leader. In Jacob and Vines, eds. *Politics in the American States*. 3rd ed. Boston: Little, Brown and Company.

National Governors' Association. 1982. *Transition and the New Governor: A Critical Overview*. Washington, DC: Office of State Services.

Rosenthal, A. 1990. *Governors and Legislatures: Contending Powers*. Washington, DC: CQ Press.

Schlesinger, Joseph A. 1957. *How They Became Governor*. East Lansing, MI: Governmental Research Bureau, Michigan State University.

Wyner, Allen. 1968. Gubernatorial Relations with Legislators and Administrators. *State Government*, 41:199–203.

ADMINISTRATIVE AND MANAGEMENT ROLES

Abney, Glenn, and Thomas P. Lauth. 1983. The Governor as Chief Administrator. *Public Administration Review*, 43, 1:40–49.

Flentje, H. 1981. The Governor as Manager. *State Government*, 42, 2.

Haas, Peter, and Deil S. Wright. 1989. Public Policymaking and Administrative Turnover in State Government: The Role of the Governor. *Policy Studies Journal*, 17, 4:788–803.

Hale, G. 1977. Executive Leadership vs. Budgetary Behavior. *Administration and Society*, 9, 4.

Hebert, F. Ted, Jeffrey L. Brudney, and Deil S. Wright. 1983. Gubernatorial Influence and State Bureaucracy. *American Politics Quarterly*, 11:243–64.

Hedge, David M. 1983. Fiscal Dependency and the State Budget Process. *Journal of Politics*, 45, 1:198–208.

Lauth, Thomas P. 1984. Impact of the Method of Agency Selections on Gubernatorial Influence Over State Agencies. *Public Administration Quarterly*, 7, 4:396–409.

Sharkansky, Ira. 1968. Agency Requests, Gubernatorial Support, and Budget Success in State Legislatures. *American Political Science Review*, 62, 4:1220–31.

Sprengel, Donald. 1969. *Gubernatorial Staffs: Functional and Political Profiles*. Iowa City, IA: Institute of Public Affairs.

Thompson, Joel. 1987. Agency Requests, Gubernatorial Support, and Budget Success in State Legislatures Reconsidered. *Journal of Politics*, 49, 3:756–79.

Williams, Charles. 1980. The Gatekeeper Function on the Governor's Staff. *Western Political Quarterly*, 33, 1:87–93.

Wright, Deil. 1967. Executive Leadership in State Administration. *Midwest Journal of Political Science*, 11, 1.

Index

About the Editors and Contributors

JEFFERY BEREJIKIAN is a doctoral student in the Department of Political Science at the University of Oregon.

E. LEE BERNICK is Associate Professor in the Department of Political Science at the University of North Carolina, Greensboro. He received his Ph.D. from the University of Oklahoma and publishes in the areas of the legislative process and state politics.

BRENT W. BROWN is Vice President for University Relations at Arizona State University. He received his Ph.D. from the University of Illinois and publishes in the areas of public policy, education politics, and state government.

RAYMOND COX III is Associate Professor and Director of the MPA Program in the Department of Political Science at New Mexico State University. He received his Ph.D. from Virginia Polytechnic Institute and publishes on a variety of topics relating to public administration.

MARILYN K. DANTICO is Associate Professor in the Department of Political Science and Vice Provost for Academic Personnel at Arizona State University West. She received her Ph.D. from Florida State University and publishes on topics relating to public policy.

NELSON C. DOMETRIUS is Professor and Chairman of the Department of Political Science at Texas Tech University. He received his Ph.D.

from the University of North Carolina and publishes in the areas of state politics, bureaucracy, and research methods.

DAN DURNING is Research Associate in the Carl Vinson Institute of Government at the University of Georgia. He received his Ph.D. from the University of California at Berkeley and publishes on topics of state government, bureaucracy, and selected public policy issues.

DENNIS GRADY is Associate Professor in the Department of Political Science and Criminal Justice at Appalachian State University. He received his Ph.D. from Emory University and publishes in the areas of intergovernmental relations, governors, policy innovation, and economic development.

JAMES S. GRANATO is Assistant Professor in the Department of Political Science at Michigan State University.

DONALD A. GROSS is Associate Professor in the Department of Political Science at the University of Kentucky. He received his Ph.D. from the University of Iowa and publishes on a variety of topics relating to American politics and institutions.

ERIC B. HERZIK is Associate Professor and Director of Graduate Studies in the Department of Political Science at the University of Nevada, Reno. He received his Ph.D. from the University of North Carolina and publishes on topics of state politics, governors, budgeting, and economic developing policy.

MARY D. HERZIK is a doctoral student in the Department of Political Science at the University of North Carolina. She has published in the areas of executive politics, management, and environmental policy.

JERRY MEDLER is Associate Professor in the Department of Political Science at the University of Oregon. He received his Ph.D. from the University of Oregon and publishes in the areas of environmental politics and policy.

ALVIN H. MUSHKATEL is Professor in the School of Public Affairs and Director of the Office of Hazards Study at Arizona State University. He received his Ph.D. from the University of Oregon and publishes on a range of topics relating to urban politics, emergency management, and environmental policy.

SAUNDRA SCHNEIDER is Assistant Professor in the Department of Government and International Affairs at the University of South Carolina. She received her Ph.D. from SUNY, Binghamton and publishes on topics of policy implementation, health care, and emergency management.

CHARLES W. WIGGINS is Professor in the Department of Political Science at Texas A&M University. He received his Ph.D. from Washington University (St. Louis) and publishes on topics relating to state politics, interest groups, and legislatures.